A Musician's Guide to Church Music

A Musician's Guide to Church Music

Joy E. Lawrence
and
John A. Ferguson

THE PILGRIM PRESS
New York

Library of Congress Cataloging in Publication Data

Lawrence, Joy E.
  A musician's guide to church music.

  Bibliography: p. 236.
  Includes index.
  1. Church music—Instruction and study. I. Ferguson,
John Allen, 1941-   joint author.   II. Title.
MT88.L39   783'.02'6   80-27567
ISBN 0-8298-0424-2

All biblical quotations, unless otherwise indicated, are from the *Revised Standard Version of the Bible*, copyright 1946, 1952, and © 1971 by the Division of Christian Education, National Council of Churches, and are used by permission. Scripture quotations marked ᴋᴊᴠ are from the *King James Version*.

The Pilgrim Press, 132 West 31 Street, New York, New York 10001

Contents

Foreword

A dictionary definition of "minister" is one "authorized to carry out the spiritual functions of the church . . . conduct worship, administer the sacraments, preach." Today's church musicians are called to minister to people in a unique way. They *do* preach and they *do* teach. They also comfort the bereaved and help sustain the weak. Often they counsel the troubled and the distressed, and they always assist at the distribution of the sacrament. They do all this not from the altar but from the choir loft or the organ bench. Furthermore, they do this largely in a nonverbal manner. For too long people have been led to believe that ministry is always verbal.

In order to communicate the Word in this unique way, ministers of music must be exegetes. Their interpretation, their analysis of biblical passages grows out of studies of the rich heritage left by church musicians throughout the ages. A stronger and more beautiful life emerges through their faith and understanding. In the purest sense of worship, ministers of music communicate this to their hearers who respond in a way that can only be described as *spiritual*. This "geist" involves each individually and all corporately as the hearts of people pray, praise, and give thanks. Together and with the saints above they sing the great *Te Deum*.

It is precisely this concept of church music that welcomes musicians into the service of the church. This comprehensive book will help prepare the newcomer in the ways of the church and will enrich those already active in church music. It is one thing to dispense carefully prepared music to the church; it is quite another to offer carefully prepared church music! The difference lies not only in the appropriateness but in the basis for all church art, namely, the *Word*. The music may woo the people, but it is the *Word* who will win them. This book will help to focus the thought and skills of musicians who seek to be of service to the church.

Paul Manz, Cantor
Mount Olive Lutheran Church
Minneapolis, Minnesota

Acknowledgments

Our debt is great—to our teachers while we were students; to our students, both private and those at Kent State University; and especially to the congregations, choirs, and pastors of the churches we have served—particularly, Central Lutheran Church, Minneapolis; The Church of the Covenant (Presbyterian), Cleveland; Euclid Avenue Christian Church, Cleveland Heights; Grace Lutheran Church, Cleveland Heights; Rocky River United Methodist Church, Rocky River, Ohio; and United Church of Christ, Kent, Ohio. Milo Brekke and Walter Holtkamp kindly read and critiqued certain sections of the manuscript. Patti Brestrup, Terry Lee Kuhn, David Moklebust, and Walter Watson contributed, all in their own way; Phyllis Gordon faithfully and skillfully typed the manuscript and Marion M. Meyer, Senior Editor, The Pilgrim Press, wisely counseled, encouraged, and prodded, as needed. Above all, our families graciously accepted our pangs while in creation and gently supported us throughout the entire project.

Joy E. Lawrence
John A. Ferguson

So You Want to Become a Church Musician!

So you want to become a church musician! (already are one?) Many musicians and teachers choose to expand the use of their musical talents to include serving churches as organists, choral directors, or combination organist-choral directors.

Perhaps you, the local high school choral director, have decided to apply for the position of Organist-Director of Music in the United Church in your community. You feel highly qualified, since you hold a bachelor's degree in music education, with a major in voice and a minor in organ. In addition, you have had two years' experience directing high school choruses and you enjoy working with people. Or perhaps now that your children are in school, you believe it is time to utilize that study of piano and organ and are considering applying for a job as organist. Or as a music specialist in an elementary school, you feel you could bring your skills in working with children to a local church that is looking for a director of children's and youth choirs.

To be effective and successful in such situations, you need to widen your musical and theological horizons and to examine carefully some of the qualifications for a church musician. This book is designed to answer questions posed by musicians seeking church positions—questions that perhaps were not even raised, let alone answered, during formal study of music.

To begin, let us look at a hypothetical church: It has 500 to 700 members and would like to consider itself a neighborhood church; however, most parishioners live at least 2 miles from the church and must use public and/or private transportation to attend meetings and services. The church is community-minded and offers a variety of activities that fulfill many religious and social needs. The energetic senior minister has a dynamic perspective on life and the ministry, with a commitment to developing the spiritual growth of the individual members of the church as a whole. An associate minister or part-time lay person guides the education program and works with two youth groups—a junior high fellowship and a senior high fellowship.

The church has expressed the need for a part-time person (or persons) to lead and direct a ministry of music, and several talent-mix possibilities have been identified. Generally, the musician/musicians are responsible for providing a broad, stimulating music program for the church, including music for Sunday worship services, special seasonal musical events—e.g., Christmas and Easter—and a variety of related activities— e.g., youth musicals, fine arts festivals, etc. The music selected and the level of performance are expected to reflect excellence and artistic merit, and to contribute toward deepening and intensifying the religious experience and quality of life of the music participants and the congregation. The musician/musicians work directly with the pastoral staff and are assisted by members of the music committee and the congregation. They cooperatively plan, coordinate, and implement the music program as part of the total church life. A brief list of criteria to be used as a guide in selecting a church musician/musicians for such a parish might include:

GENERAL

1. Considers music an integral part of the church's total ministry.
2. Possesses the ability to work effectively with both professional and lay leadership.
3. Exhibits creativity, energy, and enthusiasm.
4. Has the personality and ability to attract and recruit, and to develop rapport with choirs, including children's and youth choirs.

MUSICAL QUALIFICATIONS

1. Possesses the ability and skills to *develop* and *maintain,* over a sustained period of time, quality musical performance.

2. Is proficient in (a) choral conducting and rehearsal techniques, and/or organ performance and (b) program-planning for worship.
3. Is familiar with a broad range of sacred literature from all stylistic periods.
4. Is creative in playing hymns, and exhibits minimal improvisational skills.

These excerpts from a hypothetical job description indicate that there is much more to the position of organist and/or director of music in a church than appears on the surface, and yet each year thousands of performing musicians and public school music teachers assume the additional responsibility of being church musicians.

Being a church musician involves more than just taking a "church job." It means being dedicated to the excellent performance of the finest in sacred music and possessing a deep desire to serve God through a music ministry. This book is directed toward inspiring, informing, and encouraging those persons who wish to develop the art of being a church musician, and toward providing guidance for anyone involved in shaping the role of music in worship.

A Musician's Guide
to Church Music

CHAPTER 1

The Musician in the Life of the Church

INTRODUCTION

There are a great many challenges in assuming a position as church musician. One expects a musician to bring a high degree of skill as a performer in voice and/or organ and/or an orchestral instrument, and to have received academic training in conducting, theory and analysis, and music history. Most musicians have attended church and participated in worship but may never have given serious thought to the question "What is worship?" What is meant by being sensitive to worship, and how can this affect the work of the church musician? A second set of questions often raised by the musician assuming a leadership position in the church includes: What role has music played in worship traditions? What is the difference between liturgical worship and nonliturgical worship? What influences have shaped the musical practices of various denominations? The answers to such questions contribute toward an understanding of the church, its ministers, and its congregation.

WHAT IS WORSHIP?

The primary aim of worship is to lead people into the presence of God. It is our response to the Eternal. The word worship comes from "worth," which means "of value." The significance of worth lies in being, that is, what we really are. Therefore, in worship we realize our true being.

Worship may be overt or direct, unconscious or conscious. It may occur when we are alone or when we are with others. Corporate worship is perhaps the deepest, for here the individual is lifted to God through the love and support of others. The great theologian Reinhold Niebuhr said, "The Gospels and the Christian life are both born out of worshiping communities." It follows, then, that an understanding of the Christian life comes from interaction within the Christian community. Worship is essential to all religions, but a distinction of Christian worship is the quality given to the experience by the relation of God in Christ.

We glorify God, and worship for sheer delight. To stand before God with our faculties raised to the height of their acute perception is the true meaning of bliss.

Thus, a worship service is rightly termed a celebration. It is a time of adoring appreciation of God's gift of love. There is no more searching test of the music than "Does it enable the individual to focus on worship?" If the music directs thoughts to other matters, then it does not belong in a service of worship. This criterion rules out the cheap and sentimental, for prayers, hymns, and anthems are devout homage to God. Many hymns richly express the meaning of worship; for example, the magnificent paraphrase of Psalm 8 by Curtis Beach:

> O how glorious, full of wonder
>   Is thy name o'er all the earth;
> Thou who wrought creation's splendor,
>   Bringing suns and stars to birth!
> Rapt in reverence we adore thee,
>   Marveling at thy mystic ways;
> Humbly now we bow before thee,
>   Lifting up our hearts in praise.
>
> When we see thy lights of heaven,
>   Moon and stars, thy power displayed,
> What are we that thou shouldst love us,
>   Creatures that thy hand hath made?
> Born of earth, yet full of yearning,
>   Mixture strange of good and ill,
> From thy ways so often turning,
>   Yet thy love doth seek us still.
>
> Thou hast given us dominion
>   O'er the wonders of thy hand,
> Made us fly with eagle pinion,
>   Ruler over sea and land.
> Soaring spire and ruined city,
>   These our hopes and failures show.
> Teach us more of human pity,
>   That we in thine image grow.

4

O how wondrous, O how glorious
  Is thy name in every land!
Thou whose purpose moves before us
  Toward the goal that thou hast planned.
'Tis thy will our hearts are seeking,
  Conscious of our human need.
Spirit in our spirit speaking,
  Make us thine, O God, indeed![1]

Let us consider five basic elements of worship: (1) sensing God's presence, (2) instruction and challenge, (3) intercession and prayer, (4) realizing wholeness, and (5) dedication.

There are many ways of *sensing God's presence*. We may feel it as we view the wonders of nature; as we participate in the sacrament of communion; as we share in the birth of a child; or as we sing a hymn, listen to an anthem, or respond to the challenge of a sermon. Deep worship experiences are not predictable; nor are they consistent. What we bring to worship in the way of previous worship experiences, along with our human needs, often contributes to a worship experience. Such experiences may vary from deeply moving life-changing experiences to fleeting inspirations. Sensing God's presence involves stillness, a time of quiet when God speaks to us. It involves adoration, when we sense the power, love, and grace of God. It involves confession of our sins and shortcomings, with absolution for them; to carry our sins without forgiveness becomes a heavy burden. Jesus said, "Forgive us our debts, as we also have forgiven our debtors [Matt. 6:12]."

Instruction and challenge comprise a second element of worship. Through proclamation of the Word in scripture, sermon, and music, we share more deeply in an understanding of the Christian faith. We need to feel challenged to become better Christians, in a way that will govern our thoughts and actions daily, as we live and work together.

A third element, *intercession*, affects our thoughts concerning others. As individuals we may pray for strength to be given to another human being who is undergoing deep sorrow, or offer a prayer of thanksgiving for the joy and happiness experienced by a friend. The power of such intercessory action is difficult to document, but Christians believe that inner strength has come to persons who were very near death, a strength which has made the difference in their struggle to return to health, and for which medical science cannot provide an explanation. If we recall that none of us comes before God as an isolated self, but rather a "corporate self"—tied with others through families, communities, races, and

---

[1] From *Pilgrim Hymnal*, #74. Copyright, © 1958, by The Pilgrim Press. Words revised by Curtis Beach, 1980.

5

nations—it seems inevitable that our kindred neighbors and fellow Christians should be in our hearts and in our thoughts before God.

Realizing wholeness is related to the experience of holiness. It is the moment when we are confronted by God, the moment when we bare our souls to ourselves and make decisions about the kind of lives we are going to live.

Dedication involves being led from preoccupation with self to a knowledge of God. Worship enlightens, purifies, and transforms life and is therefore, in the deepest sense, creative and redemptive. Through worship we dedicate ourselves to God. When our minds and consciousness are placed in God's care, we gain new insights into the world around us, and develop new relationships with our families, friends, communities, and nations.

Let us now consider some acts of worship. There are various rituals, according to worship traditions, that accompany such events as the celebration of Holy Communion, the celebration of a marriage, and the celebration of baptism. Music can play a vital role in making these rituals more meaningful. The choice of a hymn, the expressiveness of a selection of organ music, an appropriate text of an anthem—each can contribute toward the moment of transcendence, when life is enriched.

Our desires and convictions do not become actual until they are expressed in words and deeds. It is through corporate worship and through music, art forms which speak deeply to the emotions, that the worshiper may enter more fully into life. Music that is shallow and thin seldom contributes to a worship experience full of richness and power; but music that is powerful in construction and/or text may exert a profound force on the individual worshiper.

A major portion of the traditional Sunday morning corporate worship experience utilizes music, and it is through a leadership role in worship that the church musician carries the awesome responsibility of providing opportunities, through music, for the deepest human experiences to occur. Music may be performed accurately and expressively by a first-rate musician, but to have music truly express deep religious meaning the musician must sense an inner presence of God. One cannot predict when "high moments" may occur for the worshiper or the musician; all one can do is "set the stage for God" and then release the experience to the power of God's grace and love.

ASSESSING THE ROLE OF MUSIC IN CHURCHES' WORSHIP TRADITIONS

A church musician needs an awareness of church history to be sensitive to the worship traditions of the church. To assess the role of music in churches' worship traditions, a brief discussion of the most important theological and musical developments is in order. Approached chronologically, both liturgical and nonliturgical traditions are identified, along with their musical characteristics and theological foundations. Within this limited discussion no attempt is made to probe deeply into the multitude of historical and theological issues, but rather to provide the musician working in the church with insights into how the church developed, the directions taken by music, and what meaning history may have for the present.

Music has always played a major role in human expression of religious beliefs. The Hebrews wrote psalms rich in literary beauty that contain frequent references to instruments and music in worship. Psalm 150 is an example.

> Praise ye the Lord. Praise God in his sanctuary: praise him in the firmament of his power.
> Praise him for his mighty acts: praise him according to his excellent greatness.
> Praise him with the sound of the trumpet: praise him with the psaltery and harp.
> Praise him with the timbrel and dance: praise him with stringed instruments and organs.
> Praise him upon the loud cymbals: praise him upon the high sounding cymbals.
> Let every thing that hath breath praise the Lord.
> Praise ye the Lord.
>
> *(King James Version)*

JEWISH BACKGROUND OF THE CHRISTIAN LITURGY

The local religious service of the synagogue or "assembly" was the chief liturgical invention of later Judaism: for the first time, ordered corporate worship was dissociated from sacrifice, and centered on the reading of scripture. The synagogue's influence on the development of Christian worship has probably been greater than any other single factor. The readings from the Torah and the Prophets were the heart of the service. These were surrounded by acts of adoration and thanksgiving, which were spontaneous at first and later evolved into a fixed form. The reading of the Prophets was in Hebrew, followed by a translation in the vernacular and an explanation or exposition. The Shema was a creed, a confession of faith that originally consisted of Deuteronomy 6:4: "Hear, O Israel: The Lord our God is one Lord."

Synagogal prayers were not written down until the fourth or fifth century. They were characterized by (1) praise and thanksgiving to God for mercies received, and by (2) a sense of sin expressed by confession, coupled with a prayer for forgiveness. We recognize the Kedushah (Sanctus) as it appears in the Mass:

> Holy, holy, holy, Lord God of Hosts,
> Heaven and earth are full of thy glory.

The responsive "amen" came from the temple liturgy and occurred after the utterance of each benediction.

Hebrew chants, an oral tradition, were a cantillation of the Pentateuch—the first five books of the Bible: Genesis, Exodus, Leviticus, Numbers, Deuteronomy—and the Prophets, e.g., Elijah, Elisha, Isaiah. In addition to speech-song or intonation of biblical texts, an elaborate, coloratura chant developed in which the rhythm was free and nonmetrical.

One of the basic forms taken by the music was the call-response, in which a leader intoned the first half verse and the congregation repeated it. This same procedure was used by the Puritans, when they "lined out" the singing of psalms during seventeenth-century worship in America.

THE EARLY CHRISTIAN CHURCH

About A.D. 28 there occurred a great outpouring of the Holy Spirit, called Pentecost. During this event the disciples became conscious of a new inward power that completely transformed their attitude toward life, and that they attributed to the Holy Spirit of God. This sense of power marked the beginnings of their active missionary work—the spreading of the gospel of Christ. After Pentecost, followers of Jesus exhibited a passionate conviction that conveyed to all, even to those who did not understand their language, the power of their message. Seeming fearless, they stood up and said what they wanted to say, regardless of the consequences—often torture or death. As a result, these disciples were amazingly effective. People listened and were inspired as they heard them tell the wonders and works of God. The writer of Acts used a single sentence to describe this phenomenon of communicating with people who spoke other languages: "And they were all filled with the Holy Spirit, and began to speak with other tongues, as the Spirit gave them utterance [2:4, KJV]."

Pentecost drew people together who loved and adored Jesus in a common devotion—and it has drawn Christians together ever since. The effect the power of Pentecost had on the lives of the disciples may be illustrated by drawing an analogy with a concert of music. Those who attend a concert may represent every nationality, religious belief, political

8

party, life-style, temperament, and personal taste; they come together because of a common devotion to music. If the concert is great, the audience experiences an ecstasy that may continue as an aura for hours or even days. Even the casual listener may be caught up in the spell of the moment, for each shares in some way the same experience, an enriched sense of feeling. When the moment has passed, one wants to share this experience with others and quickly tells friends about the "marvelous" concert. Events like this draw people together, and a group spirit takes hold and gives them power to communicate their joy to others. Because similar feelings were present in the disciples on the day of Pentecost, a community of believers began to emerge and the Christian church was formed.

By 180 the Christian church had been established in all parts of the Roman Empire, with Old Testament books being accepted as the rule and norm of faith. By 192 the Four Gospels and the thirteen "letters of Paul" had been codified into the New Testament; these are referred to as *canon*, that is, the books of the Bible recognized by the Christian church as being genuine and inspired. The Apostles' Creed came into being about the same time, and although not written by the apostles, it nevertheless embodied the apostles' doctrine.

Apostles' Creed

I believe in God, the Father almighty,
 creator of heaven and earth.

I believe in Jesus Christ, his only Son, our Lord.
 He was conceived by the power of the Holy Spirit
  and born of the virgin Mary.
 He suffered under Pontius Pilate,
  was crucified, died, and was buried.
 He descended into hell. (*or*, He descended to the dead.)
 On the third day he rose again.
 He ascended into heaven,
  and is seated at the right hand of the Father.
 He will come again to judge the living and the dead.

I believe in the Holy Spirit,
 the holy catholic Church,
 the communion of saints,
 the forgiveness of sins,
 the resurrection of the body,
 and the life everlasting. Amen.[2]

---

[2] From the *Lutheran Book of Worship*. Apostles' Creed prepared by the International Consultation on English Texts.

The service of worship was centered in (1) the Word and (2) the Sacrament of Holy Communion, also called the Eucharist. Within the sacrament was the theological tenet that this act represented a new covenant. The concept of a covenant or an agreement between Israel and Yahweh was basic to the Jewish faith. When Moses descended from Mount Sinai with the Ten Commandments, he threw blood on the people, thus sealing this covenant. So it was natural for Jesus to say, "This blood is the *new* covenant." The original meaning of the word covenant was "obligations sworn to by the religious community."[3]

In Old Testament traditions, covenants were a frequent basis for human relationships that were not kinship ties. The classical and probably original covenant with which Christians are most familiar is the Abrahamic covenant (Genesis 15; 17:1-4). The important fact in each of these versions is that Yahweh swore to create of Abraham a nation and to give Abraham's seed the blessing and the land.[4] This covenant tied God to people.

In New Testament narratives of the Last Supper (Matthew 26:28; Mark 14:24; Luke 22:20; 1 Corinthians 11:25), the blood of Christ is specifically related to the *new* covenant. This covenant relationship centered on Christ and his relationship to the New Testament church. It is not accidental, then, that the concept of covenant finds its deepest expression in the Eucharist. The Eucharist was regarded as the formal act that established a lasting relationship between the community and Christ. In recognition of the role this sacrament plays in Christianity, many churches celebrate the Eucharist every Sunday.

MUSIC IN LITURGICAL AND NONLITURGICAL TRADITIONS

Worship traditions evolved into liturgical and nonliturgical forms. In this book the term *liturgical* denotes a particular fixed form of corporate public worship of God, while *nonliturgical* denotes a free or nonfixed form of worship. It is important that everyone concerned with worship have an understanding of the evolution of liturgical practice, for, whether liturgical or nonliturgical, most corporate worship has its roots in liturgy.

Liturgical Worship   Liturgical churches follow an ordered form of worship, consisting of (1) readings and music, which vary according to the Christian Year, and (2) fixed events, such as Kyrie Eleison, Gloria, Creed, Sanctus, Agnus Dei, and Benedictus. As mentioned earlier, the

---

[3] *Interpreter's Dictionary of the Bible*, vol. I (New York: Abingdon Press, 1962), p. 716.
[4] Ibid., p. 718.

Eucharist was the act in which Christianity was centered; Christians celebrated both the passion and resurrection of Christ in this solemn event. The liturgy, as celebrated about mid-second century, may have included:

The Liturgy of the Word

Readings from the Prophets, Epistles, and Gospels
Instruction and exhortation
Common prayers in litany form
Psalms and hymns

The Liturgy of the Upper Room

Kiss of Peace
Offertory:
   Collection of gifts for poor
   Bringing in of the elements for the celebration
     of the Eucharist
Prayer of Consecration:
   Thanksgiving
   Invocation to bless the gifts of bread and wine
   Intercessions
   Peoples' amens
Communion
Dismissal

Two forms of prayers used in the early church were (1) those offered by the celebrant, to which all responded by saying *amen;* and (2) those said by all the worshipers together. In this early form of the liturgy, the celebrant stood behind the Holy Table, facing the people.

During the third and fourth centuries, the Salutation and the Sursum Corda, an introduction to the Prayer of Consecration, came into use. The Salutation began:

   Minister: The Lord be with you.
   People: And with thy spirit.

This was followed by the Sursum Corda:

   Minister: Lift up your hearts.
   People: We lift them up unto the Lord.
   Minister: Let us give thanks unto the Lord, our God.
   People: It is meet and right so to do.

This series of prayers was climaxed by the reciting of the Sanctus:

   Holy, holy, holy, Lord God Almighty,
   Heaven and earth are full of thy glory.
   Glory be to thee, O Lord.

Although these services lasted about 3 hours, the worship throughout was responsive and cooperative, and the general structure and emphasis permeated all later forms of worship.

The earliest liturgical churches were the Eastern Orthodox and the Roman Catholic. The liturgy of the Eastern Orthodox Church centered on the risen Christ, and was rich in symbolism and mystery. The Roman Catholic Church is a sacramental church; that is, it observes such acts as baptism, confirmation, the Eucharist, penance, marriage, holy orders, and anointing of the sick. The Mass is the fixed order of worship used by the Roman Catholic Church.

During the Reformation, traditions known as Lutheran and Anglican evolved. The rich heritage of Lutheranism affirms the importance of music, along with theology and the active participation of the congregation in the services of worship. The chorale remains a unique Lutheran musical contribution to all traditions of Christian worship.

The American Protestant Episcopal Church originated with the Church of England, a liturgical church. The most important and influential document is the *Book of Common Prayer*, which has been in use, with slight modifications, since its restoration, in 1660. There are three services: Holy Communion, Morning Prayer, and Evening Prayer. The custom of composing anthems, as begun by English Tudor composers such as William Byrd, Thomas Tallis, and Orlando Gibbons, has been a most significant musical contribution from the Anglican tradition. While the shape of Episcopal worship has changed little since the Reformation, twentieth-century composers have continued to provide new service settings and anthems, while retaining unique musical styles.

Nonliturgical Worship   Although nonliturgical churches may find their roots in the Church of England and the Church of Scotland, they do not follow a fixed form of worship, such as the Mass or Morning Prayer. However, a semifixed shape has evolved.

American churches were greatly influenced by an immigrant and rural society; and the frontier church, with its emphases on simplicity and freedom of worship, developed an autonomous system of organization and of individuality of worship tradition. Except for the singing of the psalms, traditional European music—e.g., anthems by Tallis and by Byrd, and motets by Bach and by Brahms—is little used in American nonliturgical churches.

Worship in these churches is essentially a time for coming together, a time in which people experience a unity of heart and feeling with one another and with God. Elements that make up the nonliturgical service are:

1. *Praise*. In the worship of the free churches, hymns serve as a liturgy, as a response to the gospel.

2. *Prayer*. There is no set form of prayer. Extemporaneous and improvisatory prayer is offered by the worship leader, while unison prayers may be expressed by the whole congregation.

3. *Scripture*. Nonliturgical worship traditions draw their theology directly from the Bible. Through the Bible and its varied writings, God communicates to us; therefore, the reading of the scriptures is given a major role in the service of worship.

4. *Sermon*. Preaching the gospel is essential and primary in nonliturgical churches, and except for the reading of the Bible, all else in the service is secondary. Many nonliturgical churches emphasize evangelism and social action, and often devote money and time to ministering to "unbelievers" and, through missionaries, to spreading the gospel throughout the world.

5. *Sacraments*. Sacraments are *acts* of religious observance, rather than *symbols* of religious observance. Only two are retained by most nonliturgical churches: baptism and the Lord's Supper. Both infant baptism by sprinkling and adult baptism by immersion are practiced. The Lord's Supper is celebrated as a memorial, a feast of fellowship, and is simple, spiritual, and scriptural. Reformed churches set aside the word altar and the ideas associated with it, and use "table" instead; thus, what might have been called the altar in a liturgical tradition becomes a communion table in nonliturgical worship.

For readers interested in a deeper understanding of worship traditions, brief vignettes about the role of music in major worship traditions are in Appendix B.

CHAPTER 2

Working Within
the Church

In 1972 a delightful little book by Richard DeVinney was published. The title, *There's More to Church Music Than Meets the Ear*, provides a clue to its contents.[1] In witty and informal style DeVinney develops his basic premise that nonmusical considerations often do more to determine the success or failure of a church musician than musical competencies. In a more scholarly manner a recent survey of 5,000 lay and clergy members of Lutheran churches in the United States supports this idea.[2] Even a cursory reading of the study makes clear that its authors believe a person's qualities are often more important than any specific professional competencies. As one considers the nature and responsibilities of a musician in the church, it is imperative to be aware of interpersonal dynamics that are part of such a position. Suggesting a good book on interpersonal relationships might suffice (the two already cited would be helpful), or applying the Golden Rule and "good common sense" would help; yet there are specific considerations growing out of the unique relationships of musician to colleagues and musician to congregation that deserve some exploration.

The major person/persons with which the church musician must work is/are the clergy on the staff. In some churches the senior minister is the

---

[1]Richard DeVinney, *There's More to Church Music Than Meets the Ear* (Philadelphia: Fortress Press, 1972).
[2]Milo L. Brekke, Merton P. Strommen, and Dorothy L. Williams, *Ten Faces of Ministry* (Minneapolis: Augsburg Publishing House, 1979).

most powerful person by policy and/or constitution. In all churches the senior minister is a significant figure, if only by tradition. (Many ministers, well aware of their power, are cautious about utilizing it, believing that an enabling, encouraging style of leadership is more effective in the long run than one that is autocratic and dictatorial.) In most churches the senior minister is the person responsible for shaping worship. Therefore, since the ultimate goal of the church musician is to enrich worship through music, it is essential that the musician develop a good working relationship with him/her.

A major responsibility of the senior minister is to preach the word. Preparing and delivering the sermon is a time-consuming, demanding responsibility. It should be. The proclamation of God's word is an important dimension of worship in all branches of Christendom. In fact, some churches and ministers consider the sermon so central to worship that it becomes confused with worship. Such an attitude explains an order of worship in which the sermon is placed toward the close, with all other activities becoming a kind of warm-up for the main event—the sermon. (Interestingly, little justification for such an ordering of worship can be found in the classical shapes of early Christian worship.) Whether one considers the sermon an integral part of a larger structure or an end in itself, it is, in reality, a kind of performance, with the preacher expecting the undivided attention of the gathered congregation. Performing musicians should be able to understand this concept, since they prepare music and expect the same kind of attention.

All good performers must have a bit of healthy ego in their personality, but two strong and inflexible egos on one staff can lead to tension and trouble. Effort must constantly be made to avoid ego-related problems, recognizing, however, that these problems will still appear from time to time. Accepting them as such and keeping a clear perspective usually reduce tension to a minimum.

For example, the church musician who schedules a very lengthy anthem without consulting the minister should expect a negative reaction. Such a choice will make the service longer than usual unless the time allotted for other elements (perhaps even the sermon) is shortened. Since many events are planned for the few hours available on a Sunday morning—e.g., church school classes and meetings—a service that extends overtime can throw the rest of the morning's agenda into confusion. The ego of the musician who projected and prepared the long anthem comes into conflict with the ego of the minister who prepared the sermon and who is responsible for the overall worship-planning. A conference, in advance, to consider an appropriate way to schedule such special music can lessen the possibility of a tension-producing, ego-related problem.

Most ministers who preach regularly agree that the constant pressures of their many responsibilities tend to limit the amount of time they can devote to worship-planning and sermon preparation. There is much truth in the old cliché about the Holy Spirit not speaking until the secretary needs the sermon title. One way a pressured minister can feel helped rather than threatened by a competent church musician is through *creative sharing in planning worship*. The musician must offer assistance carefully and gently. "If I could share in some of your ideas regarding Advent-Christmas this year, I could begin to plan music accordingly." The minister must not feel that his/her control of worship-planning is lost, but rather that after being given the basic ideas, the musician is ready to help work out the details. Since the senior minister is ultimately responsible for worship, the musician must be sensitive to any concern over losing control of worship-planning.

A specific area in which the musician can assist and in which assistance is often appreciated is hymn selection. Most ministers assume that they should select all the hymns. When approached, they are usually open to dialogue about their selections. "Would you mind if I choose the opening hymns for each Sunday in May, so that I may prepare organ preludes based on these hymns? It takes a while to prepare hymns properly and to find free accompaniments or descants, so knowing the first hymn earlier would help me so much." Most ministers respond positively to such proposals, especially if the proposals involve opportunity for consultation and recognize the right of the minister to make the final decision. Many times a creative team relationship in worship preparation has evolved from a trust relationship in the selection of hymns.

Frequently, a minister or a director of Christian education is charged with overall responsibility for the educational program. The musician can be of help in this area from time to time. It is wise to express interest and readiness to assist, without being dogmatic or attempting to control things that are not part of your direct responsibility. It is also important to encourage use of good musical materials in the church school as part of preparation for active participation in worship. Many fine tunes with significant but understandable texts should be part of a child's experience in church school.

With the support of the director of Christian education, the church musician might offer informal music-training sessions for teachers. Study of appropriate musical materials and opportunities for teachers to develop their music skills will contribute toward a more effective children's choir program, since many musical learnings will be reinforced.

Some churches employ business managers to oversee much of the administrative detail, thus freeing ministers for pastoral care. While such persons may possess unique organizational skills, it is important to recognize that the church is unlike other institutions or businesses. Rigid application of fiscal or personnel efficiency formulas developed in an industrial situation frequently result in a troubled church and an unhappy staff. For example, much more may be gained by the minister and the musician informally discussing the strengths and weaknesses of the music program than by instituting a formal review process involving written evaluations by members of the congregation and/or colleagues, a procedure widely used in business and in academe.

Many churches engage more than one musician. Perhaps you are the organist, and there are others directing the choirs. Before assuming a position it is essential that you have a clear understanding concerning areas of responsibility and lines of authority. When a position is accepted and these relationships are determined, they must be respected until an evaluation is undertaken. Changing the rules while playing the game is dangerous business. To be more specific, if it is agreed that the adult choir director is the musician in charge, all must operate accordingly. After a spirit of trust develops, a more informal give-and-take is possible. No matter who is in charge, it is unwise to criticize or correct each other in public—in front of the choir. If you disagree about a tempo choice, disagree in private. While *you* may consider a discussion about proper tempo nothing more than two musicians talking about musical concepts, choir members may see it as an argument. Keeping this in mind will help to avoid many unfortunate situations.

One of the most important members of the nonprofessional or support staff is the secretary to the senior minister. The secretary can often provide good advice about the personality of "the boss," and can usually judge the appropriate time to present a new idea or suggestion.

Someone within the secretarial support staff will be responsible for preparing the Sunday service bulletin. Always be sensitive to the need for lead time in meeting printing or mimeographing deadlines. Often a dittoed or mimeographed form with blanks that can be completed weekly will expedite your work as well as the secretary's. Never assume the person typing the bulletin has competence in matters of spelling or in accent placement in foreign languages. A good way to ensure accuracy is to offer to proofread the entire bulletin.

A second publication may be a weekly or monthly newsletter. An occasional article or column commenting on an upcoming anthem or a new hymn, or an announcement and discussion of special programs, provides an opportunity for the musician to communicate with the congregation. Since many parishioners seldom get to know the musician, communication through the printed word can prove helpful. Again, be aware of publication deadlines in order to get material submitted in time and also to schedule other secretarial work. The best way to make an enemy of the secretary is to arrive at the church office needing a special letter reproduced at exactly the same time the newsletter or bulletin must be completed.

Another important person on the support staff is the custodian. It is wise to inform your custodian in advance if you expect to have special needs or plan to change a routine, e.g., a rehearsal in the sanctuary on a Saturday afternoon. Remember, custodians also plan their time and work responsibilities. If possible, deal directly with the custodian if you have a complaint or problem. Of course, if troubles persist, you must take them to the person or committee responsible for the physical welfare of the church. Assist the custodian where possible, such as taking responsibility for locking doors and turning out lights. Be sure you understand what is expected of the custodian by the church. Sometimes the musician expects the custodian to do more work—such as chair-arranging—than the church leaders have indicated to the custodian. Be prepared to secure volunteer help for special rehearsal preparations or programs if such work is not clearly the responsibility of the custodian. Usually, if you do not overload a custodian, you can expect ready assistance in time of emergency.

In addition to working with the paid staff, you must develop good relationships with the members of the congregation. Remember that the church is a group of volunteers. In this context *asking, never presuming,* and *appreciating, never assuming,* become wise expressions of an attitude of respect. Because they have volunteered to be part of a given congregation, people often feel a strong loyalty to it. In each person's mind his/her church is the most beautiful. Some devoted members in leadership positions may be the most provincial in their perspectives, since their very commitment to a given congregation precludes their visiting many other churches. The same can be said of many ministers. Their experience is usually less varied than that of church musicians, who often serve different denominations while in school, if not during their careers. Especially in theologically conservative churches, clergy tend to grow up in one denomination, attend church-related colleges of the same denomination, and then enroll in denominationally related seminaries. Because of the differences in background and experience, an idea that seems not the least bit radical or new to the musician may be rejected by the parishioners or ministers of a given church. Do not be surprised if your sensible, logical, time-proven idea meets with strong opposition. If you believe you are right, keep trying—gently, of course—and in time . . . maybe . . .! Honest compliments coupled with patience will work, whereas caustic criticism, even if justified, tends to harden opposition.

One of the best ways to develop trust is to do a good job in your position. As you demonstrate your competence, your credibility will improve. Another important way to build rapport and trust is for the congregation to come to know you as a person. For most people, especially those not involved in the music ministry, you will be an unknown. You do not speak to them through the sermon or shake their hands at the door. Your means of communication is nonverbal and much more subjective. Before worship you are hard at work in a last-minute rehearsal or in playing the prelude. After worship you are playing the postlude or putting away music. The only folk who come to know you are those who sing in the choirs, and often they see just one side of you—the professional music-maker.

As a church musician, you must be alert for opportunities for church members to come to know you. Attendance at parish social events and participation in the nonworship life of the church are essential if this "knowing" is to take place. Respond to invitations to visit or to provide a program for various organizations within the church. While you must guard against exploitation, you must be ready to share some of yourself in these ways. Through such sharing, people can come to know and trust you, and when they trust you, they will respond better to what you do as a musician.

As you become acquainted with the parishioners, single out some whose judgment you respect. "Was the organ too loud on that anthem?" "Do you think the congregation is ready to face the issue of a new organ?" In most churches there is usually a small group of interested people who function as a kind of sounding board for the professional staff. The best of these tend to be committees, provided for in a church's constitution. These committees function regularly, not just in emergencies. By working together a trusting relationship is nurtured and developed before problems arise. Acquaint yourself with the organizational structure of the church, and learn how it functions. As you begin to understand the various boards, committees, and groups within the parish, and perceive the lines of authority, you will be more comfortable working within the system, for you will develop the knowledge and skills to make your concerns known in the right places.

Perhaps the most important thing to keep in mind in any church situation is this: *How* it gets done is as significant as *what* gets done. The best music made by an uncooperative, difficult, and temperamental musician is not going to be effective in the long run. One must be an encourager—always ready to lead the congregation, with sensitivity and enthusiasm, in its pilgrimage of faith. It will be hard at times, but in the end it will be effective and satisfying.

CHAPTER 3

Expressing the Word

MUSIC FOR THE CONGREGATION

A significant and important theological concept is the priesthood of all believers, which affirms the responsibility of each individual in spiritual matters. Although each of us makes a personal response to God, in corporate worship we respond to God together, primarily through singing hymns and participating in the liturgy. In a service of worship the congregation is not the audience; rather, as Kierkegaard suggests, God is the audience and we are the actors.

In a very real sense, liturgy is an experience of worship by people. As a church musician, your primary responsibility is to provide a rich environment in which an understanding of and a sensitivity to the congregation's musical needs are evident. In all Christian worship the singing of hymns is a significant act by the congregation, for hymn-singing is not only a response to God but a means of proclamation as well.

Because hymn-singing is a congregational activity, the body of music called hymnody is, by definition, music of the people. It is democratic in spirit—more like secular folk song than art song. While the text is of primary importance, the tune is often more significant in determining whether a hymn is accepted or rejected, liked or disliked. Tune styles have varied greatly throughout the history of hymnody, and most contemporary hymnals affirm this diversity by including a wide range of tunes, e.g., plainsong, chorale, folk, gospel. In a significant way a good hymnal is an ecumenical rather than a denominational book, since it contains the best texts and tunes from many periods and cultural traditions.

20

Because hymns are meant to be sung by all worshipers, their structure must be relatively simple. Most are arranged in stanzas, so that the tune may be repeated. Melodies tend to be restricted in range, and uncomplicated in rhythmic or intervallic structure. Yet, like good texts, good tunes are miniature works of art that stand on their own merits.

In most instances the tune and the text of a hymn are not produced by the same person, or even in the same century. Since tunes may stand alone, without texts, each has been given a name of its own for identification. Some hymn tune names are based on the text, e.g., ALLEIN GOTT IN DER HOCH SEI EHR, LOBE DEN HERREN, and GO TELL IT ON THE MOUNTAIN); some refer to a place, e.g., NICAEA, HANOVER, ST. PETERSBURG; others are given names by the composer, e.g., MARION (name of the composer's mother), WOODLANDS (a house of Gresham School in Norfolk, England), and KALMAN (a composer's name). Most hymnals include the name of the tune with the hymn, as well as provide an index of tune names.

Hymn texts are categorized according to the number of syllables in each line. Certain arrangements have been used so often that they have been given names. The text below, for example, is 8.8.8.8., and is organized in a structure called long meter.

From all that dwell below the skies	8
Let the Creator's praise arise;	8
Let the Redeemer's name be sung	8
Through every land, by every tongue.	8

Others are short meter, 6.6.8.6.; common meter, 8.6.8.6.; and common meter doubled, 8.6.8.6.d. The *d* indicates that each stanza has eight lines, the last four having the same metrical pattern as the first four. A study of the metrical index of a hymnal reveals many common patterns, as well as a great variety of other patterns, including some that are "irregular" or one of a kind, e.g., SICILIAN MARINERS' HYMN (9.7.6.6.10.) and ECCE AGNUS (6.6.6.4.8.8.4.). It is possible to choose a text associated with one tune, find a second tune of the same meter, and sing the text with this "new" tune. One must always make such changes cautiously, to be sure that natural accents of the text correspond to the musical accents of the tune. An example of such a "divorce and remarriage" is Harry Emerson Fosdick's famous hymn "God of Grace and God of Glory," originally conceived to be sung with the tune REGENT SQUARE, but now usually sung to the Welsh tune CWM RHONDDA.

For the serious church musician, some knowledge of the historical development of hymnody is essential. The oldest and still the most important source of hymnody for Christian worship is the Psalter. Because of the poetic beauty of the psalms and their wide range of subject matter, they were immediately adopted for use in early Christian worship. Psalm-singing is done in many and varied ways. Some psalms are sung to simple musical formulas of a few notes, one of which is a reciting tone for the variable number of syllables in each line of text. These musical formulas have taken many forms, from the simple unison of ancient plainsong to the rich Anglican four-part (SATB) chants. For the majority of congregations, the most frequent encounter with psalm texts occurs in paraphrases such as Isaac Watts' version of Psalm 90, "Our God, Our Help in Ages Past."

The oldest hymn tunes found in hymnals today are plainsong melodies dating from the sixth to the twelfth centuries. An example is the text "Veni Creator Spiritus" and its companion tune, VENI CREATOR SPIRITUS. This ninth-century Latin text in praise of the Holy Spirit is set to a typical plainsong tune, characterized by a mystical, haunting quality. Except for a long note at the end of each phrase, the melody consists of even-flowing notes of the same value. These notes group themselves into patterns of twos and threes, in contrast to highly structured duple and triple meters found in later hymn tunes. While most contemporary hymnals feature light-textured accompaniments, these ancient tunes sound best when sung in unison, unaccompanied, and in a gentle, unhurried manner. Many of these lovely tunes and meaningful texts are well within the performance capabilities of the average congregation, provided they are introduced carefully.

During the Reformation, a major emphasis was placed on providing additional opportunities for congregational involvement in worship, and hymn-writing—of both texts and tunes—received special attention. A logical extension of this idea was the development of the hymn in the language of the people. Reformer Martin Luther actively encouraged the production of hymns and hymnals, and spent much time and energy adapting Roman Catholic hymnody and contemporary folk song literature for use in worship. The music most closely associated with the Lutheran church is the chorale—the name given to the hymn style introduced by Martin Luther and his contemporaries. These chorale melodies are rhythmically vital, modest in vocal range, and have a modal flavor. A good example is Luther's stirring tune EIN' FESTE BURG, composed for his paraphrase of Psalm 46. The original rhythmic version is striking in its strength and vigor. Later many of these chorale melodies were organized metrically and provided with rich harmonizations. The best examples of these revisions are J.S. Bach's exquisite harmonizations of chorales utilized in his cantatas and passions. Unfortunately, these isometric (metered) versions, while lovely in harmony, lose much of the rhythmic excitement of the originals. Many contemporary hymnals include both versions, so one may choose and compare.

John Calvin and his followers also made a contribution to hymnody. Calvinists believed that psalms were the only hymns appropriate for worship, since they were part of God's inspired Word. New paraphrases of the psalms appeared, in simple metrical shapes, along with tunes for singing. Melodies composed or adapted by Louis Bourgeois for the *Genevan Psalter* of 1551 are still in use. While more restrained rhythmically and melodically than German chorale melodies, the balance, shape, and melodic interest of these tunes make them ideal for congregational singing. Examples of such *Genevan Psalter* tunes still in use include OLD HUNDREDTH and PSALM 42. One problem with using the Psalter as the sole source for congregational hymnody is that the psalms are pre-Christian and lack any direct reference to the New Testament gospel. In 1719 Isaac Watts published *The Psalms of David Imitated in the Language of the New Testament and Applied to the Christian State and Worship.* Watts so "Christianized" some of the psalms that few people, even those who are biblically sensitive, think in terms of Psalm 72 when singing "Jesus Shall Reign Where'er the Sun," or of Psalm 98 when singing "Joy to the World." Watts also was successful in introducing "hymns of human composure" to reformed worship, in Calvinist churches in England and in Europe. Texts utilizing new, singable tunes became popular, and many of these reflected the excitement and thrill of New Testament themes, such as Christ's birth, ministry, resurrection, and ascension. Soon Charles and John Wesley joined Watts in producing hymns that spoke clearly and inspiringly to the new individual and personalized religious theology. Because of the contributions made by these men, the triumph of the hymn as a central part of congregational worship was assured.

During the nineteenth century an emotional and pietistic flavor permeated many poetic and musical works. The strong theology of Wesleyan texts and the folklike quality of tunes used with them deteriorated into a shallow, emotional style of writing. The important balance between head and heart (intellect and spirit) declined, and florid little tunes with simple harmonies and sentimental texts regularly appeared. Later called gospel songs, some of these had their origin in the revival meetings that were so popular in America and in England during the nineteenth and early twentieth centuries. Many tunes were weak imitations of popular songs of the day, with a strong foot-tapping beat and usually a refrain to be sung after each stanza.

Early in the twentieth century new trends began to influence hymnody. In England, Ralph Vaughan Williams was asked to be music editor for *The English Hymnal* (1906). He proposed replacing the most pallid and trite of nineteenth-century hymn melodies with folk tunes, as well as with new tunes composed in a style that benefited from a study of folk traditions. Inspired by Vaughan Williams' pioneering work, American musicians launched efforts to enlarge their repertoires of tunes through utilizing American folk music sources. A significant result of these efforts was the publication of *The Hymnal 1940* (Episcopal), which contained 109 tunes composed during the twentieth century, 44 new for that book. Many have a rhythmic elasticity within the bar line, reflecting a trend in much twentieth-century music.

Editors of American denominational hymnals have become interested in the rich treasury of early American music heretofore ignored, and have rediscovered music of the nineteenth-century frontier. Tunes like JEFFERSON, which first appeared in William Walker's 1835 songbook, *Southern Harmony*, are finding a rightful place in contemporary hymnody, along with other tunes from strong ethnic or regional roots. Through the pioneering work of Ethel and Hugh Porter in the *Pilgrim Hymnal, 1958*, the spiritual has been given its just place in hymnody.

In recent years churches have been flooded with "folk hymns." Since most of these are new both in text and tune, the term folk hymn is questionable. True folk music grows out of an aural tradition and the sharing of life's experiences, rather than being composed and handed to people. Yet the bouncy tunes and informal language of the best of this material—the work of Richard Avery and Donald Marsh, for example— may well have a place in worship. The ever-present danger is that this type of music may come to dominate or replace other hymns.

A steady thread running through the history of congregational song is a reaction/counterreaction to the tastes and preferences of preceding generations. Not all Victorian hymns are bad, nor are all sixteenth-century chorale tunes so good that they should be revived. Some folk hymns and gospel songs have great integrity and should be used. But it is essential to retain a perspective leavened with a clear understanding that *when* a hymn was written—whether today or a hundred years ago—has nothing to do with its quality.

Another concept to remember is that the word old has many different meanings. When one speaks of "the good old hymns," one is not usually referring to hymns of historical antiquity, but to those hymns learned as a child and many times associated with one's personal or religious experiences. In this context, a perceptive commentary on "the good old hymns" provides a fitting conclusion.

> Hymns under the title of "the good old hymns" are often used as an escape from reality. It is easy to settle comfortably into the belief that "the old time religion is good enough for me" and to forget that God has not made [God's] final revelation to any one person or any one generation. [The] Holy Spirit still moves among us to reveal new truth to those who will hear. While the psalms are a great body of hymn literature, imagine how poor would be our worship if the early church had stuck only to the good old hymns. There would be no song of Mary (Magnificat) and no song of Simeon (Nunc Dimittis). If nothing but the "good old hymns" had been allowed during the time of Martin Luther, perhaps there would have been no Reformation and certainly not "A Mighty fortress is our God." With only the good old hymns

in the Wesleyan revival there would have been none of Charles Wesley's 6,500 hymns. Who would wish to be without Harry Emerson Fosdick's great hymn of the present century, "God of Grace and God of glory"? To stick to nothing but the good old hymns—meaning the songs one learned as a child—is to stifle the Holy Spirit.[1]

MUSIC FOR THE CHOIR

One of the chief functions of the choir is to express the word of God through performances of such choral forms as the Mass, motet, anthem, chorale, cantata, oratorio, and opera. While no attempt is made here to provide a complete historical discussion of these forms, what follows will help the church choral director to review some of the traditional characteristics associated with such forms, along with examples of compositions that might be performed in church.

Mass   The Mass is the name of the service in Roman Catholic worship which celebrates the Eucharist. The Mass consists of items that change from day to day (Proper) and others that retain the same text (Ordinary). The Proper includes the Introit, Gradual, Offertory, and Communion. These are variable, according to the season, Sunday, or festival. The Ordinary includes the Kyrie Eleison, Gloria, Credo, Sanctus and Benedictus, and Agnus Dei.

I. Kyrie Eleison

Kyrie eleison.	Lord, have mercy upon us.
Christe eleison.	Christ, have mercy upon us.
Kyrie eleison.	Lord, have mercy upon us.

II. Gloria

Gloria in excelsis Deo,	Glory be to God on high,
Et in terra pax hominibus	and on earth, peace to men
bonae voluntatis.	of good will.
Laudamus te, Benedicimus te,	We praise thee, we bless thee,
Adoramus te, Glorificamus te,	we adore thee, we glorify thee,
Gratias agimus tibi	We give thanks to thee
propter magnam gloriam tuam,	for thy great glory.
Domine Deus, Rex caelestis,	Lord God, heavenly King,
Deus Pater omnipotens. Do-	Father Almighty. Lord,
mine, Fili unigenite, Jesu Christe,	the only begotten Son, Jesus Christ;

---

[1]Austin C. Lovelace and William C. Rice, *Music and Worship in the Church* (Nashville: Abingdon Press, 1976), p. 155. Used by permission.

Domine Deus, Agnus Dei,	Lord God, Lamb of God,
Filius Patris,	Son of the Father,
Qui tollis peccata mundi,	Who takest away the sins of the world,
miserere nobis,	have mercy upon us,
suscipe deprecationem nostram,	receive our prayer,
Qui sedes ad dexteram Patris,	Who sitteth at the right hand of the Father,
miserere nobis,	have mercy upon us,
Quoniam tu solus sanctus,	For thou only art holy,
tu solus Dominus,	thou only art the Lord,
tu solus altissimus,	thou only art the most high,
Jesu Christe,	Jesus Christ,
cum sancto spiritu in gloria	with the Holy Ghost, in the glory
Dei Patris, Amen.	of God the Father, Amen.

III. Credo

Credo in unum Deum,	I believe in one God,
Patrem omnipotentem,	Father Almighty,
factorem coeli et terrae,	maker of heaven and earth,
visibilium omnium	and of all things visible
et invisibilium,	and invisible,
Et in unum Dominum, Jesu Christum,	And in one Lord, Jesus Christ,
Filium Dei unigenitum,	the only begotten Son of God,
et ex Patre natum	born of the Father
ante omnia secula,	before all ages,
Deum de Deo, lumen de lumine,	God of God, light of light,
Deum verum de Deo vero,	Very God of Very God,
genitum non factum,	begotten, not made,
consubstantialem Patri,	of one substance with the Father,
per quem omnia facta sunt,	by whom all things were made,
Qui propter nos homines	Who for us men
et propter nostram salutem	and for our salvation
descendit de coelis.	came down from heaven.
Et incarnatus est	And became incarnate
de spiritu sancto	by the Holy Ghost
ex Maria Virgine	of the Virgin Mary
et homo factus est,	and was made man,
Crucifixus etiam pro nobis	And was crucified also for us
sub Pontio Pilato,	under Pontius Pilate,

passus et sepultus est,	suffered and was buried,
Et resurrexit tertia die	And the third day he rose again,
secundum scripturas,	according to the scriptures,
et ascendit in coelum,	and ascended into heaven,
sedet ad dexteram Patris,	and sitteth on the right hand of the Father,
et iterum venturus est	and he shall come again
cum gloria	with glory
judicare vivos et mortuos,	to judge the living and the dead,
cujus regni non erit finis.	whose kingdom shall have no end.
Et in Spiritum sanctum,	And in the Holy Ghost,
Dominum et vivificantem,	the lord and life-giver,
qui ex Patre Filioque procedit,	who proceedeth from the Father and the Son,
qui cum Patre et Filio	who with the Father and the Son
simul adoratur et conglorifica-tur,	together is adored and glorified,
qui locutus est per prophetas,	who spake by the prophets,
Et unam sanctam catholicam	And in one holy catholic
et apostolicam ecclesiam,	and apostolic Church,
Confiteor unum baptisma	I acknowledge one baptism
in remissionem peccatorum,	for the remission of sins,
Et expecto resurrectionem mor-tuorum,	And I expect the resurrection of the dead,
et vitam venturi saeculi,	and the life of the world to come,
Amen.	Amen.

IV. Sanctus et Benedictus

Sanctus, sanctus, sanctus,	Holy, holy, holy,
Dominus Deus Sabaoth,	Lord God of Hosts,
pleni sunt coeli et terra	heaven and earth are full
gloria tua.	of thy glory:
Osanna in excelsis.	Hosanna in the highest.
Benedictus qui venit	Blessed is he who cometh
in nomine Domini.	in the name of the Lord.
Osanna in excelsis.	Hosanna in the highest.

V. Agnus Dei

Agnus Dei,	Lamb of God,
qui tollis peccata mundi,	that takest away the sins of the world,
miserere nobis,	have mercy upon us.
dona nobis pacem.	Give us peace.

A special form of the Mass is the *Missa Pro Defunctis* (Mass for the Dead). It is called *requiem*. In a Requiem Mass certain sections of the Proper are made invariable, and are grouped with selected changes of the Ordinary in the following order: Introit, Kyrie Eleison, Gradual, Sequence, Offertory, Sanctus and Benedictus, Agnus Dei, and Communion.

During the Renaissance (1400-1600) the term mass, in reference to music, assumed its present-day meaning, i.e., a polyphonic setting of the entire Mass Ordinary. The main types of Mass composition from this period are:

Plainsong Mass: The polyphonic setting of a Gregorian Mass Ordinary. These masses are cyclical, in that they fully correspond to one of the plainsong cycles, e.g., Christmas, Epiphany, Solemn Feasts.

Cantus Firmus Mass: A Mass in which all the movements are based on the same melody, usually in the tenor
Based on hymns: Josquin: Missa Pange Lingua
Palestrina: Missa Salva Regina
Based on chanson: Obrecht: Missa Fortuna Desperata
Freely Invented: More open form, which still utilizes a cantus firmus
Obrecht: Missa Sine Nomine
Palestrina: Missa Brevis

With the decline of Mass composition after 1600, new developments led to the use of small instrumental ensembles and the addition of sections for solo voices and choruses. Gradually, the Mass was divided into a number of contrasting movements, culminating in the monumental *B Minor Mass* by J.S. Bach. Not until Beethoven's *Missa Solemnis* did a work appear that could withstand comparison with the Bach *B Minor*. Mozart, Haydn, Cherubini, Schubert, von Weber, Liszt, Gounod, and Bruckner continued to produce masses designed for liturgical use; during the twentieth century, masses have been written by such composers as Ralph Vaughan Williams, Paul Hindemith, Igor Stravinsky, and Leonard Bernstein.

Selected Masses

Renaissance

Byrd, William	Mass for Four Voices
Monteverdi, Claudio	Parody Mass a6 (1610)
	Mass a4 (post 1613)
Palestrina, Giovanni da	Missa Brevis
	Missa Papae Marcelli (Pope Marcellus Mass)
Tallis, Thomas	Missa Sine Nomine

Baroque

Buxtehude, Dietrich	Missa Brevis

Charpentier, Marc-Antoine	Messe de Minuit pour Noel (Midnight Mass for Christmas)
Schuetz, Heinrich	Requiem
Vivaldi, Antonio	Chamber Mass

Classical

Beethoven, Ludwig van	Mass in C
Cherubini, Luigi	Requiem in C Minor
	Mass in C (Coronation)
	F Major Mass
Haydn, Franz Joseph	Missa Brevis in F
	Missa Sancti Nicolai
	Missa Solemnis in B Flat
	Third Mass (Imperial/Lord Nelson)
Mozart, Wolfgang Amadeus	Jubilate Mass in C (Coronation)
	Mass in C Minor (Great)
	Missa Brevis in F
	Requiem

Romantic

Brahms, Johannes	A German Requiem
Bruckner, Anton	Mass #1 in D Minor (Symphonic)
	Mass #2 in E Minor
	Mass #3 in F Minor (Symphonic)
Dvořak, Anton	Requiem
Fauré, Gabriel	Requiem, Op. 48
Gounod, Charles	Messe Solemnelle
Janaček, Leoš	Slavonic Mass
Liszt, Franz	Missa Choralis
Schubert, Franz	Mass in G
	Mass in A Flat
Weber, Karl Maria von	Mass in G

Twentieth-century

Bernstein, Leonard	Mass
Britten, Benjamin	Missa Brevis in D
Delius, Frederick	Mass of Life
Duruflé, Maurice	Requiem, Op. 9

Hindemith, Paul	Requiem
Kodály, Zoltán	Missa Brevis
Langlais, Jean	Missa in Simplicitate
Satie, Erik	Mass for the Poor
Thompson, Randall	Mass of the Holy Spirit
Vaughan Williams, Ralph	Mass in G Minor

Motet   The motet is one of the most important forms of early polyphonic music developed during the Middle Ages and the Renaissance. It is an unaccompanied choral composition (usually sung in Latin) based on a sacred text. During the Renaissance the ever-increasing use of imitation culminated in the approximately 120 motets by the great Franco-Flemish composer Josquin des Prez. He often composed a separate motive, or melody, for each section, phrase, or sentence of text, and employed "word painting," in which a word was given vivid and symbolic treatment.

Interest soon spread; in Italy, motets sprung from the pens of Andrea Gabrieli, Giovanni da Palestrina, and Giovanni Gabrieli; in Spain, Christóbal Morales, Tomás Luis de Victoria; in England, Thomas Tallis and William Byrd; and in Germany, Ludwig Senfl, Jacob Handl, and Hans Leo Hassler. The motet reached new heights at St. Mark's in Venice, where Adrian Willaert (c. 1490-1562) served as *Maestro di capella* for 35 years (1527-62) and founded a style of music later called Venetian. This style, characterized by the use of a double choir, achieved its highest point of development in the works of Giovanni Gabrieli (c. 1557-1612), a composer whose imaginative use of tone color—both instrumental and vocal—movement from texture to texture, and use of short incisive phrases alternating with long melismata, exploited the use of contrast. In England, Thomas Tallis and William Byrd composed motets of rare beauty, characterized by heightened sensitivity to the meaning of texts.

During the baroque period (after 1600) compositions called motets introduced solo voices and independent instrumental accompaniment. Heinrich Schuetz's *Symphoniae Sacrae* (1629, 1647, 1650) are a treasure of masterpieces written in a variety of styles—some incorporating instruments or solo voices and alternation between singers and instruments. While Johann Christoph Bach, Johann Michael Bach, Dietrich Buxtehude, and Johann Pachelbel continued to write motets, the style did not reach its zenith until J.S. Bach's six motets were composed. Four of these are written for a double chorus of eight voices; *Jesu, meine Freude* is for five voices; and *Lobet den Herrn* is written for four voices and continuo.

The use of chorale melodies and their texts was a common feature of the German motet during the early eighteenth century. In a number of motets the chorale material is framed by choral settings of biblical text, upon which the chorale comments. Many of these motets are strophic (several verses), with the first verse set note against note and the remainder of the verses in imitative polyphonic style.

After J.S. Bach, the most significant composer of motets was Johannes Brahms, whose works display a heightened sensitivity to and mastery of the unaccompanied vocal style. Two of his motets frequently performed by church choirs are *Es ist das Heil uns kommen her* (Salvation Is Come unto Us) and *O Heiland, reiss die Himmel auf* (O Saviour, Rend the Heavens). The first work is in two sections: (1) a chorale setting of a single verse of the text, and (2) a series of fugal expositions using phrases from the chorale as subjects. The upper of two bass parts carries the melody in augmentation at the close of each exposition. The latter composition is a five-stanza poem set for four voices. The soprano carries the melody in verses one, two, and five, while the melody appears in the tenor in verse three and in the bass in verse four. The use of diminution in the three-note motif sung by the tenor at the beginning, contrasts with the chorale melody being sung by the soprano. Word-painting is employed in verse three, with staccato, jagged melodies alternating with long, legato phrases, extending the melody with triplet figures. Verse four contains increased use of chromaticism, and culminates in the final section marked allegro, which features a return to the polyphonic, melismatic style of the baroque.

French composers of motets include Jean Baptiste Lully (1632-87), Marc-Antoine Charpentier (1634-1704), André Campra (1660-1744), and Jean Philippe Rameau (1683-1764). The motets of Camille Saint-Saëns (1835-1921) include seven for solo voice and organ, five for two voices and organ, three for trio, one for treble quartet, and only four for chorus and organ. These functional pieces mark a return to simplicity, and utilize various vocal combinations.

Selected Motets

Renaissance

Byrd, William — Bow Thine Ear

Croce, Giovanni — Cantate Domino (O Sing Ye to the Lord)

Des Prez, Josquin — Miserere
O Domine Jesu Christe
Veni Sancte Spiritus

Gallus (Handl), Jacobus — Haec Est Dies (Easter)
Palestrina, Giovanni da — Hodie Christus Natus Est
Victoria, Tomás Luis de — Ne Timeas Maria
Jesu Dulcis Memoria (Advent)
O All Ye That Pass By (Lent)
Hosanna Filio David (Palm Sunday)

31

Baroque

Lotti, Antonio (ed. Dickinson)	Joy Fills the Morning
Praetorius, Hieronymous	Oculi Omnicum (We Turn Our Eyes to Thee)
Schuetz, Heinrich	I Am the Resurrection and the Life
	Lift Up Your Heads, O Ye Gates
Sweelinck, J.P.	Hodie Christus Natus Est

Classical

Haydn, Johann Michael	Plange Quasi Virgo (Son of God)
	O Vos Omnes (O Ye People)
Mozart, W.A.	Ave Verum

Romantic

Brahms, Johannes	Let Nothing Ever Grieve Thee
	O Saviour, Rend the Heavens
	Create in Me a Clean Heart, O Lord
Bruckner, Anton	Christus Factus Est (Christ Was Made Obedient)
Mendelssohn, Felix	Grant Us Thy Peace
Stanford, Charles Villiers	Three Motets (Latin)

Twentieth-century

Bender, Jan	Hosanna to the Son of David
Durufle, Maurice	This Day a Child
Hovhaness, Alan	Three Motets Op. 259 (Peace Be Multiplied, God Be Merciful unto Us, Wisdom)
Pinkham, Daniel	Behold, How Good and How Pleasant
Poulenc, Francis	O Magnum Mysterium
	Quem Vidistis Pastores Dicite
	Videntes Stellam
	Hodie Christus Natus Est
Vaughan Williams, Ralph	O Clap Your Hands
Zimmerman, Heinz Werner	O Sing unto the Lord

Canticle   The Roman, Anglican, and Lutheran liturgies include opportunities for the singing of certain canticles. A canticle is a hymnlike text, similar to a psalm but taken from a book of the Bible other than the book of Psalms. It is usually identified by the first few words of the Latin version of the text. The three *Cantica majora*, or greater canticles, are taken from the New Testament. These are the *Magnificat* (Song of Mary), from Luke 1:46-55; *Benedictus* (Song of Zechariah), Luke 1:68-79; and the *Nunc Dimittis* (Song of Simeon), Luke 2:29-32. The fourteen *Cantica minora,* or lesser canticles, are from the Old Testament. Certain psalms are suggested for use in the liturgies as well, and are often confused with the canticles, because their Latin names are used for identification. These include the *Venite* (Psalm 95) and the *Jubilate Deo* (Psalm 100). The *Te Deum,* which is not from the Bible but is an early Christian hymn, often is considered to be one of the major canticles.

All the canticles have been set to music in a variety of styles and lengths for use in worship. Many are relatively brief and could be used as anthems in nonliturgical situations. Throughout the history of music, certain canticles have been singled out for more elaborate settings. These include the *Magnificat* and the *Te Deum.* The others—*Jubilate Deo, Venite, Benedictus,* and *Nunc Dimittis*—also have been set extensively but usually in a less elaborate manner, since they are intended to be sung as part of the liturgy.

Magnificat

1. Magnificat anima mea Dominum.

My soul doth magnify the Lord,

2. Et exsultavit spiritus meus in Deo salutari meo.

And my spirit hath rejoiced in God my Saviour.

3. Quia respexit humilitatem ancillae suae: ecce enim ex hoc beatam me dicent omnes generationes.

For he hath regarded the low estate of his handmaiden: for behold, from henceforth all generations shall call me blessed.

4. Quia fecit mihi magna qui potens est: et sanctum nomen ejus.

For he that is mighty hath done to me great things; and holy is his name.

5. Et misericordia ejus a progenie in progenies timentibus eum.

And his mercy is on them that fear him, from generation to generation.

6. Fecit potentiam in brachio suo: dispersit superbos mente cordis sui.

He hath showed strength with his arm; he hath scattered the proud in the imagination of their hearts.

7. Deposuit potentes de sede, et exaltavit humiles.

He hath put down the mighty from their seats, and exalted them of low degree.

8. Esurientes implevit bonis: et divites dimisit inanes.

He hath filled the hungry with good things; and the rich he hath sent empty away.

9. Suscepit Israel puerum suum, recordatus misericordiae suae.

He hath holpen his servant Israel, in remembrance of his mercy;

10. Sicut locutus est ad patres nostros, Abraham et seminiejus in saecula.

As he spake to our fathers, to Abraham and to his seed for ever.

11. Gloria Patri, et Filio, et Spiritui Sancto.

Glory be to the Father, and to the Son, and to the Holy Ghost;

12. Sicut erat in principio, et nunc, et semper, et in saecula saeculorum. Amen.

As it was in the beginning, is now, and ever shall be, world without end. Amen.

Selected Magnificats

Renaissance

Byrd, William	Magnificat and Nunc Dimittis (Great Service)
Gibbons, Orlando	Magnificat and Nunc Dimittis
Monteverdi, Claudio	Magnificat #2
Tallis, Thomas	Magnificat and Nunc Dimittis
Weelkes, Thomas	Magnificat and Nunc Dimittis

Baroque

Bach, J.S.	Magnificat in D Major, BWV 243
Charpentier, Marc-Antoine	Grand Magnificat
Pachelbel, Johann	Magnificat in C Major

Twentieth-century

Lechner, Leonhard	Magnificat primi toni für vierstimmigen chor
Petrassi, Goffredo	Magnificat
Pinkham, Daniel	Festival Magnificat and Nunc Dimittis
Vaughan Williams, Ralph	Magnificat

Te Deum

We praise Thee, O God; we acknowledge Thee to be the Lord.
All the earth doth worship Thee, the Father everlasting.
To Thee all angels cry aloud; the heavens and all the powers therein.
To Thee cherubim and seraphim continually do cry,
Holy, holy, holy, Lord God of Sabaoth;
Heaven and earth are full of the majesty of Thy glory.
The glorious company of the apostles praise Thee;
The goodly fellowship of the prophets praise Thee;
The noble army of martyrs praise Thee;

The holy Church throughout all the world doth acknowledge Thee;
The Father of an infinite majesty;
Thine adorable, true, and only Son;
Also the Holy Ghost, the Comforter.

Thou art the King of glory, O Christ,
Thou art the everlasting Son of the Father.
When Thou tookest upon Thee to deliver man, Thou didst humble
Thyself to be born of a virgin.
When Thou hadst overcome the sharpness of death, Thou didst open the
Kingdom of Heaven to all believers.
Thou sittest at the right hand of God, in the glory of the Father.
We believe that Thou shalt come to be our Judge;
We therefore pray Thee, help Thy servants whom Thou hast redeemed
with Thy precious blood;
Make them to be numbered with Thy saints in glory everlasting.

O Lord, save Thy people and bless Thine heritage;
Govern them and lift them up for ever.
Day by day we magnify Thee,
And we worship Thy Name ever, world without end.
Vouchsafe, O Lord, to keep us this day without sin.
O Lord, have mercy upon us, have mercy upon us.
O Lord, let Thy mercy be upon us, as our trust is in Thee;
O Lord, in Thee have I trusted, let me never be confounded.

Selected Te Deums

Renaissance

Anerio, Felice	Te Deum
Kerle, Jacobus	Te Deum
Palestrina, Giovanni da	Te Deum

Baroque

Charpentier, Marc-Antoine	Te Deum in D Major
Scarlatti, Alessandro	Te Deum

Classical

Haydn, Franz Joseph	Te Deum in C Major

Romantic

Berlioz, Hector	Te Deum
Dvořak, Anton	Te Deum
Verdi, Giuseppe	Te Deum

Twentieth-century

Britten, Benjamin	Festival Te Deum
Kodály, Zoltán	Te Deum
Mathias, William	Festival Te Deum
Pepping, Ernst	Te Deum
Persichetti, Vincent	Te Deum
Titcomb, Everett	Festival Te Deum
Vaughan Williams, Ralph	Te Deum

Jubilate Deo

O be joyful in the Lord, all ye lands; serve the Lord with gladness, and come before His presence with a song.

Be ye sure that the Lord He is God; it is He that hath made us, and not we ourselves; we are His people and the sheep of His pasture.

O go your way into His gates with thanksgiving, and into His courts with praise; be thankful unto Him, and speak good of His Name.

For the Lord is gracious; His mercy is everlasting; and His truth endureth from generation to generation.

Glory be to the Father, and to the Son, and to the Holy Ghost; as it was in the beginning, is now, and ever shall be, world without end. Amen.

Venite

O come, let us sing unto the Lord;
let us heartily rejoice in the strength of our salvation.

Let us come before His presence with thanksgiving;
and show ourselves glad in Him with psalms.

For the Lord is a great God and a great King above all gods.

In His hand are all the corners of the earth;
and the strength of the hills is His also.

The sea is His and He made it;
and His hands prepared the dry land.

O come, let us worship and fall down,
and kneel before the Lord our Maker.

For He is the Lord our God;
and we are the people of His pasture,
and the sheep of His hand.

O worship the Lord in the beauty of holiness;
let the whole earth stand in awe of Him.

Glory be to the Father, and to the Son, and to the Holy Ghost;
As it was in the beginning, is now,
and ever shall be, world without end.   Amen.

Benedictus

Blessed be the Lord God of Israel; for He hath visited and redeemed His
    people:
And hath raised up a mighty salvation for us in the house of His servant
    David;

As he spake by the mouth of His holy prophets, which have been since
    the world began:
That we should be saved from our enemies, and from the hand of all that
    hate us;

To perform the mercy promised to our forefathers, and to remember His
    holy covenant;
To perform the oath which He sware to our forefather Abraham, that he
    would give us;

That we, being delivered out of the hand of our enemies, might serve Him
    without fear,
In holiness and righteousness before Him, all the days of our lives.

And thou, child, shalt be called the prophet of the Highest: for thou shalt
    go before the face of the Lord to prepare His ways;
To give knowledge of salvation unto His people for the remission of their
    sins,

Through the tender mercy of our God; whereby the Dayspring from on
    high hath visited us,
To give light to them that sit in darkness and in the shadow of death, and
    to guide our feet into the way of peace.

Glory be to the Father, and to the Son, and to the Holy Ghost;
As it was in the beginning, is now, and ever shall be, world without
    end.   Amen.

Nunc Dimittis

Lord, now lettest Thou Thy servant depart in peace according to Thy
word.

For mine eyes have seen Thy salvation,

Which Thou hast prepared before the face of all people;

To be a light to lighten the Gentiles and to be the glory of Thy people,
Israel.

Glory be to the Father, and to the Son, and to the Holy Ghost;

As it was in the beginning, is now, and ever shall be, world without
end.   Amen.

Anthem   The anthem grew out of the motet and became a choral
composition in English, based on words from the Bible or another
religious text. Originating in England, the anthem utilized short phrases
and was generally syllabic. The verse anthem, introduced by William
Byrd at the end of the sixteenth century, contained choruses that
alternated with sections for a single voice or solo voices. While
Elizabethan anthems were polyphonic and, with the exception of verse
anthems, usually sung a cappella, anthems composed during the
seventeenth century became more homophonic, declamatory, and
frequently utilized accompaniments. During the latter part of the
seventeenth century, Henry Purcell (1659-95) and John Blow (1648-1708)
introduced instrumental interludes, which separated the solos and
choruses. Thus, the anthem came to resemble the cantata somewhat. A
unique characteristic of some English anthems was the use of alternating
halves of the choir—*decani* on the south, or dean's, side; and the *cantoris*
on the north, or precentor's, side.

Worship in the king's chapel (Chapel Royal) and in other royal estates
frequently included extended verse anthems composed for choir,
soloists, and orchestra. Henry Purcell, musical genius of the Restoration,
brought the verse anthem to its height, utilizing solos, ensembles,
choruses, and instrumental accompaniment.

The Chandos and Coronation anthems by baroque composer George
Frederick Handel (1685-1759) are examples of the more highly developed
choral-cantata anthem, which contained brilliant choruses punctuated by
instrumental flourishes, and remarkable examples of word-painting.
Following Purcell and Handel, church music in England declined, and
only a few composers, such as Maurice Greene (1694-1735) and William
Boyce (1710-79), continued the English anthem tradition.

In the music of Samuel Sebastian Wesley (1810-76) a momentary spark
of quality can be found in what was for English church music a rather
dismal period. Today Wesley is remembered chiefly for his beautiful
shorter anthems and for his stubborn pursuit of musical excellence in the

face of almost impossible circumstances. Toward the end of the nineteenth century the music of Charles Villiers Stanford (1852-1924), especially his six motets (a type of anthem given the name motet), provided another brilliant moment, but it was not until well into the twentieth century that any significant number of quality anthems began to appear.

After 1900 a fresh new style, inspired by sixteenth-century Tudor polyphony and traditional English folk music, provided the impetus for a new era of English contributions to church music. Anthems by Gustav Holst and Ralph Vaughan Williams soon had companions in the works of Herbert Howells and Benjamin Britten. Rhythmic activity and freedom, along with new post-Romantic but not atonal harmonic ideas, characterized much of this music.

Some of the first American anthem composition occurred when a group of Pietists, later to be called Moravians, settled in Bethlehem, Pennsylvania. Moravian composers John Frederik Peter (1746-1813) and John Antes (1741-1811) produced some of the first significant American church music. Lowell Mason (1792-1872), the well-known music educator, composed pieces called anthems, although these were shorter and less complex than their English counterparts from the same period.

By the late nineteenth century, especially in America, the term anthem had lost much of its earlier musical and liturgical connotation (originally a piece to be sung at a specific place in the Anglican liturgy for Evening Prayer). American composers of anthems at the turn of the century include Mrs. H.H.A. Beach, Dudley Buck (1839-1909), Horatio Parker (1863-1919), and Harry Rowe Shelley. Almost all their anthems feature a solo voice or a quartet, and have become known as "anthems for solo voices" or "anthems for solos with mixed quartets," rather than anthems for mixed chorus. While this style of composition no longer dominates American church music, in many places the taste for this type of anthem remains strong.

American composers of the early twentieth century who have contributed to the sacred choral anthem repertoire include Seth Bingham, F. Melius Christiansen, Joseph W. Clokey, Clarence Dickinson, Helen A. Dickinson, Harold W. Friedell, Leo Sowerby, Everett Titcomb, and David McK. Williams.

Another type of anthem that evolved late in the nineteenth century and that has become increasingly popular is the hymn anthem, a composition which usually quotes a hymn tune and text, sometimes in conjunction with a free polyphonic texture reminiscent of chorale-based cantata movements of earlier times. Other hymn anthems employ a variation technique, in which each stanza of the hymn is given a new setting, frequently with organ interludes. Early examples can be found in the work of Stanford, Vaughan Williams, and Holst. F. Melius Christiansen's settings of *Beautiful Saviour* and *Wake, Awake* are examples of a cappella hymn anthems, and Heinz Werner Zimmermann's settings of Psalm 100 (quoting OLD HUNDREDTH) and Psalm 23 (quoting ST. COLUMBIA) are complex, rhythmically invigorating, jazz-inspired compositions.

During the second half of this century, choral compositions based upon a religious text of any length and for any combination of voices are now called anthems. There has been a rise in the use of gospel songs and gospel styles, as well as an increase in various popular idiomatic conventions, e.g., irregular rhythms, syncopation, "blues" patterns, and use of guitar and folk instrument accompaniments. Composers such as Alan Hovhaness, Jean Berger, Richard Dirkson, and Healey Willan have retained the classic anthem tradition, while others, e.g., John Gardner, John Rutter, and Walter Watson have incorporated jazz rhythms and sophisticated popular techniques into their works. A few composers, such as Leslie Basset and Daniel Pinkham, have introduced electronic tape and avant-garde vocal sounds as innovative musical expression of religious texts.

Selected Examples of the Anthem

English Tudor

Byrd, William	I Will Not Leave You Comfortless
	Look Down, O Lord
	Sing Joyfully unto God
Gibbons, Orlando	Almighty and Everlasting God
	Hosanna to the Son of David
	O Clap Your Hands
Weelkes, Thomas	Alleluia, I Heard a Voice
	Hosanna to the Son of David

Restoration

Blow, John	I Was Glad
	The Lord Is My Shepherd
Purcell, Henry	Hear My Prayer, O Lord
	O Sing unto the Lord (verse anthem)
	Rejoice in the Lord (verse anthem)

Baroque

Boyce, William	O Sing unto the Lord a New Song
	Turn Thee unto Me

Greene, Maurice	Acquaint Thyself with God
	Blessed Are Those That Are Undefiled
Handel, George Frederick	Six Chandos Anthems
	Three Coronation Anthems

Classic/Romantic

Stanford, Charles Villiers	The Lord Is My Shepherd
Wesley, Samuel Sebastian	Cast Me Not Away
	Thou Wilt Keep Him in Perfect Peace

Moravian

Antes, John	Go, Congregation, Go
Geisler, Johann	Glory to God in the Highest
Peter, John Frederik	Blessed Are They
Peter, Simon	Behold a Sight

Twentieth-century

Basset, Leslie	Collect
Beach, H.H.A., Mrs.	Hymn to the Sun
Berger, Jean	I Will Lift Up Mine Eyes
	A Rose Touched by the Sun's Warm Rays
Britten, Benjamin	Antiphon
	Hymn to St. Peter
Christiansen, F. Melius	Beautiful Saviour
	Lamb of God
	Wake, Awake
Dickinson, Clarence	Christmas Story
	O Nightingale, Awake
Dirkson, Richard	Christ Our Passover
Finzi, Gerald	God Is Gone Up
Friedell, Harold W.	Draw Us in the Spirit's Tether
	For This Cause
	Jesus, So Lowly
Gardner, John	Five Hymn Anthems in Popular Style
Holst, Gustav	Christmas Day
	Let All Mortal Flesh (hymn anthem)
	Turn Back, O Man (hymn anthem)

41

Hovhaness, Alan	Out of the Depths
Howells, Herbert	Like as the Hart
	A Spotless Rose
Joubert, John	Torches
Noble, T. Tertius	Souls of the Righteous
Pelz, Walter	At the Lamb's High Feast
Pinkham, Daniel	In the Beginning
Rutter, John	O Praise the Lord
	Shepherd's Pipe Carol
Sowerby, Leo	I Will Lift Up Mine Eyes
	Now There Lightens upon Us
Thiman, Eric	Fight the Good Fight
	Immortal, Invisible
Vaughan Williams, Ralph	Miles Lane (hymn anthem)
	O How Amiable
	O Taste and See
	Old Hundredth (hymn anthem)
Watson, Walter	Gloria, Gloria, Praise Be to God
Willan, Healey	Behold the Tabernacle of God
	Rise Crowned with Light (hymn anthem)
Williams, David McK.	In the Year That King Uzziah Died
Zimmerman, Heinz Werner	Psalm 100
	Psalm 23

Passion   A passion is a setting of the text of the Passion of Christ according to one of the four evangelists—Matthew, Mark, Luke, or John. It is a dramatic form that usually includes among its participants Jesus, Peter, Pilate, Judas, the mob (chorus), and a narrator, who tells the story. The magnificent Bach passions—*Passion According to St. John* and *Passion According to St. Matthew*—utilize recitatives and short choruses to express the biblical text. Poetic texts are used for the arias and large choruses. Various settings of *The Seven Last Words*, such as that of Heinrich Schuetz (1585-1672), fall into the same category as the passions. Passions by Schuetz include that of *St. Matthew*, of *St. John*, and of *St. Luke*. Common characteristics of his passions are (1) absence of any instrumental music; (2) strict adherence to the biblical text, with the exception of the *Exordium* and the *Conclusio;* (3) restriction of the dramatic roles to unaccompanied solo-singing; and (4) all the crowd scenes are set for SATB.[2] While no less dramatic, the passions of Schuetz are much more restrained than the great Bach passions, and are generally much shorter. After Bach, few

---

[2] Elwyn A. Wienandt, *Choral Music of the Church* (New York: The Free Press, 1965), p. 302.

composers were attracted to the form, although the classical composer Haydn and the romantic French composer Theodore Dubois also wrote settings of *The Seven Last Words*.

During the late nineteenth century Sir John Stainer (1840-1901) composed his popular *The Crucifixion*, a work that was unchallenged for many years. Each quotation from scripture is sung in recitative, and poetry is used for solo arias, ensembles, or choruses. The five hymns used throughout the work serve a function similar to the chorale in German passions. The chromatic tunes and straightforward harmonies, along with catchy rhythmic devices, held the interest of English-speaking congregations in Great Britain and in America.

Two leading composers of the twentieth-century liturgical revival are Hugo Distler and Ernst Pepping. Distler's affinity for the baroque and for Heinrich Schuetz is reflected in his *Choral-Passion*, where his unaccompanied treatment of text drawn from all four Gospels is a direct descendant from the passions of Schuetz. The passion chorale serves as a unifying feature, framing each of the seven sections. Ernst Pepping's *Passion According to St. Matthew* was composed in 1949-50 and is a motet passion; thus it has no soloists. The text is divided between two choruses; one telling the Gospel version of the Passion and the other commenting on or intensifying the text of the first chorus.

Among composers considered avant-garde, Krzysztof Penderecki, of Poland, has produced a work of enormous scope and power called *The Passion and Death of Our Lord Jesus Christ According to St. Luke*. His incorporation of new sonorities and contemporary compositional techniques serves to heighten the dramatic impact of this extraordinary work.

Selected Passions

Renaissance

Victoria, Tomas de	St. Matthew Passion

Baroque

Bach, J.S.	St. John Passion
	St. Matthew Passion
	St. Luke Passion
Schuetz, Heinrich	St. Matthew Passion
	St. Luke Passion
	St. John Passion
	The Seven Last Words
Telemann, George Philipp	St. John Passion
Walther, Johann	St. Matthew Passion

Classical
Haydn, Franz Joseph   The Seven Last Words

Twentieth-century
Dubois, Theodore   The Seven Last Words

Cantata   The cantata is a short, dramatic choral work developed during the baroque period, and consists of a number of movements, such as arias, recitatives, duets, and choruses. Cantatas for the church are based on religious texts: biblical, poetical, dramatic. During the baroque period, cantatas often included an instrumental introduction and closed with a stanza of a chorale. Dietrich Buxtehude (1637-1707) wrote more than 120 cantatas of all types and styles, from simple choral cantatas to those with elaborate solos and choruses accompanied by orchestral instruments. These cantatas are rich in text interpretation and romantic lyricism.[3]

The greatest composer of chorale cantatas was Johann Sebastian Bach (1685-1750), who wrote more than 300 cantatas—188 of them, sacred—of which over 200 have been preserved. The majority of these cantatas are set for soloists, a four-voice choir, and orchestral accompaniment. The great emphasis on instrumental music during the baroque is evidenced through such devices as fugal passages appearing as concertato choruses, melismatic vocal melodies highly expressive of the text, extended choruses approaching a choral fantasia style, and increasing use of obbligato instruments and orchestral accompaniments. What makes Bach's cantatas stand out from all others is not their musical artistry, but rather "their intellectual penetration, the facility of their word interpretation and the breadth of vision, which never loses sight of the totality of text and its connotations."[4]

With the rise of the oratorio, the smaller church cantata fell into decline, and few composers of the eighteenth and nineteenth centuries chose to write in this form. During the twentieth century there has been renewed interest in writing church cantatas, as evidenced by the compositions of Benjamin Britten, Zoltán Kodály, Ralph Vaughan Williams, Alan Hovhaness, Aaron Copland, Dave Brubeck, Daniel Pinkham, and others.

Selected Cantatas
Baroque
Bach, J.C.   THE CHILDHOOD OF CHRIST
Bach, J.S.   #79 GOTT, DER HERR IST SONN' UND
                               SCHILD (Reformation)

---

[3] Friedrich Blume, *Protestant Church Music* (New York: W.W. Norton, 1974), pp. 274-75.
[4] Ibid., p. 282.

	#4 CHRIST LAG IN TODESBANDEN (Easter)
	#80 EIN' FESTE BURG (Reformation)
	#142 UNS IST EIN KIND GEBOREN (Christmas)
	#106 GOTTES ZEIT IST DIE ALLERBESTE ZEIT
	#140 WACHET AUF (Advent)
	#41 JESU, NUN SEI GEPREISET (New Year's)
Buxtehude, Dietrich	COMMAND THINE ANGEL THAT HE COME
	OPEN TO ME, GATES OF JUSTICE
	REJOICE, BELOVED CHRISTIANS
	REJOICE, EARTH AND HEAVEN
	SING TO THE LORD (solo cantata)
Pachelbel, Johann	WHAT GOD ORDAINS IS ALWAYS GOOD

Twentieth-century

Barber, Samuel	PRAYERS OF KIERKEGAARD
Britten, Benjamin	REJOICE IN THE LAMB
	ST. NICHOLAS
Debussy, Claude	L'ENFANT PRODIGUE (A Lyric Scene)
Distler, Hugo	A LITTLE ADVENT MUSIC
Gardner, John	CANTATA FOR EASTER
Honneger, Arthur	CANTATE DE NOEL (Christmas Cantata)
Hovhaness, Alan	GLORY TO GOD (Christmas)
	I WILL LIFT UP MINE EYES
	IN THE BEGINNING WAS THE WORD
	MAKE A JOYFUL NOISE
	PRAISE THE LORD WITH PSALTERY
Kirk, Theron	NOËL
Lekberg, Sven	LORD OF THE EARTH AND SKY
Lockwood, Norman	CHOREOGRAPHIC CANTATA
	THE HOLY BIRTH
Pinkham, Daniel	EASTER CANTATA
Siegmeister, Elie	CHRISTMAS IS COMING
and Wheeler, Rufus	(Customs and Traditions)
Sowerby, Leo	CHRIST REBORN
Thiman, Eric	THE EARTH IS THE LORD'S
	THE FLOWER OF BETHLEHEM (2 parts)
	THE NATIVITY
Vaughan Williams, Ralph	DONA NOBIS PACEM
	HODIE CHRISTUS NATUS EST

Oratorio   An oratorio is a large dramatic work based on a religious text, which is performed in concert, without costumes or scenery. In an oratorio there is often a narrator, who introduces the various characters. During the early seventeenth century G. Carissimi (1605-74) wrote *Jeptha*, his masterpiece in miniature, which was characterized by tersely dramatic scenes and brilliant use of rhythm. Alessandro Scarlatti and Marc-Antoine Charpentier, two of Carissimi's students, also wrote in this form.

The first German composer of oratorios was Heinrich Schuetz. In his *Christmas Story*, Schuetz exhibits a rich use of musical symbolism: rising melodic figures expressive of angels call Joseph to arise; moving rhythmic figures represent the wise men coming to the manger, and florid melodies portray such active verbs as "fly," "go," and "run."

To many people the term oratorio is synonymous with the oratorios of Handel, especially *Messiah*. These works were written for the concert hall rather than the church, and *Messiah* is atypical, since it includes little dramatic action. Of the many oratorios composed by Handel, those particularly worthy of mention are *Judas Maccabaeus, Saul, Israel in Egypt, Samson, Belshazzar,* and *Jeptha*.[5]

During the eighteenth century, choral music was no longer solely identified with the church, and composers wrote lengthy works on biblical texts for chorus and orchestra. One of the greatest of these is Haydn's *The Creation*, a work of large dimensions that utilizes many fine choruses and solos, which reflects Haydn's debt to Handel and to the English tradition. Beethoven wrote only one oratorio—*The Mount of Olives*—and while it has some great moments, it lacks a certain sensitivity to vocal materials.

With Felix Mendelssohn (1809-47) the oratorio was revived, and once again it became a viable sacred form. His *Saint Paul*, a work that is of uneven quality, contains many beautiful choruses and arias, such as "How Lovely Are the Messengers," that are familiar to many church musicians. *Elijah*, which was composed ten years after *Saint Paul*, is operatic in style and dramatic in effect. Familiar excerpts from this oratorio include "If with All Your Hearts You Truly Seek Me," "O Rest in the Lord," "Lord God of Abraham," and "Ho, Everyone That Thirsteth"—standard repertory for many soloists and church choirs.

Franz Liszt's only oratorio composed for the church is *Christus*, a Latin

---

[5] For a thorough discussion of Handel's oratorios, see *Handel: A Symposium*, ed. Gerald Abraham (New York: Oxford University Press, 1954).

work that draws its text directly from the Bible and from Roman Catholic liturgical texts. Hector Berlioz continued the concert tradition with his *L'Enfance du Christ*. "The Shepherds' Farewell" is a well-known choral excerpt from this large dramatic work. Camille Saint-Saëns (1835-1921) wrote a *Christmas Oratorio*, a short work employing the harp as accompaniment. The closing chorus, "Praise to the Lord of Hosts," is performed frequently by both church and high school choirs.

A significant recent work in the French dramatic idiom is Arthur Honegger's *Le Roi David* (King David). It is so close to being a theatrical work that it is sometimes difficult to place it in the oratorio tradition. Its 27 sections give the impression of a series of unrelated episodes, although its dramatic impact cannot be overlooked.

The oratorio *Dies Irae* (Auschwitz Oratorio), by Krzysztof Penderecki, is a strong and significant concert work from this influential contemporary Polish composer.

Other Choral Forms   Composers since the Renaissance have used poetry, biblical texts, and literary writings—often in combination—to produce a variety of other works. Certain Latin hymns and liturgical texts have received special attention by many composers. Among these are the *Gloria in Excelsis* (A Hymn of Praise from the Mass) and the *Stabat Mater* (a thirteenth-century sequence). Twentieth-century composers have created an assortment of shorter choral works frequently set for soloist, chorus, and instrumental accompaniment.

Selected Examples of the *Gloria in Excelsis*
(See pp. 25-26 for text)

Poulenc, Francis
Rutter, John
Vivaldi, Antonio

The *Stabat Mater*, a thirteenth-century sequence based on the following text, has been set by composers from most of the periods in history.

Stabat Mater	*Tribulation*
Stabat mater dolorosa Juxta crucem lacrymosa, Dum pendebat Filius.	Lord most holy! Lord most mighty! Righteous ever are Thy judgments. Hear and save us, for Thy mercies' sake.

47

Cujus animam gementem
contristantem et dolentem
  Pertransivit gladius.
O quam tristis et afflicta
Fuit illa benedicta
  Mater Unigeniti;
Quae moerebat, et dolebat
Et tremebat, cum videbat
  Mati poenas inclyti.

Quis est homo quin non fleret
Christi matrem si videret
  In tanto supplicio?
Quis non posset contristari
Piam matrem contemplari
  Dolentem cum Filio?

Pro peccatis suae gentis
Vidit Jesum in Tormentis,
  Et flagellis subditum.
Vidit suum dulcem natum
Morientem desolatum
  Dum emisit spiritum.

Eia, mater, fons amoris,
Me sentire vim doloris
  Fac, ut tecum lugeam.
Fac ut ardeat cor meum
In amando Christum Deum,
  Ut sibi compaceam.

Lord! vouchsafe Thy loving-
kindness,
Hear me in my supplication,
  And consider my distress.
Lo! my spirit fails within me,
Oh! regard me with compas-
sion,
  And forgive me all my sin!
Let Thy promise be my refuge,
Oh, be gracious and redeem me,
  Save me from eternal death!

Power eternal! Judge and Father!
  Who shall blameless stand
before Thee,
    Or who Thy dreadful anger
fly!
Hear, and aid us strength to
gather
  To obey Thee, still adore
Thee,
    In hope and faith to die!

Through the darkness Thou wilt
lead me,
In my trouble Thou wilt heed
me,
  And from danger set me free.
Lord! Thy mercy shall restore
me,
And the day-spring shed before
me,
  All salvation comes from
Thee!

Thou hast tried our hearts to-
wards Thee;
but if Thou wilt not forsake us,
our souls shall fear no ill.
  Lord! we pray Thee, help Thy
people;
save, O save them; make them
joyful, and bless Thine inheri-
tance.

Sancta mater, istud agas,
Crucifixi fige plagas
  Corde meo valide.
Tui nati vulnerati,
Tam dignati pro me pati,
  Poenas mecum divide.
Fac me vere tecum flere
Crucifixo condolere,
  Donec ego vixero.
Justa crucem tecum stare,
Te libenter sociare
  In planctu desidero.
Virgo, virginum praeclara,
Mihi jam non sis amara,
  Fac me tecum plangere.

Fac ut portem Christi mortem,
Passionis ejus sortem,
  Et plagas recolere
Fac me plagis vulnerari,
Cruce hâc inebriari,
  Ob amorem Filii.

Inflammatus et accensus
Per te, Virgo, sim defensus
  In die judicii.
Fac me cruce custodiri,
Morte Christi praemuniri,
  Confoveri gratiâ.

Quando corpus morietur,
Fac ut animae donetur
  Paradisi gloria.

In sempiterna saecula. Amen.

I have longed for Thy salvation, and my hope was in Thy goodness! Blessed be Thy Name, O Lord, for ever!

Now and henceforth, we beseech Thee, turn our hearts to Thy commandments, and incline them evermore to keep Thy law.

Give Thy servants understanding, so that they may shun temptation, and in all things follow Thee.

Oh! vouchsafe us true repentance, teach us always to obey Thee, and to walk the way of peace.

Let Thy light so shine before us,
  And Thy mercy be upon us,
    Ev'n as is our trust in Thee.

I will sing of Thy great mercy, for I was in deep affliction, and Thou didst deliver me. I will call unto the people, and the nations all shall hear me, and shall praise Thy holy Name!

When Thou comest to the judgment, Lord, remember Thou Thy servants! None else can deliver us.

Save, and bring us to Thy kingdom, there to worship with the faithful, and for ever dwell with Thee!

Hear us, Lord! We bless the Name of our Redeemer! and His great and wondrous mercies now and ever glorify!

To Him be glory evermore. Amen.

Selected *Stabat Maters*

Renaissance
Des Prez, Josquin
Lassus, Orlando
Palestrina, Giovanni da

Baroque
Pergolesi, Giovanni
Scarlatti, Alessandroni
Scarlatti, Dominico

Romantic
Dvořak, Anton
Rossini, Gioacchino
Schubert, Franz
Stanford, Charles Villiers
Verdi, Giuseppe

Twentieth-century
Persichetti, Vincent
Poulenc, Francis
Thompson, Randall

Other Choral Forms

Medieval

Maastricht Easter Play (Liturgical Drama, ed. Wilbur W. Hollman)

Baroque
Buxtehude, Dietrich   The Little Newborn Jesus Child
Charpentier, Marc-Antoine   Song of the Birth of Our Lord
                             Jesus Christ
Schuetz, Heinrich   Psalms of David

Classical
Mozart, W.A.   Litany in B Flat, K.125
                             Vesperae Solennes de Confessore, K.339

Romantic
Brahms, Johannes   Alto Rhapsody
Mendelssohn, Felix   Hymn of Praise
Rachmaninoff, Sergei   Songs of the Church

Twentieth-century

Berger, Jean	Vision of Peace
Britten, Benjamin	Ceremony of Carols
	Canticle II: Abraham and Isaac, op.51
Fetler, Paul	A Contemporary Psalm
Hanson, Howard	The Cherubic Hymn
Peeters, Flor	Song of Joy
Respighi, Ottorino	Laud to the Nativity
Sowerby, Leo	Forsaken of Man
Thompson, Randall	The Nativity According to St. Luke
Vaughan Williams, Ralph	Benedicte
	A Song of Thanksgiving
Zimmerman, Heinz Werner	Psalmkonzert

Opera

Britten, Benjamin	The Burning Fiery Furnace
	Curlew River
	Noye's Fludde
Mayer, William	One Christmas Long Ago (based on "Why the Chimes Rang")
Menotti, Gian-Carlo	Amahl and the Night Visitors

The Sacred Solo   In many nonliturgical traditions, musical selections for the worship service often include an anthem by the choir and a solo by either a professional or nonprofessional singer. Much of this stems from the choir-quartet era, when some churches used a professional quartet in place of a volunteer choir. Today large churches often try to have the best of both worlds by using members of a professional quartet to serve as section leaders in the choir and also as soloists for either regular services or special musical presentations.

One of the problems facing the choral director has been to find solo music of good quality that is suitable for worship services. A few musicians who have composed in this genre include Charles Ives, Leroy H. Baumgartner, Samuel Barber, Aaron Copland, Josef Freudenthal, Alan Hovhaness, Michael Head, Ralph Vaughan Williams, and Eric Thiman.[6]

MUSIC FOR THE ORGAN

For centuries the organ has been the major instrument used for leading congregational music in worship, therefore, a brief overview of the long

---

[6] A list of selected solo literature may be found in Appendix C.

history of the instrument, in relation to its extensive repertoire, may be useful both for the organist and for one who is not trained as an organist. The musician who has had extensive study of organ literature will recognize immediately that what follows is, of necessity, highly condensed. Chapter 9, "Designing, Purchasing, and Maintaining the Organ," contains a more detailed discussion of the organ's mechanical aspects.

The origin of the organ can be traced to the pre-Christian cultures of the Near East. Descriptions of ancient organs may be found in writings from Greece, Rome, and Byzantium. In the West, Emperor Constantine Copronymus is said to have presented an organ to Pepin, king of the Franks, in A.D. 757. Such royal gifts helped establish the organ as part of Christian culture. The organ was also used in England, and much has been written—and even more speculated—about the famous Winchester Cathedral organ, supposedly extant toward the end of the tenth century. According to legend, it was a noisy, raucous instrument that could be heard for miles.

As the organ evolved—becoming more manageable and, at the same time, larger—it was adopted for church use. By the beginning of the Renaissance, some multimanual instruments with primitive pedals were in use; those found in the Netherlands were the most advanced. By the beginning of the sixteenth century, distinct national "schools" of organ-building and literature began to emerge. These schools took shape during the seventeenth and eighteenth centuries, a period now considered the golden age for the organ and its literature.

In Italy the development of the organ reached a climax early, and there was little change over the next three centuries. Sixteenth-century Italian organs were among the first to have stops, although few had more than one keyboard. Pedals, if provided, tended to be coupled permanently to the manual. While they had no mixtures, Italian organs did have many higher unison and mutation registers which, because of their high pitch, often broke back to lower octaves as the pipes became smaller, thus functioning in the ensemble like mixtures. The tone of Italian organs tended to be warm, fluty, and gentle.

Significant composers of the Italian school include Andrea Gabrieli (1515-86), Claudio Merulo (1533-1604), Giovanni Gabrieli (c. 1555-1612), and Girolamo Frescobaldi (1583-1643), who wrote in such forms as canzone, ricercar, and toccata. The Italian musical culture of the time was of such importance that these forms played a strong, influential role in the development of organ literature throughout Europe.

Like the Italian school, Iberian organ-building enjoyed an early and vital development. As Spanish organs developed they became larger and more powerful than contemporary Italian instruments. Even though they too had primitive pedals—usually playing certain low manual pipes—

52

they evolved into two- and, in some cases, three-manual instruments, with keyboards often divided at middle C.[7] Some of the instruments included a device that controlled the loudness of certain pipes—especially a reed stop—which was placed inside a small box with a hinged lid that could be opened and closed by the organist. This device is the first known example of a kind of swell box. From the middle of the seventeenth century, a unique characteristic of the Iberian organ was its large number of reed stops, many of which were mounted horizontally from the front of the case (en chamade), creating an impressive visual and aural effect. Following their introduction to French organs by the nineteenth-century builder Aristide Cavaillé-Coll, horizontal, or en chamade, reeds spread to other countries, and today may be found throughout Europe and America. Organ literature from the Iberian school remains somewhat of a mystery, much of it being lost. Yet surviving works, like the tientos of Cabinilles (1644-1712) and the concertos for two organs of Antonio Soler (1729-83), reveal a style of great charm and character.

The Netherlands school of organ-building was the first to develop a large organ with more than one keyboard, an independent pedal division, and a variety of stops, including flutes and reeds, as well as principals. The many significant schools and famous families of builders from this period inspired the work of later builders, such as the Compenius family, and Gottfried and Andreas Silbermann.

The work of the Netherlands school culminated in the North German school, led by the builder Arp Schnitger (1648-1719). His instruments are considered to be perfect examples of high baroque North German organs. Each of the three, four, or five independent divisions (Pedal, Hauptwerk, Oberwerk, Rückpositiv, and Brustwerk) was an organ in itself, with a complete principal chorus, including mixture or crown, gedackts and flute foundations, some mutations, and a variety of reeds. The ensemble was clear, brilliant, and cohesive—ideally suited to projecting polyphonic textures and for leading congregational music. Indeed, many believed that the concern of the Reformers for congregational participation through singing hymns and liturgy did much to stimulate the art of organ-building.

The impetus of the Reformation and the challenge of the evolving organ inspired a steady flow of organ music. Just as the Netherlands provided the basis for the brilliant German schools of organ-building, so it provided a foundation for the literature. The works of Jan Pieterszoon Sweelinck

---

[7] A divided keyboard, or manual, is a clavier with a separate stop action for bass and treble portions of the compass, usually divided at about middle C. Thus, the organist may draw separate stops in bass and treble—4 and 2 in bass against 8 solo register in treble—to play both solo and accompaniment on the same keyboard.

(1562-1621) and of his most famous pupil, Samuel Scheidt (1587-1654), stand at the forefront of the most significant body of literature ever composed for the organ, a corpus of music crowned by the work of J.S. Bach.

The music of the German schools of organ composition encompassed a wide range of styles, from preludes, toccatas, and fugues to works both simple and complex based upon existing melodies. As they evolved, each of the German schools developed its own character. Composers of the North German organ school include Franz Tunder (1614-67), Dietrich Buxtehude (1637-1707), and Vincent Lubeck (1654-1740). They wrote in free and in cantus-based forms, and their literature is characterized by florid, virtuoso writing. Their music typically utilizes the pedals as an equal polyphonic voice, with active, often virtuoso, figuration.

Composers of the South German school include Johann Pachelbel (1653-1706), Johann Jacob Froberger (1616-67), and Georg Muffat (1653-1704). Although some cantus-based literature was composed, especially by Pachelbel, most of the literature in Roman Catholic southern Germany was adopted from the nonliturgical, Italian toccata, canzone, ricercar, capriccio, fantasia, and fugue. The music is simpler in conception than that of the contemporary North German school, with polyphonic textures less complex and pedal passages much less difficult. In many compositions the pedals are not used at all, reflecting the more primitive state of the pedal divisions in the typical South German organ of the time.

In the heartland of Germany, Thuringia and Saxony, the Middle German school absorbed features of style and form from the North and the South. Leading composers include Michael Praetorius (1571-1621) and Johann Gottfried Walther (1684-1748). Generations of the Bach family lived in central Germany, and from this family came Johann Sebastian Bach (1685-1750), the greatest German composer for the organ. Most organists agree that his organ compositions are the most significant in history and probably will never be surpassed. Bach's organ works, which covered the gamut of forms developed to his time, resulted in a style made remarkable by its fusion of elements utilized by composers and schools that preceded him. Yet his music has a unique and special quality that transcends all that went before. A significant portion of Bach's music is based on chorale melodies, and all his organ music is appropriate for use in worship, if only because Bach considered it to be an offering to almighty God. The construction of organs and organ composition in Germany suffered a decline after Bach. Although recital programs often included music by Haydn and Mozart, these compositions (with the exception of Haydn's organ concerti) were not written for the organ, but rather for small mechanical "musical clocks," which used pipes as their sound source.

Felix Mendelssohn (1809-47) composed six sonatas and three preludes and fugues for organ, while Franz Liszt (1811-86) composed literature designed to produce spectacular virtuoso effects ideal for the German Romantic organs of his time. Max Reger also produced a large corpus of work, much of it rather tedious and complex. The chorale fantasias, especially WACHET AUF (Opus 52, No. 2), are among his most successful compositions; however, the short chorale preludes, Opus 79b and Opus 135a, are most useful for the parish organist.

In the twentieth century, German organ-builders, organists, and composers played a significant and leading role in the organ reform movement, which, by returning to the tonal and engineering practices of the seventeenth century, attempted to discover the true nature of the instrument and its literature. Hugo Distler (1908-42) is perhaps the most significant composer of organ music to appear in this century. While his output is not large, it is well crafted, and ranges from short chorale preludes to two major works based on the chorales WACHET AUF and NUN KOMM DER HEIDEN HEILAND.

The organ and its music also has a long, extensive history in France. By the early seventeenth century a unique and flexible style of organ-building was flourishing and continued to do so until the late eighteenth century. The typical instrument had a complete Great organ, with a colorful Positive organ as well. The Great (Grand Orgue) usually included a complete principal chorus, flutes 16-8-4-2 with mutations, a cornet, and chorus reeds 8 and 4, as well as a Vox Humana or other gentle solo reed. The Positive was a miniature Great, with its own principal chorus, flutes with mutations, and at least a Cromorne, if not additional reed stops. An additional manual (sometimes manuals) was often found, although it was usually limited, specialized, and short of compass. While these instruments possessed pedal divisions, they never developed to the extent of those found in the German organs to the north. A climax to this style of building was reached in the magnificent work of builders François Henri Clicquot (1728-90) and Andreas Silbermann (1678-1734).

Literature worthy of these instruments was produced by many fine composers, including François Couperin (1668-1733), Pierre duMage (c. 1676-1751), Nicolas de Grigny (1672-1703), Jean-François Dandrieu (1682-1738), and Louis-Nicolas Clerambault (1676-1749). Their organ masses, suites, hymn variations, and noels thoroughly exploited the silvery ensembles, splendid reeds, and piquant mutations typical of the instrument. The music was so closely tied to the tonal palette of the instrument that individual pieces often were named for specific combinations of stops, e.g., Basse de trompette (trumpet solo in the bass voice, accompanied by flues in the upper parts), Cromorne en taille (cromorne solo in the tenor, accompanied by flues), or Dialogue sur les grands jeux (Dialogue alternating between two large ensembles, flues, mutations, and reeds—usually between the Great and the Positive organs). Such was the total unity and fusion of organ-building and organ composition of this period that it has come to be called the French Classical school.

Stimulated by the brilliant talent of Aristide Cavaillé-Coll (1811-99), a second great period of organ-building and organ literature began. In 1841, Cavaillé-Coll completed a large four-manual organ for the basilica of St. Denis, near Paris. This instrument and the one built in 1859 at St. Clotilde, where César Franck (1822-90) was organist, changed the entire nature of French organ-building. Instruments became larger and louder, and included brilliant reeds. Manual registers included harmonic flutes, strings, and orchestral solo reeds, while the pedal division was expanded by adding many lower-pitched registers. This led to a greater frequency of playing the bass voice in the pedals, a trend that eventually became common practice in France. The reaction of composers to these new ideas was swift and dramatic. The symphonic style of César Franck, Charles Marie Widor (1845-1937), and Louis Vierne (1870-1937) was in direct response to the rich, orchestral tonal resources of the Cavaillé-Coll organ. This style of organ-building has continued to influence French organ literature and organ-building of this century. Such composers as Jehan Alain, Marcel Dupré, Maurice Duruflé, and Olivier Messiaen continue to conceive literature and propose registrations for instruments essentially like those envisioned and constructed by Cavaillé-Coll.

In England, organ-building was interrupted during the Commonwealth period, and little remains of sixteenth- or early seventeenth-century instruments. After the monarchy was restored, in 1660, the eighteenth-century English organ became much like the French Classical organ, although not as intense in sound. Besides being smaller, with much less emphasis on reed color, there was a major difference between it and its contemporary continental instruments: the absence of pedals. Literature from composers like William Boyce and John Stanley was written for manuals without pedals, and consisted almost solely of voluntaries and other compositions in a variety of forms and styles. Some were slow moving and included free counterpoint; others were bright, sparkling duos, featuring echo effects and solo sonorities.

In the nineteenth century the English organ expanded rapidly and rather abruptly into the large, romantic, cathedral organ, known to most American organists because of its strong influence on American organ-builders. The great organs of Henry Willis I (1821-1901), constructed in the middle to late nineteenth century, still influence English organ-building. These instruments made loud, colorful sounds, which were ideally suited to the accompaniment of the Victorian, Anglican worship then evolving. The famous English "full Swell" of reeds with mixture was perfected, if not developed, by Willis. He was instrumental in expanding the size of the typical English organ, and encouraged the development of a Pedal division with a range of registers, both flue and reed, from 32' up.

There is little significant organ literature inspired by this style of organ-building, perhaps because the instrument's main role was the leading of congregational worship and accompaniment of the choir in anthems and psalms. A few interesting works have remained in the repertoire, especially by composers from the early twentieth century, of whom Herbert Howells may well be the best known.

In America, organ-builders tended to copy the various European styles with which they were familiar. Three major early centers of organ-building can be identified, the earliest being in Pennsylvania. German immigrant David Tannenberg (1728-1804) produced many instruments of high quality; some survive to this day. Later, especially after the War of 1812 limited the possibility of importing organs, New York and New England became centers of activity. In New York, Henry Erben (1800-1884) and George Jardine (1801-83) directed establishments more like some of the organ firms in operation today. In Boston the firm of E.G. Hook and Co. was active from the mid-1800s to the early twentieth century, when the company was known as Hook and Hastings. By midnineteenth century such builders had the capability of producing from 10 to 20 organs a year.

Toward the end of the nineteenth century, the Romantic movement in European organ-building was reflected in the work of both New York and New England builders. Lists of specifications grew longer, and powerful registers with more unison stops became common.

By the early 1900s the perfection of electropneumatic action had encouraged builders to increase the size and complexity of their instruments. Ever-larger instruments were produced, culminating in the monster six-manual organ of 469 ranks, 30,067 pipes for the Grand Court of the John Wanamaker department store in Philadelphia (1930), and the seven-manual instrument of 455 ranks, 33,112 pipes built in Convention Hall in Atlantic City, New Jersey. While most large organs could only claim size as a virtue, some did achieve artistic stature, especially in their warm, orchestral solo stops, e.g., English Horn and French Horn. The work of Ernest Skinner is especially notable, in that the many large instruments he made for significant and prestigious institutions—especially the later ones (1920-30) reflect a remarkable degree of quality in construction and a cohesion in tonal design.

By 1930 the organ reform movement that had begun in Germany attracted the attention of G. Donald Harrison, artistic director of Aeolian-Skinner, in Boston, and organ-builder Walter Holtkamp, in Cleveland. These men led a return by American organ-builders to some of the concepts of design and voicing that were part of the Golden Age of the organ in Europe. Renewed interest in a cohesive, clear ensemble and a smaller more intimate instrument has characterized the work of these pioneers and their many followers. Since 1950 there has been increasing interest in mechanical action instruments, and many small firms specializing in the construction of encased mechanical action organs have been established.

American organ literature also tended to model styles found in Europe and especially in England. Early American composers, like William Selby (1738-98), produced voluntaries much like the English voluntaries of the same period. Later a strong German influence can be noted, as many Americans went to Germany and to Austria for their musical training. *Variations on the Austrian Hymn* by John Knowles Paine (1839-1906) is a good example, as is the *Organ Sonata* (1908) of Horatio William Parker (1863-1919); both these composers completed their musical education in Germany.

Most of the American organ literature inspired by the Romantic instrument of the early twentieth century is relatively insignificant, although a few interesting works remain in the repertoire, especially those of Leo Sowerby. His work ranges from useful, accessible hymn preludes to concert pieces of extreme difficulty. With the renaissance of organ-building in America has come a new interest by composers in writing for the instrument. Important major works are being contributed to the repertoire by respected avant-garde composers, such as William Albright and William Bolcum; however, the length and difficulty of these works tend to limit their usefulness for the church musician.

Throughout all its history, most organ literature has been influenced by the style of organ-building practiced at the time of its composition. In addition, two types of organ compositional techniques should be identified: one uses an existing melody as the basis for a new composition; the other does not utilize any extant material to construct a new composition.

Organ compositions based upon a *cantus firmus* (preexistent melody) tend to use hymn or chorale tunes and for this reason are especially useful to the church musician, who can often select a work for a prelude, voluntary, or postlude that incorporates a cantus (hymn) to be used during the same service. The range of cantus-based compositions is very wide—from simple reharmonizations of chorale and hymn melodies, and short polyphonic works based upon a psalm tune, to extensive works either in variation form or in free fantasia forms. The cantus-based form most useful for the church organist is the chorale or hymn prelude. This form reached its peak in the compositions of North German baroque composers, especially J.S. Bach. Often between 2 and 7 minutes in length, a chorale-prelude usually quotes the tune once during the composition. Sometimes the chorale appears in augmentation, normally in soprano or bass, while a rich texture is woven around it. At other times the melody may appear as a highly decorated solo line, usually in the soprano. Composers of almost every generation have produced cantus-based literature, some of great complexity. From time to time tiny masterpieces, like the *Eleven Chorale Preludes* of Johannes Brahms, appear.

In this century, and especially in America, the concept of the chorale-prelude has expanded to include other hymn tunes, and a wide variety of literature—difficult to easy, compositionally conservative to avant-garde—is available. Major and significant works from composers of stature, like Hugo Distler, as well as less significant but equally useful works are very important to the church musician. With the postwar publication of many new denominational hymnals and the renaissance in American organ-building, many composers have exhibited a resurgence of interest in writing cantus-based chorale or hymn preludes, thus enhancing the potential for the organ to play a more effective role in worship.

The other large body of organ literature encompasses works that do not utilize any extant material on which to construct a composition. Music for organ has been produced employing almost every form developed throughout the history of music, from trio sonata to symphony. A form that frequently provides an opportunity for the exploitation of the facility and flexibility of the organ is the toccata—often referred to as a "touch piece"—which is generally virtuosic in character. Other forms, such as the fugue, provide opportunities for creative use of polyphonic textures. Polyphony sounds especially well on the organ, since if all voices are played on the same keyboard, the unity of timbre highlights the differences in the individual lines. The wide range of repertoire is such that an organist can find much that is appropriate for worship and/or concert.

CHAPTER 4

The Musician Leads
in Worship

PLANNING AND SELECTING MUSIC

Finding and selecting music for worship is one of the chief tasks of the church musician. In the liturgical tradition the musical portions of the liturgy—items that might be called responses in a nonliturgical context—are predetermined; some are invariable and some change from season to season and day to day. The texts for the variable items—e.g., in the Lutheran tradition, alleluia verses, psalms, and offertories—would be sung by the choir, while invariable portions of the liturgy are sung by all. The choir director determines if the choir will attempt to do the specially appointed variable items, and if so, which of the available versions will be used.

In the nonliturgical tradition, choral responses generally consist of an introit, call to prayer (sometimes called an orison), and responses after the pastoral prayer and the closing benediction (usually an extended amen). Other choral music includes an anthem or vocal solo, usually before the scripture and/or during the offering.

Increasingly, nonliturgical churches are discovering the rich heritage of liturgical music, and are utilizing such literature at various times during worship; e.g., the Gloria Patri is used as a response to a psalm; a setting of the Kyrie Eleison or the Agnus Dei is utilized on a Sunday when communion is observed. Many churches find that hymns sung during the distribution of the communion elements provide additional stimulus for meditation and reflection on the part of their congregations, and they now alternate vocal selections with organ selections. Because some parishioners may at first be disconcerted, it is also helpful to plan for *silence* during such times as the absolution, the distribution, or before a prayer.

Traditionally, an instrumental prelude and postlude have been part of Christian worship. There are two types of preludes: one is based on a cantus firmus, most generally called a chorale-prelude, and the other is any form that is not based on a cantus firmus, e.g., toccata, elevation, pastorale, aria. There may be times when the organist will want to choose an organ prelude that is directly related to a hymn to be sung in the service. At other times, selections of other forms may be equally appropriate. No matter what type of music is selected, the organist should always remember that it must contribute to the worship experience and should never become a recital or exhibition of technical prowess.

The postlude should serve as a musical benediction. (Unfortunately, in most churches the postlude's function is that of exit music, rather than being an integral part of the worship service.) Thus, one should expect a postlude to continue the mood of the service. For instance, it would be as inappropriate to play Louis Vierne's *Carillon de Westminster* as a postlude to a Maundy Thursday or Tenebrae service as it would be to play the Max Reger setting of the PASSION CHORALE at the close of an Easter service. An organist must be sensitive to the mood and focus of worship, carefully planning music to be used as preludes and postludes. Do avoid playing extended, loud preludes *every* Sunday, and *do* choose a variety of music from the pens of many different composers. A mixture of Bach, Mendelssohn, Vierne, and Messiaen is preferable to a steady diet of Couperin, Bach, Walther, and Frescobaldi. Likewise, it is well to avoid programming all twentieth-century composers on a consistent basis, e.g., Distler, Messiaen, and Sowerby.

A word is also in order concerning the selection of organ music to be used for Holy Communion. Most ministers request organists to play "soft music" during the distribution of the elements. There are two choices: (1) music with a familiar text (e.g., "Bread of the World, in Mercy Broken") that is perceived by the worshipers and guides their meditation, or (2) abstract music (e.g., Couperin: *Elevation;* Dupré: *Antiphon III*) that is used to provide a quiet background for the worshiper's reflections and meditation. Much can also be said for the use of *silence* as another way to encourage personal worship. When choosing organ music, one should select literature that is meditative in nature. However, at certain times, such as Easter, the nature of the sacrament of Holy Communion is such that a mood of celebration and joy is more appropriate. Of course, even on such an occasion the excessive use of loud, brilliant, and flashy sounds or repertoire would be inappropriate.

The major items of music to be selected for worship include hymns, anthems, choral responses (in nonliturgical), prelude, postlude, and communion music. It is desirable and important to relate these items of music to the theme of a given day. In a nonliturgical church the theme is usually determined by the sermon topic, and the scripture is related to that topic. Many ministers employ the discipline of an ordered pattern of lessons, called a *lectionary* or *pericopes*, which assures the use of a wide range of scripture. Most of these ordered sets of lessons also relate to the liturgical or Church Year. If the music is to be coordinated with the scripture/sermon, it is essential for the musician to consult with the minister to ascertain how sermon topics and themes for specific Sundays will be determined.

The liturgical year is a twelve-month cycle structured through a system of Sundays and special holidays related to the history of salvation in Jesus Christ. In this sense the liturgical year is truly a Christian year. Traditionally, the Christian Year begins with Advent, with the prophecy of the coming of Christ. Advent is considered a penitential time, a time for the preparation of hearts and minds for the glorious event of Christmas, and for reflection on the mystery of Christ's continued presence with us and eventual return to earth.

The four Sundays of Advent are followed by the first major holiday, the feast of Christmas. Christmas begins with Christmas Day, and the most obvious Christmas music should be saved until Christmas Eve. The tradition of beginning major holidays on the eve of the feast day can be traced to the Hebrew custom of worship from sundown to sundown, beginning on the eve of the Sabbath. Christmas continues to Epiphany, and many liturgical churches extend Christmas music and themes into Epiphany.

Epiphany—January 6—is the day when the coming of the wise men, led by a star, is celebrated. The scriptures record that these men went out and told abroad what they had seen and heard. Thus, a central theme of this season is the telling of the good news of Christ's birth (hence the continuing Christmas emphasis) and of his ministry while on earth. Epiphany, the season to tell, is often a time for emphasizing the mission of the church, and the symbolism of light—Christ, as the light of the world, and the light of the star—plays an important role.

Lent is the next major division of the year, and is the second penitential time in the calendar. Lent begins on Ash Wednesday. During this season, human sinful nature and eventual redemption through Christ's death and resurrection is celebrated. Frequently, Lent is considered a time for renewal and reflection, with many churches scheduling extra services.

Lent ends with Palm Sunday (sometimes called Passion Sunday), Christ's triumphal entry into Jerusalem; followed by Maundy Thursday, Christ's institution of the Last Supper; and Good Friday, Christ's crucifixion. The solemn, somber mood of Lent, and especially Good

Friday, is transformed by the exuberant joy of Easter day. The word alleluia—that marvelous ejaculation of praise—traditionally banished from the liturgy during Lent, returns to remind us that we do have something special about which to sing.

The joyful season of Easter continues through Ascension Day— Christ's ascension into heaven—and ends with the day of Pentecost. On this feast the coming of the Holy Spirit to empower the original disciples and all Christians is remembered. Pentecost begins the longest season of the year (sometimes called Trinity), and continues until Advent marks the beginning of the new liturgical year, four Sundays before Christmas. During this yearly cycle, certain other liturgical feast days/holidays may or may not be observed, depending on local custom.

Knowing the ideas to be used in forthcoming sermons and understanding the spirit of the seasons of the Church Year, make the selection of appropriate music much easier.[1]

The following suggestions will enable the director to organize the music to be performed and yet remain flexible to the changes that occur during the year.

1. Compile a notebook, dividing the pages by the months of the year.
2. Enter all dates and musical requirements of the service, e.g., prelude, offertory, postlude, anthem, responses. Enter all the special services: Reformation, Advent, Christmas Eve, Palm Sunday, Easter. (See the "Sample Planning Chart" on page 64.)
3. Select music that is appropriate to these days from your choral/organ library or choose new music.
4. Enter the selections on a chart (see "Service Plan" on page 65) taking care not to schedule too many "big" pieces in a row for either organ or chorus. Try to select music that reflects a variety of styles and moods. Difficult pieces for the choir should alternate with some that are easier, and loud, with soft. Avoid music that all sounds alike.

While this outline may take many hours to create, having done it, you then have a guide for the music during the year and are not frantically trying to decide what to do from one week to the next.

PLAYING HYMNS

As one develops an understanding and appreciation of congregational music, especially hymns, one must also develop and perfect techniques

---

[1] A unique tool for helping the busy choral director locate titles of selected choral octavos is *Choralist*, a computer-based program at Kent State University.

(Sample Planning Chart)

November

Nov. 4
  Sermon Theme:

Prelude:

Responses:

Anthems:
           Title: Composer:
               (Text source:)

Communion:

Hymns:

Postlude:

Notes:

for leading the congregation in its worship through this music. Since it is an area in which the organist carries the prime responsibility, it is wrong to underestimate the potential influence for meaningful worship that the organist exerts. A service well played leads the congregation in worship without their being aware of the skillful work of the organist. A service poorly played calls attention to the organist, because rather than worshiping, the congregation is disturbed and distracted.

On assuming a position, the organist must study the tonal possibilities of the organ. It is important to explore the total instrument, trying each stop at various octaves of the keyboard. A 2′ stop might be a beautiful solo register played one or two octaves lower. Check to be sure that all mechanical aids, e.g., couplers, pistons, expression pedals, are understood so that they will assist and not confuse. This process of orientation should be *repeated yearly*, the organist attempting to hear the organ as if for the first time, in order to assure that the approach to the instrument remains fresh. Some organists have been heard to observe that a given instrument is hopeless, and that it is "impossible to do anything with it." Such an attitude is unprofessional and intolerable if one has accepted the position. At the same time, one may tactfully identify tonal or mechanical difficulties, and make suggestions for their correction or improvement, for it is also the organist's responsibility to keep the congregation informed about the true state of the instrument.

After carefully assessing the tonal possibilities of the organ, a basic

Service Plan (nonliturgical)
November

Scripture Reference/ Sermon Theme	Prelude	Responses	Anthem	Offertory Anthem	Postlude	Communion	Hymns	Other Service Music
Old Test. Prophets. "New Wine in Old Wineskins"	By the Waters of Babylon (John Huston)	Introit: "O God, Our Help" (vs. 1) Prayer: "May the Words" (UCC #347) Closing: "Shalom" (UCC #368)	Kyrie (Missa Brevis) Gabrieli Text: 3/30/78	By the Waters of Babylon (Philip James) Text: 10/6/79	"Praise to the Lord" (Johann Walther)	Meditations on Communion Hymns (Leo Sowerby)	Pro: "God of the Prophets," Toulon Prep: "Comfort Ye My People," Psalm 42 Re: "O God, Our Help"	
"We Do Believe"	St. Catherine (McKinley)	Introit: We Believe in One True God Prayer: Let the Words of My Mouth (UCC #344) Closing: Father, Give Thy Benediction (UCC #367)	Credo, Wir Glauben (Gretchaninoff) Text: New*	Victory Te Deum (Everett Titcomb) Text: UCC #369	"We Believe in One True God" (J.S. Bach)		Pro: "On God the Spirit We Rely," Truro Prep: "We Believe in One True God," Ratisbon Re: Lord, Dismiss Us	
Thanksgiving Sunday	Now Thank We All Our God (J.S. Bach)	Introit: "Come, Ye Thankful People, Come" (handbells) Prayer: "For All the Blessings," Oldridge Closing: "For All the Blessings of the Year"	"Sing to the Lord of Harvest"(Healey Willan) Youth Choir Text: New*	Jubilate Deo (Dale Wood) Text: UCC #371 (Children's Choir)	"Now Thank We All Our God" (Karg-Elert)		Pro: Old Hundredth** Prep: We Gather Together Re: Now Thank We All Our God	Old Hundredth (Vaughan Williams) Intro to Hymn: "We Gather Together" (Wilbur Held)
"A World Awaits"(Prelude to Advent)	Wachet Auf (J.S. Bach)	Introit: "Ye Watchers and Ye Holy Ones" Prayer: "Saviour of the Gentiles, Come" Closing: "God Be in My Head"	Solo: Prepare Thyself Zion (Christmas Oratorio) (J.S. Bach) Text: 11/30/80	"Lo, How a Rose" (Michael Praetorius) Text: New*	Prelude and Fugue in A Major (J.S. Bach)		Pro: "Lift Up Your Heads," Truro Prep: "The King of Glory Comes," Promised One (UCC #75) Re: "Come, Thou Long-Expected Jesus"	

* Text not printed in past; must be given to secretary.
**Processional: Old Hundredth, Vaughan Williams Trumpets/Festival Processional/Banners. Choir enters and sings stanza 2 in aisle before proceeding into chancel.

registration scheme for hymns should be prepared. If the organ is large enough to have general pistons, set two or three that will provide basic combinations to be utilized for hymn-playing. The first combination might include some flute and principal tone of 8' and 4' pitch, as well as a gentle 2'; all manuals coupled to the Great, some coupled to the Pedal, with pedal 16' and 8' (occasionally 4') tone. The second might combine the Great principal chorus (with mixture) and additional pedal (principal 8', octave 4'). The third might include some reed tone and additional mixtures to add brilliance, but not yet utilizing full organ. As the complexity of the combinations increases, avoid excessive doubling of pitches, and make sure that each stop drawn makes a distinct contribution to the total ensemble. If it can barely be heard going on or off, it probably should be left off. If the organ is of reasonable size, the third combination might include some 16' manual tone, especially a buzzy or bright reed weak in fundamental pitch, or a 16' light flue, e.g., quintaton. However, *avoid heavy 16' manual stops, sub-16' and super 4' couplers*, unless you are absolutely sure that using such couplers will not make the ensemble too bottom-heavy or too top-heavy. Neither a thick, heavy sound nor a brilliant "screaming" sound is effective or acceptable to lead a congregation in singing hymns.

The first and most important concept to remember in playing hymns is that one must lead rather than follow the congregation, at the same time remaining sensitive to it. Although the organist must not allow the flow of the music to be interrupted, conversely, the organist should not rush the tempo of the hymns to the point of leaving the congregation struggling to catch up. Hymns should be played in such a way as to support and encourage the congregation to sing.

To provide effective musical leadership, it is essential to find the appropriate tempo for each selection. Many external factors must be considered, e.g., size and acoustics of the building, size of the congregation, and even the time of day; but none is as vital as a careful analysis of the music to be sung. Questions to be raised include: Is the text complex? How active is the melodic line? Does the phrase end with a long note? Does the hymn begin with an upbeat? What seems to be the basic pulse of the tune? Many tunes notated in 4/4 or 6/8 meter need to be felt in a pulse of two, while some 3/4 tunes are felt in a pulse of one. Before determining the tempo of any tune, think and sing it through, so that the physical motions of fingers and feet do not overrule musical judgments.

Once established, maintain the pulse! One must communicate a sense of rhythmic stability and poise if a congregation is to feel secure enough really to sing with confidence; an insecure congregation is a bashful congregation. Play accurately and with confidence. All notes in a single vertical sonority must sound at the same time. Since hymn tunes are vocal compositions, play the melodic line carefully. All repeated notes in the melody must be observed, usually giving half the written value to any repeated notes. In the other voices it is not always necessary to observe every repeated note. Consider lifting every other note of successive repeated vertical sonorities, e.g., a group of four repeated chords, in 4/4 meter, might best be played with soprano and tenor as notated, and alto and bass as half notes. Always restate any repeated notes over a bar line. An examination of the hymn tune below, where all repeated notes to be played have been marked with a vertical slash, should make the above discussion clear.

The Church's One Foundation   (AURELIA)

Mentally sing the text of the hymn as you play, breathing with the congregation. As indicated before, hymns and liturgy are vocal compositions. The spirit and shape of the text often determine the appropriate places to breathe, rather than the shape of the musical line. This same spirit and shape of the text also reveal places where minute stretching or contracting of the musical flow (subtle rubato) can contribute to increased sensitivity to and understanding of the text.

A frequent problem is the relationship between one stanza and the next. While there is much difference of opinion over the most effective method to end one stanza and begin the next, a widely used and logical approach is to complete the first stanza as written, take a breath, and begin the next. Hymn tunes in 4/4 meter that end on the third beat may need extra time on the last chord. Hymns that begin with an upbeat, especially in 3/4 meter, also may require a bit of additional time at the end of each stanza. Of course, there should be no ritards except perhaps at the end of the final stanza.

When an amen is used it should be sung in the spirit of the text and in the tempo of the hymn. A joyous hymn of praise is destroyed by a long amen. Some organists choose to tie the last note of the soprano line with the first note of the amen; others prefer a clear articulation preceding the amen. Whatever the choice, there should be consistency.

Variety in hymn-playing is encouraged. Some congregations and organists enjoy and indeed are inspired by a significant utilization of free accompaniments and other techniques to achieve variety; however, there are some who prefer a more conservative approach. Whatever the preference, all decisions to vary the rendition of a hymn tune should grow out of a consideration of the text. Perhaps the best way to gain insight into employing variety in hymn-playing is to seek out and attend a church where this practice is encouraged (or different techniques are used). Another way is to attend hymn festivals or purchase recordings of hymns, and study what is done.

Techniques for providing variety either involve (1) those that are utilized by the organist or (2) those that involve the congregation. The organist may simply play the tune in unison, alternate between unison and four-part harmony (e.g., LASST UNS ERFREUEN), play certain stanzas on manuals only, play the tune as a solo on another manual, or utilize a free accompaniment. If the latter is selected, using one of the many published free accompaniments is recommended. In choosing these, it is well to begin with those that clearly retain the tune in the soprano. Only later, after a congregation is comfortable with the idea of free accompaniments, is it wise to select ones in which the tune "disappears" into the texture of the accompaniment. Another way to achieve variety is to employ intonations to introduce hymns, instead of the more conventional method of playing the entire hymn as an introduction. Again, many collections of intonations are published. These short pieces, usually based on a striking feature of the melody, can do much to set the spirit and feel of the text. When initiating this technique be sure the intended tempo for the hymn is established; after a congregation becomes accustomed to the idea of intonations, this is not always necessary. In essence, the word intonation implies the giving of pitch. Therefore, it is even possible to utilize nonrelated material (perhaps a brass fanfare in the key of the hymn to follow) to set the mood for a favorite, well-known hymn on a festive Sunday.

Techniques that involve the choir and/or the congregation include singing a stanza a cappella; men and women singing alternate stanzas; choir and congregation singing alternate stanzas. Of course, these latter methods assume that a system of communication is devised, to inform the worshipers of what is going to happen. Usually the best method is to print instructions in the service bulletin. In addition, any planned changes in hymn accompaniment, except perhaps registrational ones, must be communicated to the choir during preservice rehearsal. Hymn descants sung by the sopranos also can add variety to hymn-singing, and usually are most effective when the rest of the choir and the congregation are instructed to sing in unison.

From this brief discussion one can sense that leading a congregation in hymn-singing can be an exciting, creative activity for the organist, work full of joy and musical satisfaction.

PLAYING ACCOMPANIMENTS

Another responsibility of the organist is to play accompaniments of choral, vocal, or instrumental music that is rendered to enrich congregational worship. While some of this music may be written for the organ, especially any that involves other instruments, most is written for the piano or is a piano reduction of an orchestral score.

Arranging piano or orchestral scores for the organ is a challenge. Much piano music contains figurations and patterns devised to maintain sound and energy (arpeggios, Alberti figuration, and/or repeated chords), none of which is indigenous to the organ. It is best to rearrange such textures to include some sustained sounds. For example, hold some notes in repeated chords while repeating others; revise Alberti figures to include movement while sustaining other pitches.[2]

---

[2]Some might question the quality of the music, but few organists would quarrel with the excellent transcription by Carl Weinrich of the original piano accompaniment for Albert Hay Malotte's The Lord's Prayer. Anyone interested in learning how to rearrange piano textures for organ should make a careful comparison of both versions as published by G. Schirmer.

In general, registrations for choral accompaniment should be clear and transparent. Combinations of gentle 8' Gedackt with a 4' Principal or Gemshorn work much better than combinations of 8' pitches. The choir sings at 8' pitch, so only 8' pitch from the organ is difficult to hear. Support for the singing may be effectively achieved by using gentle, clear 16' tone in the Pedal, and some brighter color above—4' and even 2' tone in the manuals. In forte sections, buzzy and rich, but not thick or loud, reed stops are very effective (Dulzian, Krummhorn, Fagott, Hautbois, for example). They contribute a feeling of excitement without covering the singing, and their rich harmonic structures enable them to be easily heard by the choir. (An especially useful combination for forte effects would comprise 16' and 8' reeds, as described above, with 8' Gedackt, 4' and 2' Principals, and perhaps a light mixture, all coupled to the Pedal.)

Registration of an orchestral reduction is difficult. Since the organ is not a surrogate orchestra, most attempts to "orchestrate" an oratorio chorus are doomed to failure. However, one can gain important insights into the music by studying the full score. It is also helpful to listen to a recording of a given chorus or aria to gain a feel for any instrumental solo sonorities, as well as for the qualities of sound that could be approximated on the organ. Careful listening would help to prevent mistakes, like utilizing full organ for the dark and rich opening measures of the Fauré *Requiem*, even though there are fortissimo marks in the piano reduction.

PLAYING INTERLUDES (IMPROVISATIONS)

The organist also has the responsibility of providing interludes and/or modulations, as well as other incidental music during the service. Such music performed well makes a beautiful contribution to a worship experience. Such music performed poorly becomes obtrusive and can ruin a fine service. When in doubt about using a bit of incidental music or doing a modulation, consider silence. Often the best modulation technique is to finish one piece, pause, and then begin in the new key without any attempt at a musical connection. Silence is the bridge!

While some have cultivated their skills in improvising modulations and small interludes, others may feel uncomfortable doing this. One should not be embarrassed to use any of the many published modulations, interludes, or short compositions that could function as interludes, e.g., Flor Peeters' *Sixty Short Pieces*. Although the best incidental music should be related to the musical event adjoining it, and may well be most effective if improvised, silence or short, composed selections is preferable to the idle wanderings on a celeste stop that frequently pass for "improvisation."

70

PLAYING/DIRECTING THE "FIRST" SERVICE IN A NEW CHURCH

Services of worship are either liturgical or nonliturgical. For the musician trained in a nonliturgical tradition, playing/directing the music in a liturgical service is vastly different from previous experience. Conversely, the liturgical musician may also experience great differences in a nonliturgical setting. It is impossible within this limited discussion to raise, much less answer, all the questions related to playing and/or conducting these services, but a careful look at several potential problems and some suggested solutions may prove helpful.

As stated in chapter 1, liturgical churches (Roman Catholic, Protestant Episcopal, Lutheran) follow prescribed liturgies based on historic practices—e.g., Matins, Morning Prayer, Vespers, Mass—with worship organized around the Church Year; nonliturgical churches (Methodist, Presbyterian, Baptist) follow a freer structure of worship, and may or may not observe the Church Year.

At first the nonliturgical musician may say, "Why is the liturgy so different? After all, I have been playing services of worship all my life." The chief difference lies in an ordered liturgy. Most of it is sung, and consists of chants, responses, hymns, canticles, and anthems. There are various prayers prescribed for different seasons of the year, and certain responses may be added or deleted, e.g., the *Alleluia* is not sung during Lent. Familiar musical portions in the nonliturgical service, e.g., *Doxology, We Give Thee but Thine Own, Gloria Patri* (Meineke, 1844), are rarely used in the liturgy. Instead, the musician is called on to play/lead the singing of chants/canticles/psalms, e.g., *Gloria Patri, Te Deum, Venite, Jubilate Deo*. The first time a nonliturgical musician encounters sixteen verses of the *Te Deum* and all the liturgical responses, he/she may feel slightly overwhelmed. Many choir members have sung these chants for years, and they know how long to hold certain words, where they are going to breathe, and which verses are sung softer or louder. But the new musician is unfamiliar with these little things that could affect the mood of the service. To give or not give the pitch for a response; to play or not play the first or last phrase as an introduction; to play when the minister moves from altar to pulpit or allow for silence; to allow time for the congregation and the choir to turn toward the altar when singing the *Gloria Patri*—all these decisions the musician must make in order for the service to proceed smoothly. Many times the texts and tunes are radically different from those with which the nonliturgical musician is most familiar—from unmetered plainsong hymns to irregular rhythms of Reformation hymns and contemporary hymnody. Just having the right music ready, e.g., liturgy, hymns, organ voluntary, anthems, communion music, often

71

makes the nonliturgical musician feel like he/she needs three hands and two heads.

To assist the nonliturgical musician in the transition, some differences between liturgical and nonliturgical worship practices are identified below:

Liturgical	Nonliturgical
1. The congregation stands, sits, and *kneels*. Time must often be allowed for kneeling or rising, before going on with the liturgy.	1. The congregation stands and sits; *it seldom kneels.*
2. A minister chants and the congregation sings the responses.	2. The choir generally sings the "liturgy," consisting of the Introit, Call to Prayer, and Responses after Prayers and Benediction.
3. There is active participation by the congregation throughout the liturgy.	3. The chief musical participation by the congregation is hymn-singing, along with singing the *Gloria Patri* and the *Doxology.*
4. Readings from the Bible (Psalms, Epistle, Gospel) are followed by appropriate musical responses.	4. Musical responses by the congregation are rare, unless perhaps, during communion.
5. Musical portions of the liturgy vary a great deal, depending on the Church Year and also on such feast days as Pentecost and All Saints.	5. Nonliturgical congregations frequently frown on the use of Latin texts (even with a translation).
6. Usually there is only one anthem.	6. Many times there are two anthems: one frequently occurs before the scripture and the other at the offertory.
7. Acolytes and crucifer are used in significant roles, e.g., leading the processional, lighting/extinguishing the Gospel and Epistle candles (Episcopal), etc.	

Frequently, the nonliturgical musician has difficulty with the musical portions of the liturgy because of not understanding the significance of certain terms. A detailed discussion of terms and functions that are important in the liturgy of the Lutheran tradition (of special interest to liturgical musicians as well) may be found in the *Manual on the Liturgy, Lutheran Book of Worship.*[3]

The Episcopal Church has revised the language of the Prayer Book and is assembling material for a new hymnal. Supplements to *The Hymnal 1940* are being used now by many Episcopal churches in an effort to meet contemporary interests and needs.

There are several steps the musician can take to become successful and effective quickly in a new situation, whether liturgical or nonliturgical.

Musical Preparation

1. Study the various liturgies; e.g., Matins, Morning Prayer, Vespers, etc. Read the prayers, responses, canticles.

2. Sing/play all the chants and responses. Breathe with the punctuation. Choose organ registration that reflects the spirit of the chant, e.g., *O Lamb of God* would be played using a softer combination than the *Gloria Patri*.

3. When playing the canticles, e.g., *Te Deum* (16 verses), prepare changes in organ registration to reflect the verses of the text.

Example

Te Deum

1. We praise thee, O God; we acknowledge thee to be the Lord. All the earth doth worship thee: the Father everlasting.	*8'4' Principal tone with mixtures*
2. To thee all angels cry aloud; the heavens and all the powers therein. To thee cherubim and seraphim continually do cry,	*8'4' Principal tone without mixtures*
3. Holy, holy, holy, Lord God of Sabaoth; heaven and earth are full of the majesty of thy glory.	*Lighter, flues, small mixtures* *Swell box closed*
4. The glorious company of the apostles praise thee; the goodly fellowship of the prophets praise thee;	*Light, flues* *Swell box opened*
5. The noble army of martyrs praise thee; the holy church throughout all the world doth acknowledge thee;	*Swell, Light 16', 8', 4' reeds*

---

[3]Philip H. Pfatteicher and Carlos R. Messerle, *Manual on the Liturgy, Lutheran Book of Worship* (Minneapolis: Augsburg Publishing House, 1979).

6. The Father, of an infinite majesty; thine adorable, true and only Son; also the Holy Ghost, the Comforter.	*Swell, light flues mixtures*
7. Thou art the King of glory, O Christ, Thou art the everlasting Son of the Father.	*Full organ without mixtures*
8. When thou tookest upon thee to deliver man, Thou didst humble thyself to be born of a virgin.	*Swell, light flues without mixtures*
9. When thou hadst overcome the sharpness of death, Thou didst open the kingdom of heaven to all believers.	*Swell, Full with mixtures, reeds*
10. Thou sittest at the right hand of God, in the glory of the Father.	*Swell, mixtures, reeds*
11. We believe that thou shalt come to be our judge;	*Swell, off mixtures, reeds*
we therefore pray thee, help thy servants whom thou hast redeemed with thy precious blood;	*Swell, flues only*
12. Make them to be numbered with thy saints in glory everlasting.	*Swell, add mixtures*
13. O Lord, save thy people and bless thine heritage: govern them and lift them up forever.	*Swell, full*
14. Day by day we magnify thee, and we worship thy name ever, world without end.	*Diminish swell to principals and flues*
15. Vouchsafe, O Lord, to keep us this day without sin. O Lord, have mercy upon us, have mercy upon us.	*Diminish swell to flues*
16. O Lord, let thy mercy be upon us, as our trust is in thee; O Lord, in thee have I trusted, let me never be confounded.	*Close swell box*

4. Study various hymn-settings of both texts and tunes. Become aware of how texts differ from those with which you are familiar.

Before the First Service
1. Discuss with the minister the history of this particular congregation, as well as the history of the denomination in general.
2. Go over the liturgy with the minister, noting the breath marks and pointing of the chants. Decide how the responses are to be introduced, e.g., single pitch, phrase, unison, harmony.
3. Rehearse the service with the minister/ministers, and two or three

members of the choir, who may also play the role of the congregation. This should be scheduled early in the week.

4. The first rehearsal should be followed later by a second, with the full choir. If these two rehearsals take place, everyone will breathe easier on that first Sunday.

(a) Start at the beginning of the service. Play and time the prelude. Be sure that you know where the ministers and choir are going to assemble before you begin the opening hymn. Also, make certain that you know which parts of the service will be announced (if any).

(b) Practice playing all stanzas of the opening hymn as the choir processes. This is imperative if you are to know how long it takes for the choir to arrive in the chancel/choir loft.

(c) Rehearse the *entire service* precisely as it will be on Sunday morning. Include when the choir stands, sits, or kneels.

5. Rehearse the procedure and timing for movement of the ministers from one location to another. Do they speak from the altar, pulpit, front of the chancel?

6. Rehearse the offertory (sometimes the trickiest part of any service, liturgical or nonliturgical). Do you play when the ushers come to the altar to receive offering plates? What is the signal for them to return? When do you play the offertory hymn (Doxology or other)? Do you modulate into another hymn or play walking music at the close of the offering? This is a well-known place for panic to set in, as the new organist asks frantically, "Where are the ushers?"

Be conservative on your first Sunday. Save the free accompaniments for a future date; after all, you have enough music to juggle without free accompaniments adding to the confusion. It is better to play everything just as it is; there will be plenty of time to get fancy later on.

General Questions

1. Where will the minister be at the beginning of the service?
2. What is your signal to begin the opening hymn? Clock? Flasher?
3. What portions of the service are announced?
4. Will there be special events? (baptism, installation, new members)
5. What will the minister do if your offering music is too long/too short? How will you know? Who will signal you to begin the Doxology/offertory response?
6. How many prayers requiring musical amens will be used?

The liturgical organist who moves into a nonliturgical service may need to adjust to the additional music performed by the choir, and also may be disturbed by the informality of many such services. As in any job, it takes a full year before you really feel at home, but thinking through the service, along with much practice and careful planning, will make your transition to that new job successful and rewarding.

CHAPTER 5

The Adult Choral Program

OUR HERITAGE OF CHORAL MUSIC

The choral program lies at the heart of music in the church, for it is through choral music that many individuals may share as leaders in worship. For nearly 3,000 years, groups of dedicated people have been trained to sing services of worship. King David commissioned the leaders of the Levites "to appoint their brethren as the singers who should play loudly on musical instruments, on harps and lyres and cymbals, to raise sounds of joy [1 Chron. 15:16]." The joyous procession, led by David, of the Ark of the Covenant to Jerusalem provided another opportunity for the Levites to appoint a leader to "direct the music, for he understood it [1 Chron. 15:22]." David may have been the first "choir director," since he organized 288 musicians, who participated in 24 choral groups, singing various liturgical works. For months these singers prepared the services that were to initiate temple worship. We read of this spectacular consecration of Solomon's temple in 2 Chronicles 5:11-14:

> Now when the priests came out of the holy place (for all the priests who were present had sanctified themselves, without regard to their divisions; and all the Levitical singers, Asaph, Heman, and Jeduthun, their sons and kinsmen, arrayed in fine linen, with cymbals, harps, and lyres, stood east of the altar with a hundred and twenty priests who were trumpeters; and it was the duty of the trumpeters and singers to make themselves heard in unison in praise and thanksgiving to the Lord), and when the song was raised, with trumpets and cymbals and other musical instruments, in praise to the Lord,
>> "For he is good,
>> for his steadfast love endures for ever,"

the house, the house of the Lord, was filled with a cloud, so that the priests could not stand to minister because of the cloud; for the glory of the Lord filled the house of God.

During the Christian era, liturgical choirs existed in almost every chapel and cathedral, along with many monasteries, especially those of the Benedictine Order. In Rome the *Schola Cantorum* has existed continuously since the sixth century. Later, in the Reformation, choirs were formed to assist and lead the congregation in a new liturgy that included the singing of hymns. This German tradition was continued by J.S. Bach, cantor at the St. Thomas Kirche, in Leipzig. In the English cathedrals, choirs of men and boys were trained in the choir school. Some of the finest choral music was written for these choirs by Tallis, Byrd, Weelkes, and others. During the eighteenth and nineteenth centuries, composers such as Haydn, Mozart, Schubert, and Bruckner continued to write choral works to be sung in the church.

In America, singing schools were organized to improve the singing of hymns in churches, and many of the singers who trained in these schools eventually formed choirs. The volunteer choir is an American phenomenon, and grew out of the nonliturgical traditions. During the late 1800s and early 1900s, the quartet choir and the quartet anthem—an outgrowth of the English anthem, with solo sections—became common. Many churches were built with a choir loft capable of housing no more than twelve singers.

Gradually, the concept of a paid quartet who served as the choir was replaced by the concept of a volunteer choir, a group of church members who gathered to enjoy singing church music and who wished to serve in this way. While some churches pay members of a professional quartet to serve as leaders in vocal sections, others expect trained singers to sing "for the glory of God," without remuneration. A strong case may be made for the professional singer; if the minister, the custodian, the secretary, and (hopefully) the organist and choir director are to receive remuneration for their professional services, the singers should not be denied equal consideration, especially since they, as section leaders, provide the same kind of catalytic leadership as other paid staff. The same argument might be used for highly trained educators in the church school, but it is not within the scope of this book to enter into such debate.

The four main functions of choirs are:

1. *To supply musical leadership in the morning worship service.* The choirs are responsible for leading the congregation in hymn-singing and responses, and for preparing all appropriate choral responses and one or two anthems. In addition, they may prepare special musical services, such as a cantata or an oratorio. Increasingly, these presentations are

77

being incorporated into the morning worship service, rather than as an afternoon or evening service, although this becomes a matter of individual church preference. Services of Evensong and Vespers continue to be observed in many liturgical traditions.

2. *To provide opportunity for musical expression through developing musical skills*, e.g., sight-reading, choral tone, and intonation. The development of such skills should contribute toward a greater appreciation of the musical heritage of sacred choral music. Every effort must be made to select music from a broad spectrum of historical periods and styles.

3. *To give members of the congregation an opportunity to meet together and enjoy social interaction with one another.* This should not lead to a clique, but rather to a Christian fellowship experienced through sharing a common effort of making music together.

4. *To provide opportunities for individuals to give of themselves through the sharing of their musical talent,* an exercise in Christian stewardship. These individual contributions, modest as some may be, can produce a combined result that frequently exhibits a musical stature far beyond the sum of its individual parts.

THE ADULT CHOIR

In most churches the adult choir is the primary choral group. It usually consists of volunteer singers from within the congregation, who meet once a week for rehearsal and who sing at least one anthem in the Sunday morning worship service. The size of the choir may vary, depending on the size of the congregation. Other influential factors are the minister's attitude toward the importance of music, the value placed on music by the congregation, the musical skill and effectiveness of the choir director and/or organist, and the esprit de corps of the choir.

An adult choir in a church is very different from a high school a cappella choir. In the first place, an adult choir usually has a wide range of ages and musical talent. Choral tone produced by such a group has great diversity, and the director is challenged to create blend, good intonation, and accuracy of rhythms. Most volunteer singers come to choir rehearsal after working all day. Choir rehearsals are held most often during the evening; thus the director must work with the element of fatigue that is present at day's end.

Many churches have a program of choirs for all ages. (Chapter 6 discusses youth and children's choirs.) Some churches have begun to experiment with a newer idea—ad hoc choirs that do not serve regularly.

The *festival choir* is usually formed for the purpose of performing a larger choral work than is possible with the membership of the regular Adult Choir. Singers who do not feel they can give their time on a regular weekly basis are often interested in singing in special musical events. They are willing to give five or six weeks to rehearsals, and often provide those extra voices needed to present a major work.

The *family choir* is increasing in popularity as an alternative to no music the week after Christmas or during the summer months. Families are invited to participate together (changed voices only). The music selected is generally easy, and rehearsals are held prior to the morning worship service. People may come for one Sunday only or for as many as they wish.

The *choir-for-a-day* may be organized for a special event, such as Lay Sunday or Youth Sunday. An example of this type of choir is a men's chorus (TTBB), which would hold one rehearsal and provide the music for a single Sunday's worship service.

The Warm-up   The warm-up is most important for people who do not sing every day. It should be a time for releasing tensions encountered during the day, and for preparing body and mind for the evening's musical experience.

The first activity involves loosening the muscles in the shoulders and neck. This may be accomplished by:
- moving the head slowly in a circle, and then up and down
- rolling the shoulders forward and backward
- letting the arms hang loosely at the sides and then shaking them gently
- stretching the arms straight up, above the head
- placing the hands behind the head and drawing up to full height
- exaggerating facial expressions to loosen up facial muscles
- placing hands on the hips and moving the body slowly in an arc.

No dancer or athlete would think of performing without an adequate warm-up, and yet many church choirs begin their weekly rehearsals by singing the opening hymn for the next Sunday morning service.

The second step in the warm-up procedure should be vocalises. These vocalises should be selected effectively to diminish the familiar problems found in many adult church choirs: wide vibrato (wobble); scooping and sliding; hooty, nasal, breathy sounds; intonation problems; rhythmic insecurity; and lack of choral blend. Reasons for some of the vocal problems and suggestions for dealing with them follow.

The vibrato. The wide vibrato is one of the most common problems found in volunteer choirs. While it may occur in the male voice, more frequently it is a problem of the female voice. Contrary to popular opinion, it is not a special possession of the *older* female voice; it can afflict the high school voice as well. Generally, it is caused by a lack of breath support, and is induced by poor coordination and muscular tension. The vibrato of a trained singer has a regular, smooth variation of approximately six or seven vibrations per second. A vibrato that is wider than this causes such strong variance in pitch, e.g., above or below the pitch by a quarter to a half step, as to render the pitch indistinguishable, and makes blending the voice with others almost impossible. This problem may be countered (although probably not remedied completely) by using breathing exercises that will enable the singer to produce a smooth, even tone. The following procedures should help to reduce a wide vibrato.

1. *Insist on good posture.* Ask singers to reach for an imaginary bar above the head and to pull the body upward; then let arms hang at sides, with palms facing outward; push out and up in an arc, coming to rest in an upright and comfortable position. Avoid saying, "Let's have better posture, folks," or telling a choir to sit up. Guide people into the proper position for singing; let them experience the feel of the body. As the body that houses the vocal instrument becomes ready to produce a tone, and as blood circulation increases, fatigue drops away and one feels refreshed. Singers should leave a rehearsal exhilarated rather than exhausted.

2. *Assist singers to develop the correct placement of tone.* Many tremolos are caused by a high larynx. Pressure on the tongue or on the larynx can cause a slow vibrato; ng, m, or n can be used to relax the throat muscles. Placing the tone in the mask of the face may be aided by positioning the fingertips over the face, like a mask, and focusing the tone into the hand; then removing the hand and trying to create the same feeling.

3. *Instruct singers to focus on the center of the pitch* by singing *nn* and sustaining it for several seconds. Move from this sustained sound to the vowels, e.g., nnn-a, nnn-ah, nnn-ee, nnn-oh, nnn-oo.

4. *Insist that singers breathe through the nose* rather than through the mouth. The latter method dries the vocal cords and causes a dry, raspy sound.

5. *It does not help to tell singers to improve their breath support.* Rather, give some specific suggestions.
- Breathe as if you were startled or amazed. Keep the shoulders down and expand the rib cage.
- Breathe in, and feel an inner smile as you exhale.
- Expand the rib cage as you breathe in, and let the breath out on a hissing sound. Try not to sound like a radiator springing a leak.
- Expand the belt line when breathing. Don't gasp, but fill the entire chest cavity with air.

- Lean over from the waist. Let the arms hand loosely. Breathe deeply, expanding the rib cage. Straighten up, and exhale slowly and steadily.
- Repeat the breathing exercises, and release the breath on a pitch, using a neutral syllable, e.g., noo, nee. Avoid the sound of ah in these exercises, since this sound is a breathy sound and encourages wasting air.
- Think of singing on the breath as riding a wave into shore. The pitch production must be timed so that the vocal sound rides on top of the breath.
- Yawn. It is almost impossible without taking a deep breath. Just before the yawn occurs, be aware of the open throat.
- Place a hand in front of the mouth. Sing various vowel sounds—ah, a, ee, i, oh, oo. Only the warmth of the breath should be felt, not the air escaping.
- Blow on the fist with a hard *ssss* sound.
- Begin counting mentally on a single pitch, and keep going until you are out of breath. Try to lengthen the time to achieve more control.
- Sing before a cold window so that no fog or moisture collects.

Proper breathing improves the voice with a wide vibrato or tremolo.

The scoop/slide. Another vocal problem that appears frequently in the adult church choir is the scoop or slide. High school choirs are also plagued by scooping and sliding, since so many students imitate pop singers. While this type of singing may be appropriate for folk music, it is not desirable when performing traditional choral repertoire. Most scooping is caused by the singer's inability mentally to hear the pitch to be sung. The singer may also lack proper breath support and proper focus of the tone. Solutions include (1) focusing the tone by singing doo, poo, too; (2) inhaling and expanding the rib cage before singing a pitch; (3) articulating clearly, e.g., doot, doot, doot; and (4) sight-singing intervals, e.g., 1-2-1, 1-3-1, 1-4-1.

Hooty. Generally, this sound is a straight tone, lacking vibrato, and is placed far back in the mouth. Remedies include avoiding the oo sound, and singing lots of ee, ay, and ah. The technique of singing with a smile is particularly helpful in dealing with this problem.

Wandering voice. The "wandering" voice may be found in any amateur vocal ensemble. The singer may wander on a unison passage but more frequently wanders when singing harmony. Most of the time, unless there is a major deficiency in being able to differentiate among pitches, the singer has not learned to hear harmonic relationships or developed a melodic memory. Singing close harmonic progressions and sight-singing intervals will improve this singer's ability to carry his/her own part.

Practice in echo-singing short musical phrases (taken from the music being rehearsed) is also effective in improving the wandering singer's ear.

Diction (singing in English and Latin). The two languages used most frequently by choirs are English and Latin. English, being the vernacular, is most common, although a knowledge of Latin pronunciation is essential if a choir expects to sing any masses or motets from the Renaissance. A choir is always involved in communicating a text to the congregation. The intelligibility of this text is critical to the listener if the music is going to mean anything. This requires the director to deal effectively with vowels and consonants. A soprano section that pronounces "world" as woild, wuhld, or whirrld creates a word which is highly unintelligible to the listener. Although there are great differences in accents throughout the United States, singing diction should be nondistinctive.

It may take a major effort on the part of the director to overcome these local accents, but a good choir should sing with a uniformity of sound and pronunciation. No choir can sing as "it speaks," for no person really speaks the same as another; the choral sound of a group must be homogenous.

International Phonetic Alphabet (IPA) Symbols are useful to the director. The application of these principles is the best possible way to ensure consistent and correct pronunciation. Single vowels are a, e, i, o, u; diphthongs are syllables that have two sounds—know (kno-ooo), go (go-oo), faith (fa-eeth). Vowels must be created by sustained singing, without the slightest change in mouth shape, and all consonants and vanishing vowels must be sounded quickly—loa-d (ah), not lo-*oo*-dah.

Improving vowel pronunciation. When rehearsing a choir it is often effective to use only *one* vowel in order to achieve smoothness, a relaxed jaw, and frontal tonal placement. The neutral syllable doo is useful in accomplishing this, with the correct vowels and consonants returned to the musical line at a later time. The elongation of vowels—such as joining two vowel sounds together, e.g., cle-ear—often improves vowel pronunciation.

Consonants may be voiced or breathed. Voiced consonants include d, b, g, th, j, v, z; breathed consonants, include t, p, k, ch, f, s, sh, th. Other consonants are m, n, ng, l, and r. These latter often cause much trouble, either from being overemphasized, such as r's, or receiving little emphasis, such as m's. To avoid scooping, the subvocal consonants b, d, j, and g must be sung in tune on a given pitch at the beginnings of words. Initial consonants should be delivered as quickly as possible, so that the vowel is reached immediately. Generally, the final consonant is allotted to the first word, rather than the word following.

Sing my soul of wondrous love = wondrous love, *not* wondru-slove
The Lord is my shepherd = Lord is, *not* Lor-dis

Intonation. A basic element in producing an acceptable choral sound is good intonation. Perhaps no other segment of the choral art is as difficult to accomplish or as unpleasant and abrasive when it does not occur. Singing out of tune can become a habit, and a musician must insist that the choir work for good intonation. A congregation cannot be lifted into a worship experience by a choir singing out of tune.

Let us consider some of the problems of intonation. First, the human voice is subject to limitations of range, fatigue, and illness, and is unable to adjust to poor acoustic conditions. The body is the musical instrument, and is not dependent on keys, valves, or strings. Earlier in this chapter the importance of correct breathing and mentally hearing the pitch were discussed. Pitches will be in tune (1) if the singer hears the pitch in his/her mind before singing it, (2) if there is enough breath support and air pressure to produce a clear sound, and (3) if good diction is used. Singing with an unrelaxed jaw, insufficient breath, poorly placed tone, and a wide vibrato all contribute to out-of-tune singing. Physical fatigue and psychological stress are also major contributors to poor intonation and faulty singing.

A lack of intensity and energy in pianissimo passages will almost guarantee flatting, as will singing too loudly or singing with a chest voice. Good intonation happens when there is resonance, energy, a relaxed tone, and proper pronunciation and articulation. Avoid a heavy hand on the piano when rehearsing the choir. A choir can only stay in tune when each member can hear the other singers; if each individual is singing forte, or the accompaniment is drowning out the singers, this is not possible.

These reminders will pay dividends in improved intonation:
- Rehearse without the piano.
- Rehearse with moderate dynamics, preferably *mp* to *pp*.
- Rehearse on neutral syllables to learn the notes.
- Rehearse descending passages, taking care to sing each descending step close to the previous one.
- Rehearse ascending skips by pretending they are far apart.
- Change the tempo of repeated passages in rehearsal.
- Maintain vitality on repeated notes or sustained phrases.
- Don't allow heavy vibratos or scooping.
- Sing through the note on dotted, half, and whole notes.
- Avoid selecting compositions that are outside the range or ability of the choir.
- Tell the singers to think ahead and not just follow one note at a time.
- Ask choir members what is happening in other voice parts.

Identify where there is (1) imitation, (2) a return of the melody, or (3) harmonic changes.

Rhythm. Perhaps more musicians have trouble with rhythm than with any other musical element. Because many choir members do not understand music notation, directors must devise other ways of teaching intricate rhythm patterns. One of the best ways is to have the choristers feel the beat. As they raise and lower their hands in a 1 2 1 2 pattern, they are more likely to feel the pulse of the music. Many singers learn to perform notes quite well but ignore the rests. Use devices such as 1 2 sh / 1 2 sh / or 1 2 clap 4 / 1 2 clap 4 / instead of 1 2 3 4 in teaching the importance of rests in a composition. Verbal devices, such as speaking "Mississippi" in eighth notes and pizza pie for dotted notes, make

Mis-sis-sip-pi   Piz - za Pie

the singer aware of rhythmic patterns. Identifying and clapping rhythm patterns that recur, along with developing a feeling for pulse will soon improve the choir's ability to sing rhythms correctly and easily.

Teaching a harmonic sense. Developing a sense of harmony is essential for good intonation and blend. The warm-up period is excellent for working on this problem.

1. During the warm-up, instruct the choir to sing a major triad: Soprano—8, A—3, T—5, B—1. On cue, move up and down by whole or half steps, correcting parts that become out of tune.
2. Place hands together, fingers of right hand pointing to fingers of left hand. Raise either or both hands to indicate a whole or half step—wide movement for whole step, narrow movement for half step.
3. Sing the triad: 1 3 5 (8); on cue, indicate which part should move up or down a prescribed interval, e.g., 1—up a second, 8—down a third, etc.
4. Sing the triad: 1 3 5 (8); on cue, indicate a complete change of parts, e.g., 1 becomes 5, 3 becomes 8, 5 becomes 1, 8 becomes 3.
5. Write S A T B on a chalkboard, along with intervals. Begin on a unison pitch, and pointing to the selected part, indicate what interval choristers are to sing:
   S   A   T   B
   M2 M3   P5   P8
6. Sing a descending scale. Each part stops on a selected note.

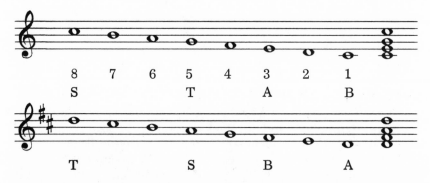

Teaching a Choir to Sight-read   The majority of choristers, regardless of what type of choral organization they sing with, have difficulty sight-reading. In contrast, their instrumentalist counterparts may read fluently, whether they play an orchestral instrument or the keyboard. What are some differences between the problems encountered by the singer and those of the instrumentalist? First, the instrumentalist relies on an instrument outside the body to produce the quality of tone and the pitches. By placing fingers on certain valves or keys, e.g., C E G, a melody or a chord is created. While an instrument is subject to pitch changes due to varying temperatures and humidity, an instrumentalist can play a given pitch on an instrument without necessarily hearing it in the inner ear first. But the singer must hear the pitch and then properly prepare the body to produce it. Sight-reading fluently as an instrumentalist does not always guarantee effective vocal sight-reading.

A chorister, then, whether trained as an instrumentalist or not, must have a system for mentally identifying pitches, intervals, and harmonic relationships. The limitations of this discussion prohibit presenting the many arguments supporting the use of numbers, movable Do, fixed Do, letter names, etc.; however, it is essential for the church choir director to decide on one method or a combination of methods that will enable the choir to learn to read music, thus reducing the necessity for rote teaching. The following outline may help clarify the strengths and weaknesses of each approach.

The four methods generally used to teach sight-reading are (1) note names, (2) numbers, (3) movable Do, and (4) fixed Do. Sight-reading by using note names requires a knowledge of letter names and a keyboard sense of tonal relationships, especially between whole and half steps. Materials used in this approach include a series of pitch patterns that occur frequently, e.g.:

C   E   G

Singers may be asked to fill in a missing pitch in a given sequence, e.g.:

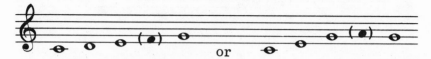

The number system is based on a seven-note scale, and has the advantage of simplicity and direct relationship to the scale degrees, e.g., 1-5-1, 1-6-5-3-1. One disadvantage is the use of two syllables, such as *sev-en*, or the unpleasant sound of *five* or *nine*. A second difficulty is the lack of any chromatic capability. An attempt to remedy this has been the use of inflected scale numbers, e.g., 1, 1 sharp, 2 flat, 2, 2 sharp, etc.

The oldest method of sight-reading is the system of movable Do. This is based on a tonal center and developing the ability to hear and sing pitches in relationship to the tonic. Most musicians are familiar with the famous Guidonian hand and the subsequent use of the syllables Do (Ut), Re, Mi, Fa, Sol, La, Ti, Do. The use of these neutral syllables provides a choral sound that is pleasing to the ear, and contributes toward legato and expressive singing. One of the chief problems with the movable Do system is the complexity of accidentals with which the singer must deal—Do, Di, Re, Ri, etc.

In the fixed Do approach to sight-singing only seven syllables are used. To express a sharp or flat, the singer adjusts the pitch but uses the same syllable. Thus, both C and C♯ are called Do. An advantage of this system is the consistency of always calling C *Do*, G *Sol*, etc. Constant adjustment is not required of the singer, other than to apply the system to chromatics.

Recognizing that rehearsal time is extremely limited, instruction in sight-reading techniques should be integrated into a variety of activities. For example:

1. Practice hymns using your chosen method. In learning an anthem, rehearse problem intervallic leaps, as well as difficult harmonic passages, not only on a neutral syllable, but also using one of the systems for sight-reading.
2. Create a series of charts with common intervallic difficulties. These might evolve into handouts for choir members, who then may drill themselves.
3. Incorporate some sight-reading of new material into every rehearsal.
4. Avoid using the piano when learning to sight-read.
5. Do not underestimate how much subliminal learning can occur during the course of a year.
6. Begin rehearsals by asking the choir to think the pitch A (440). To encourage development of the concept of hearing a pitch in the

inner ear, insist that no one hum. Then ask the choir to sing the pitch they think is A.

7. Next, ask the choir to sing an M2 or M3, P4 or P5.
8. Sing a simple and familiar tune, and analyze the intervallic relations. Example:

9. As the group improves and as time permits, add more complex patterns.

Pacing the Rehearsal   As stated earlier in this chapter, most volunteer singers come to choir rehearsal with a certain amount of fatigue from the day's activities. Pacing the rehearsal to provide interest and variety pays off in increased musical productivity and a rewarding musical experience. Some reminders:

1. Plan the rehearsal carefully.
2. Have all music, books, materials in place before the choir members arrive.
3. Know the music yourself. Do not expect to learn it along with the choir.
4. Begin with a careful warm-up, including physical exercises and vocalises.
5. Alternate difficult pieces with easier pieces. Avoid singing every piece all the way through without good reasons for each repetition.
6. Be innovative in teaching melodic problems, rhythmic problems, and diction.

Coping with the midweek rehearsal blahs: fatigue, family conflicts, absenteeism. Two major nonmusical choir problems encountered by most church choral directors are fatigue and conflicts in time. Fatigue may be overcome by careful planning, interesting music, good ventilation and lighting, pacing of the rehearsal, and an energetic and musically talented director. Factors that enter into the fatigue level include major weather problems (fighting snow in winter), extreme heat and humidity in summer, physical ailments (colds), and pressure of job and/or family. Every director develops a sensitivity for choir fatigue and takes countering steps to overcome it.

Conflicts with family activities and social commitments that interfere with a chorister's attendance at the weekly rehearsal and/or Sunday service cause many a choir director to have ulcers and/or a massive headache. The priorities of present-day living seem to take precedence over church commitments, and the time allotted to the choir is last, not first, in planning a schedule. Some directors insist that a chorister attend the weekly rehearsal or not sing on Sunday morning. For other directors, the solution is found in providing a makeup rehearsal. Whatever the decision, it must be applied equally to all choir members. Just because a chorister may be the chairperson of the Music Committee does not entitle him/her to sing Sunday morning without having attended a rehearsal. The quickest way to upset choir members is to make rules that only apply to certain singers and not to others. Before a person is "admitted" to choir membership, he/she must understand the few rules by which the choir is run and must agree to abide by these rules. Dependability is the most important requirement for choir membership, followed by talent and dedication.

The Use of Vestments Vestments bring people together, mask individuality, and convey a sense of unity in the task of leading the congregation in worship. They should add to the beauty of the worship setting. Vestments that are flashy, dramatic, and gaudy have no place in a service of worship; it is not their purpose to focus attention on the choir. To this end, it is necessary and appropriate to have a dress code for choir members when they wear vestments, for example:

1. Robes should be approximately the same length from the floor (8" to 10").
2. Robes should fit the shoulders; they should not droop.
3. Dark shoes should be worn by both men and women, especially if there is a processional.
4. High turtlenecks, and bright ties and shirts should be avoided.
5. Choristers should not wear flashy earrings or jewelry.

There are those who believe that dress codes or guidelines are not necessary, but if one adopts the view that the purpose of the vestment is to create uniformity and a sense of oneness, then these suggestions are appropriate.

Recruiting Choristers Recruiting members for the various choirs is a major task of the church musician. The first requirement is that you believe in the choir program yourself, and are willing to give the time to build it.

Begin as far ahead of the first rehearsal as is practical (4 to 6 weeks) to inform people of the musical activities that are planned for the year. Advertise the music to be sung, special musical events (cantatas, festival with other churches), and social events. Build your recruiting around a central theme, e.g., "Joyfully Sing" or "Sing Praise to God," and use visual media (colorful posters, slide show, banners).

If there has been a choir in previous years, obtain a list of former members. Send them a letter of invitation for the new season, and follow this up with a personal telephone call. Ask members and leaders of youth activities for additional names, and personally contact each person on the list. It is important that you (along with the minister and/or the Music Committee) decide on the requirements for membership. Some churches believe that all who indicate an interest should be allowed to sing, whether they have any musical ability or not. While you as a director may not elect to use the strict audition procedures of an advanced high school ensemble, or college or symphony chorus, some musical ability must be a prerequisite. The choice often must be made between the person with little musical ability having a valuable social experience, and the musically talented person who has a great deal to gain and to give to a choir. There is nothing more frustrating for anyone who is musical than to sing next to someone who is always on the wrong pitch or who is singing the wrong rhythm. As a director, you need to ask yourself, "Would I give my time to sing in a choir and experience this kind of frustration?"

A simple tryout policy is often desirable. If an applicant shows great deficiency in aural and rhythmic skills, suggest that you work with him/her on an individual basis until he/she is ready to join the choir. There are a number of sources to which the church musician can turn to recruit choir members.

Printed Publicity
Church bulletin
Weekly church paper or newsletter
Letters of invitation to former choir members
Letters of invitation to potential choir members
Booklet or folder explaining the choral program and the various choirs (if more than one)
Personal Contacts
Telephone follow-up to letters
Visits to church school classes, adult study groups
Visits to local school choral directors and ensembles
Visits to Boy Scouts/Girl Scouts, 4-H clubs, and other service organizations to tell them about the choral program
Encourage everyone in the church to give you names of potential choir members.
Telephone or personally call on new church members. Their names can be supplied by the minister.
Visit youth, women's, and men's groups in the church.
Have a song-writing contest. Give guidelines concerning length,

and use nursery or folk tunes (because these are familiar to most people). Appoint a committee of adults, teenagers, and children to choose the winner. Feature the song at the first rehearsal.

CHOIR ORGANIZATION

It is very important to keep records of choir membership, attendance, music purchased, music used, special programs, etc. Every choir member should have the following information on file with the director:

Adult Choir

Name _____ Date _____

Address _____ Telephone _____

Occupation _____ Place of business _____

Business telephone _____

Are you a member of <u>(church's name)</u> ? _____

Are you a member of another church? _____ Name of church _____

_____ Have you ever sung in a church or community choir?

_____ What part do you sing? _____

Do you play an instrument? _____ Instrument played _____

Private study? _____

* * * * *

General Musical Information
(Scale: 5 high 4 3 2 1 low)

Range _____   Tone quality _____ (full ____ soft ____)

Intonation _____   Volume of tone _____

Breathing _____   Rhythm _____

Sight-reading _____   Tonal memory _____

Harmonic sense _____

It is imperative that the director keep accurate records of attendance. These may be entered as follows:

P . . . . Present for entire rehearsal
L . . . .Present, but late
INC . . . Present, but left early
EX. . . .Excused because of illness
A^n . . .Absent with notification[1]
A . . . .Absent

THE MUSIC LIBRARY

The choral director is responsible for choosing and ordering choral music and maintaining the music library. Following these few simple procedures will save an enormous amount of time and energy.

1. Catalog each set of music as soon as it is received. Stamp each copy with the church's name, and give each set a number for filing purposes. The anthem then may be filed alphabetically in drawers or by filing number in boxes. Two file cards should be completed for each selection: one listing the title first and the other listing the composer first.

2. Assign a number to each copy in the set. This number will correspond to a numbered choir folder, thus enabling a given singer to use the same copy of music for as long as the singer remains in the choir. Such a system encourages the careful marking of music by the singer and enables the director to locate missing copies.

3. Record the date for each performance. Many congregations appreciate having the text of the anthem printed in the Order of Service, if copyright laws allow. Maintaining a file of all services simplifies the process of text preparation, because once printed, the person typing the Sunday bulletin can refer to a previous performance for the text.

See the sample below for cataloging music.

Choral Library

File Number _____

Title: Be Ye Followers of God   Composer: Leo Sowerby
Text: Ephesians 5:1-2; 6:10, 13   Voicing: SATB
Classification: Confirmation, General
Publisher: H.W. Gray/Belwin CMR 2790   Copies purchased: 25
Performance: 10/26/80   Date: August 1980

---

[1]While people will miss a rehearsal for reasons other than illness, such absences should be discouraged without the director appearing unsympathetic or insensitive to conflicting schedules.

CHAPTER 6

The Youth and Children's Choir Program

DEVELOPING YOUTH CHOIRS

One of the chief concerns of churches is to provide for the Christian education of children and youth. The youth choir movement began in the 1920s, and many attribute its growth to the work of John Finley Williamson, organist-choirmaster of Westminster Presbyterian Church in Dayton, Ohio, and founder of the Westminster Choir College. He gave impetus to the graded choir system—that is, a choir for every age-group—and youth choirs began to appear in even the smallest churches. In the larger churches, choirs for junior high mixed voices, senior high mixed voices, junior high girls' voices, and junior high boys' voices were organized. Smaller churches often combined junior and senior high school students. During the 1950s, as bellringing became popular, many churches substituted youth bellringing groups for youth choirs. Today, many directors experience competition with public school music programs for students' time. However, those churches that offer a strong music program remain in the best position to attract youth to their choirs. For the sake of discussion, a youth choir is defined as a choral organization for junior and senior high school students. It will be considered as one choir, although we recognize that in many larger churches several such choirs exist.

The purpose of the youth choir is similar to that of the adult choir: (1) to serve as a leader in worship, (2) to develop musical skills, (3) to provide opportunity for social interaction, and (4) to share musical talent. Like other choral organizations, a choir must rehearse and sing regularly if interest and motivation are to remain high. Therefore, it is important to schedule the youth choir for regular services, such as once a month; or if there are two Sunday morning services, for one of the services. Care should be taken to provide the entire congregation with the opportunity to hear the youth choir; thus, avoid having these young people always sing at the early service. (Like adults, youth are not always at their vocal best early in the morning.)

It is equally important to decide on a regular rehearsal time. Some churches have found that a midweek youth activities program, with the youth choir as a central interest group, is highly successful. A dinner immediately before or after rehearsal allows for important socializing at a time other than during the rehearsal. With a minimum of supervision, the youth often can prepare the supper themselves. Saturday rehearsals, Sunday morning or evening rehearsals, or early evening rehearsals are all probably used throughout the country. Whatever time is best for your community and your church *is* the *best* time. While you, as the director, are agonizing over finding just the right time, keep in mind that no time is perfect for all youth and their parents. Choose the time that involves the fewest conflicts, and then stick to it for at least one year. Changing the day and time of the rehearsal is a fast way to lose the interest of any singer.

A word may be in order concerning the role of parents in the youth choir. *No youth choir can be successful without the support of parents!* It is absolutely essential that parents be involved and committed to the youth choir program of the church. In our mobile society, young people are often dependent on private transportation, and when there are several children in the family, it takes a great deal of flexibility to get Judy to youth choir by 6:30 on Wednesday night. After all, Richard gets home from football practice about 6:30 and is starved for supper. Cooperation between families (car pools are essential), patience, and understanding by members of families are major contributing factors to a successful youth choir program.

A youth choir rehearsal should be more than just gathering together to sing an anthem. It should involve musical training in producing expressive choral tone, sight-reading, hymn study, church history, and music history. We recognize that the youth choir rehearsal is not a school situation; nevertheless, if it is to have individuality, if it is to be different from the school choir, then there must be some identifiable differences. Unless the youth choir tries to compete with the school, it should concentrate on sacred music. Little enough sacred music is performed in public schools today, and singing secular music adds just one more pop group to an already burgeoning number.

Every youth choir should study hymns. This does not mean that the young people sit down with pencil and paper to take notes, but rather the vibrancy and joy of the Christian tradition is communicated through the singing of hymns. The director should share a knowledge of the great chorales, folk hymns, plainsong hymns, contemporary social gospel hymns, early psalmody, and the heritage of John and Charles Wesley, Isaac Watts, and others.

A national organization devoted to the study of hymnody is The Hymn Society of America, Wittenberg University, Springfield, Ohio 45501. This organization publishes papers, provides leadership for hymn festivals, and encourages research in hymnody.

Developing the Teenage Singing Voice   A major difference between rehearsing the adult choir and rehearsing the youth choir is the changing voice. This is also one of the major reasons for *not* including junior and senior high students (except for juniors and seniors) in the adult choir. Voices in this age-group are generally light and have a limited range, and few students are musically mature enough to sing with a resonant, full tone. The exception to this is the unchanged voice of the boy soprano or the boy alto, which will be discussed later.

A girl's voice generally begins to change between the ages of 10 and 12. Her voice is soft, breathy, and childlike, even after she has begun to mature physically. Her range diminishes, and she often refers to the pitch G^2 as "too high." While this particular attitude has always been present, the imitation of pop singers by teenagers has contributed further to this view. The approximate voice ranges of early teenage girls are

First Soprano   Second Soprano   Alto

By the end of seventh grade (age 12) and throughout much of eighth grade (age 13), a girl's voice remains thin and light. Except for vocal range, few girls at this age may be truly classified as sopranos or altos. Pushing voices too hard at this point can be extremely dangerous to later vocal development, especially if improper vocal production and tensions are encouraged by asking them to "sing louder."

The changing boy's voice is usually given greater attention than that of a girl's, simply because it is much more dramatic. Most adults are familiar with the cracking voice of a young teenage boy. American music educators have long adopted the view that boys should be kept singing

94

through the voice change. Boys do not stop talking or stop athletics while their bodies mature; therefore, there is no valid reason why they should stop singing.

There are two ways in which a boy's voice changes. First, it may suddenly drop an octave. Parents may think their son has a cold, and then realize that the "cold" is rapidly becoming permanent. The muscles holding the thickening vocal cords have not matured enough to control them. At this stage of the voice change, the boy frequently will try to match a tone either an octave higher than his speaking voice or an octave lower. Most boys have to learn to hear the new pitch; after all, for 12 or more years they have been singing in a treble range.

The other way that a voice changes is called the slow slide. Often there is little dramatic change, nor is there the uncontrolled cracking characteristic of the sudden drop. These boys' voices tend to slide downward, plateau by plateau, until they arrive at their adult destination. Sometimes they remain at a given level for 6 months to a year; at other times they change every few months. It must also be added here that, after the voice reaches its lowest point in the descent, it begins to rise again; thus, a boy who is a baritone in high school may well become a tenor in college. It is most important for the choral director to check boys' voices frequently at this age and reassign them to another part, if necessary. Approximate ranges for the boy's changing voice are

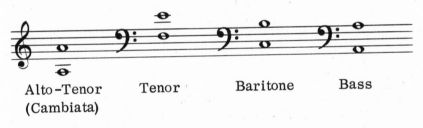

Alto-Tenor   Tenor   Baritone   Bass
(Cambiata)

These ranges are far more limited than those of the mature male voice. Because of these limitations, music must be selected carefully. American boys have a compulsive desire to sing bass, even though their voices may not have begun to change, and care must be taken to protect them from trying to sing too low. This is generally far more injurious to a boy's voice than striving for the higher pitch, which a boy is more apt to reject.

In choosing music for youth choirs, close attention must be paid to the voice ranges. Some SAB compositions are impossible for junior high voices, since the alto may be too low for the girls or too high for the alto-tenors, and the bass may be out of range for the young baritones. Easier four-part music is much less taxing on young voices. Singing remains the most individual of all musical activities, and the voice needs to be nurtured and encouraged.

The same basic techniques of choral training used with adults may be used with youth; however, modification in range, dynamic level, and choral expectations must be made. Young people in junior and senior high school choruses are frequently capable of a much higher level of performance and repertory than directors expect. While many public school choruses seem to focus on light, popular music, the church youth choir should offer an alternative and provide opportunities to sing some of the finest sacred music. To continue to do the same type of folksy, popular tunes with the jiggy rhythms is to deny young people in the church their true heritage. It raises the question, "Why go to the church choir and do exactly the same thing that I'm doing in the school choir with twice as many singers?"

There are, however, unique problems with the teenage voice, some of which have already been mentioned. First, the tone is breathy and thin; second, the range of the voice is narrower than an adult's; third, the younger student has developed little harmonic sense or ability to sing a part independent of another; and fourth, unless the student has studied an instrument privately (and that in itself is no guarantee), there is an inability to read music notation.

Warm-ups and vocalises for the youth choir are extremely important. To overcome breathiness, exercises in breathing and in focusing the tone are most important.

Breathing.

1. Inhale, and expand the rib cage like a basketball being blown up. Exhale on *sssss,* like there is a slow leak.
2. Inhale quickly, as if you see a fumble by your team on the 1-yard line. Feel the body expand.
3. Place the palm of the hand on the diaphragm, and practice pushing the hand out with the breath.

4. Inhale, and sing on the neutral syllable *mee.*

Sustain for 4 counts, then 8, then 16, etc. Move head gently, keeping the tone going. Try to avoid any changes in tone quality.

Focusing the tone.

1. Sing into hand placed in front of face. Use *nee, na, nah, noh, noo.*
2. Tip head slightly downward, and vocalize on rhythmic patterns. Use both staccato and legato articulation.

Create similar patterns, and move upward and downward by half steps.

Resonance may be achieved when the tone is properly placed in the natural resonating chambers. To accomplish this, the mouth must be open. This is particularly difficult for teenagers, who often have a mouth full of braces and rubber bands and who feel foolish when asked to drop their jaws or open their mouths. Rather than resort to the futility of such directions, suggest that singers

- sing as if you have a small egg in your mouth
- sing as if you are about ready to yawn
- use your mouth, lips and tongue as if leading a cheer at a basketball or football game
- sing as if whispering exciting news to a friend

To create a physical condition for resonance

- hum into your hand until your face tickles
- as you hum, fill all the holes in your head
- expand and contract the sound of *eee*, controlling the breath and trying for maximum sound
- use the following exercises

Forward placement

May – nee   Hing – yee

Expansion of range is critical for teenagers. As stated earlier in this chapter, boys tend to try to sing lower pitches too soon, while girls view everything as too high. Although adult choirs easily sing in unison, this should be avoided with youth choirs. Increasing the range should be done by working with an entire vocal section, even with individuals, rather than the entire choir. Long, sustained vocalizing at an extreme range must be avoided, and while singers should be encouraged to expand their ranges upward and downward, care should be taken to use only short phrases for ascending and descending patterns.

Yah - ha - ha - ha - ha - ha - ha - ha   Yo

Yah - ha - ha - ha - ha - ha - ha - ha   Yo

Yah - ha - ha - ha - ha - ha - ha   Yo

Yah   ha   ha   ha   ha   ha   ha   ha   Yo

Yah - ha - ha - ha - ha - ha - ha - ha - ha - ha - ha - ha   Yo

Yah - ha - ha - ha - ha - ha - ha - ha - ha - ha - ha - ha   Yo

Harmonic Sense/Independence of Parts   Developing a harmonic sense is particularly difficult for boys with newly changed or changing voices. They must learn to hear the pitches in their new register and then to match those pitches with their voices. Many choral directors tend to use unison arrangements and/or popular-type music. Both these choices may lead to poor musical results. The teenage choir usually has such a narrow range that unison singing is almost impossible; many of the popular arrangements which utilize very close harmony are equally disastrous. The youth choir director's first task is to develop a tonal and harmonic sense, employing wide, clearly defined intervals. Try having the singers stop before a pitch; think the pitch; then sing it.

Sing   5   4   3 2 Stop; Think; Sing 1   Sing 5   3 Stop; Think; Sing 1

The same technique should be applied to a passage in an anthem or a hymn tune.

Stop; Think; Sing

Young singers find it impossible to sing harmony if they cannot hear it. Drowning them out by pounding the piano, in hopes that they will learn their part, only adds to their inability to hear themselves in relation to the whole. Many harmonic problems occur because the range of music is too wide for the choral group. If the notes are in the singer's range, the singer does not need piano reinforcement; however, when those pitches are outside the range, the director, not wanting to really hear what the singers are doing, plays a little bit louder, usually out of desperation. Such a director is only kidding him/herself.

One of the most popular activities of youth choirs is the folk musical. Often young people who do not usually participate in church activities are attracted by the preparations involved in presenting such a musical. Also, these productions provide an opportunity for them to sing "their kind of music." Many times one can augment the choir by enlisting singers from the local junior or senior high school. Public school instrumentalists may also assist in such performances. (Be sure, however, that they have adequate rehearsal time.) Choosing a "good" musical takes a great deal of time; the ultimate choice is dependent on the size, capabilities, and interest of the choir. However, there are several criteria that can help in this selection process.

1. Is the musical crafted well?
2. Does it wear well? Can you rehearse it over a long period of time without tiring of it?
3. Is the text appropriate for teenagers?
4. Does it have catchy melodies, interesting and varied rhythms?
5. Do you have the instrumental forces available? (Avoid using a piano in place of an electric guitar.)
6. Can you afford to purchase the necessary copies?

After you have decided on the folk musical, plan and publish the rehearsal schedule. This is especially important if you are going to have any extra rehearsals. Enlist the help of other organizations within the church (parents, committees, etc.) to assist with publicity, dramatic effects (lighting, costumes, sound equipment), tickets (if used). Schedule the use of the rehearsal area well in advance of when you wish to use it. There is nothing like announcing a rehearsal of the folk musical in the sanctuary for Wednesday evening, only to find that it is going to be used by another church organization for a special program. Think and plan ahead, involving the minister and all appropriate committees. Such a presentation is frequently performed on Youth Sunday. Publicity in the local papers, church newsletter, and bulletins, along with posters and enthusiasm generated by the youth themselves, will almost guarantee a full house. Among musicals/cantatas that have been performed successfully by youth choirs are:

Bobrowitz, David and Porter, Steven	The Creation (Walton)
Draesel, Herbert	Rejoice (Marks)
Gravitt, John W.	The Hallelujah Mass (Flammer)
Johnson, David	Folk Gloria (Augsburg)
Landgrave, Philip	Purpose (Broadman)
Red, Buryl	Celebration (Broadman)
Smith, Tedd	New Vibrations (Lexicon)
Wilson, Richard	He Lived the Good Life (Augsburg)

DEVELOPING CHILDREN'S CHOIRS

The purpose of children's choirs is to provide the child with opportunities to learn about and express the Christian faith through music. On the one hand, a choir may be an adequate instrument for guiding the development of Christian character but may be poor in its expression of music. On the other hand, a choir may be well controlled, beautifully vested, and a model of tonal perfection but may lack the development of Christian character. One need not be sacrificed for the other; good music well performed is compatible with Christian education. Children are entitled to more than being cute and growing up with the feeling that no one cares or knows the difference whether they perform well musically or not. It is important that children take pride in their choir, in themselves, and in their church, and efforts directed toward attaining quality musical performances will certainly contribute toward this pride.

There are two basically different functions that a children's choir may serve, and these usually determine the nature of its organization. The first is to provide a musical activity for all children enrolled in the church school, and these might well be called church school choirs. There are no attendance requirements and no tryouts. The "choir" may rehearse during an activity hour on Sunday mornings but rarely has a separate rehearsal time during the week. The church school choir generally has more modest musical expectations than a children's choir, since a wide range of musical talent and interest is represented. Occasionally, such a choir appears in a morning worship service or church school activity, e.g., Christmas pageant, Thanksgiving dinner, etc.

A second type of choir aims to develop musicianship more fully, leadership in worship, and an understanding and appreciation of sacred music. Membership in this type of choir usually involves a simple tryout and requires a commitment of interest, time, and talent. Rehearsals are held during the week, and to the traditional musical experiences of singing, listening, moving, playing instruments, and creating music is added the dimension of hymn study, education for worship, and study of the role music has played in our Christian heritage.

The choir usually participates in the morning worship service several times a year, especially during the major festivals, e.g., Thanksgiving, Christmas, Lent, and Easter, and many also present a yearly musical. In addition, local chapters of the Choristers Guild[1] plan and sponsor festivals offering further opportunity for motivating and sustaining high interest in a choir program.

A church must decide which of these organizational plans it wishes to use and then build a music program accordingly. It is not within the scope of this book to discuss all the views for or against each form of organization, only to call attention to both. The following discussion is devoted to the children's choir concept and form of organization, although many methodologies may be applicable to the church school choir.

Organization   Children's choirs should be organized around maturation levels. It is as unrealistic to put 6-year-olds with 11-year-olds in a choir as it is to expect them to compete in baseball. Not only is there a huge psychological difference, but the differing physical and mental capabilities make it impossible to maintain interest. In an effort to have "numbers," many churches try to organize a choir with too wide an age span. Decide whether the choir is to be a "primary" choir or a "junior" choir, and choose from the following groupings:

[1]The Choristers Guild was founded by Ruth Krebiel Jacobs in 1948. A national organization with over 10,000 members, it plays a dynamic role in the continuing development of children's choirs. The monthly letters contain teaching strategies, music, and special articles of interest.

101

Primary
   Kindergarten, grades 1 and 2
   Grades 1, 2, and 3

Junior
   Grades 2, 3, 4, and 5
   Grades 3, 4, 5, and 6
   Grades 4, 5, and 6
   Grades 5, 6, 7, and 8

It is important for a children's choir/choirs to have a name. Such names as John Knox, John Wesley, Bethany, Aldersgate, Matins, Joyful Noise, Chi Rho, Chapel, and Westminster are some that have been used. Identification with a major Christian event or personage gives status to the choir and encourages pride.

RECRUITING OF CHILDREN'S AND YOUTH CHOIRS

In addition to the recruitment procedures for adult choirs, given in chapter 5, church musicians may wish to add special touches for children's and youth choirs.

Have a special ice cream party for all those who enroll on Choir Registration Day. Give out blue ribbons with name and "First Prize" on them.

Send a puzzle with the letter of invitation, e.g.:

1. An insect that stings............................
2. The edge of a knife.............................
3. The opposite of leave..........................
4. The number after one..........................
5. Rhymes with tire................................
BE SHARP, *C O M E   T O   C H O I R*

When new members are received into the children's/youth choir, a Letter of Welcome, and a Chorister's Pledge and Reminder should be sent. A similar letter might also be sent to adults.

Dear _____,

Welcome to membership in the _____ [*name of choir*] which rehearses _____ [*time and day.*]. Choir members are responsible for all information sent in the monthly choir letter. When schedules of services and special rehearsals are given, they should be posted where you and your parents will have a reminder of when you are to rehearse and sing. It is essential that you be dependable and punctual in attending the rehearsals and the services. If for any reason you must be absent, please be courteous and responsible by letting [*choir mother or director*] know of the intended absence. No choir can sing well if it has no-shows. Membership in the _____ [*name of choir*] involves such a commitment.

We of the church staff are delighted that you have joined the _____ choir, and we look forward to getting to know you and your parents in this new relationship.

Sincerely yours,[2]

The Chorister's Pledge[3]

I pledge myself
1. To be loyal to the _____ [*name of choir*]
   . . . through attending all rehearsals and services
   . . . by obeying the rules and requirements
   . . . by being dependable and responsible
2. To treat all choir members as I would have them treat me.
3. To be reverent in thought and action as I worship and lead others.

_____   _____
Date   Chorister's Signature

Chorister's Prayer

Keep your heart a-singing,
Let others hear the song.
Make your cheerful music.
Help the world along.

A Chorister's Reminder

Name _____ Choir _____

Director _____ Church _____

Telephone _____ [*of director*]

Choir Mother _____ Telephone _____ [*of choir mother*]

Fall		Spring	
Dates of Rehearsals	*Services*	*Rehearsals*	*Services*
_____	_____	_____	_____
_____	_____	_____	_____
_____	_____	_____	_____

---

[2]Used with permission of Choristers Guild, Dallas, TX.
[3]Used with permission of Choristers Guild, Dallas, TX.

Registration Form
Youth Choir/Children's Choir

Name _____ Address _____ Date _____

Telephone _____ Age _____ Grade in school _____

Father's name _____ Address _____ Telephone _____

     Business address _____ Telephone _____

Mother's name _____ Address _____ Telephone _____

     Business address _____ Telephone _____

Brothers? _____ Ages _____ Sisters? _____ Ages _____

Person to contact in an emergency _____

     Address _____ Telephone _____

What church do you attend? _____

What church does your father/mother/parents attend? _____

Do you sing in a school choral ensemble? _____

     Name of ensemble _____ Part sung _____

Do you play in a school instrumental ensemble? _____

     Name of ensemble _____ Instrument played _____

Do you take private lessons? ____ How long have you studied? ____

Name of private teacher _____

     Address _____ Telephone _____

* * * * *
General Musical Information
(Scale: 5 high 4 3 2 1 low)

Range _____	Rhythm _____
Tone quality _____	Tonal memory _____
Intonation _____	Harmonic sense _____
Volume of tone _____	Sight-singing _____

Voice change: beginning ____partial____complete____

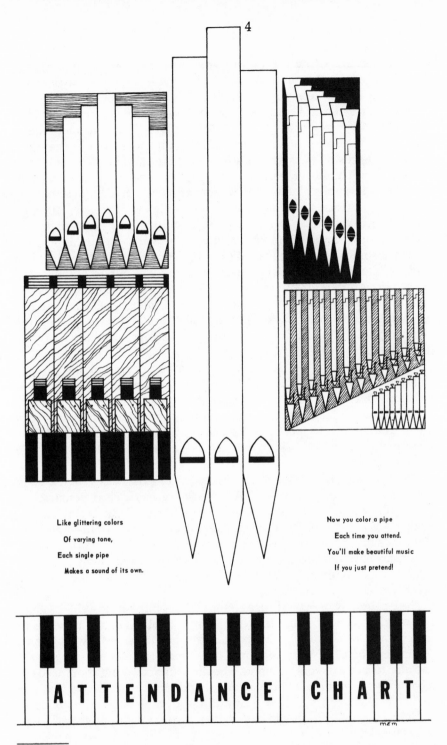

4

Like glittering colors
Of varying tone,
Each single pipe
Makes a sound of its own.

Now you color a pipe
Each time you attend.
You'll make beautiful music
If you just pretend!

ATTENDANCE CHART

Developing the Child's Singing Voice   The child's voice differs dramatically from that of the teenager or of the adult. Its quality is much thinner and the tessitura is higher. As with most other motor coordination skills, it is essential that the child learn to use his/her singing voice early, certainly by the age of 9. Authorities are in agreement that if children do not learn to match tones and sing phrases in tune by the age of 9, their chances of ever achieving this skill are minimal. This does not mean that *no* child ever learns to sing past the age of 9, but rather that attaining a level of skill after 9 becomes far more difficult. Research has shown that musical aptitude changes very little after this age, although musical achievement may increase throughout most of a lifetime.

At a time when children are greatly influenced by popular singers, what are some of the characteristics of the American child's voice? Is it truly different from the "boy choir" voice or are our techniques and expectations different? Why are boy choirs—e.g., Vienna Choir Boys—as well as children's choirs—e.g., Oberkirchen Children's Choir—capable of singing major choral works of Byrd, Tallis, and Monteverdi, while the average children's choir director in America is struggling to teach a hymn like "Away in a Manger"?

One of the major differences between a boy choir and the average children's choir is the selectivity and training found in the boy choir system, where boys must pass stringent tests in musical skill, aptitude, and musicianship before they are accepted. Their daily academic work includes a significant period of formal music study, in contrast to the twenty-minute music lesson two times a week found in many American elementary schools.

Another major difference is the quality of the girls' voices compared to the quality of the boys' voices. A boy's voice has a clear penetrating, translucent quality, generally devoid of breathiness. Because of its clarity, a boy's voice can easily be projected into a large space. In the American children's choir there are usually more girls than boys. Unfortunately, American boys are less inclined to sing than girls, and because of this, girls' voices dominate most children's choirs, thus contributing to a breathy, light, and thin tone.

The real quality of soprano or alto sound does not exist in a child's voice before adolescence. While the vocal range of a child may be wide or narrow, the basic voice is light, flutelike, and clear. Many children's choirs develop a harsh, forced tone, due in part to imitating pop singers and also to a lack of vocal training. The director of a young choir needs to recognize the children's vocal potential and have expectations that will challenge them to the fullest. Flat and out-of-tune singing, inability to sight-read, inability to sing in parts or to sing phrases, sloppy attacks and releases need *not be the norm*. How, then, does a director approach the task of drawing a pure choral sound from children?

Teaching intonation. The basic rules for singing in tune may be applied to children's choirs but need to be "packaged" differently. Telling a child to "sing high" means little, but telling a child to sing up to the window in the back of the church almost always raises the pitch. When working with pitch problems the director must create a framework for the child to

- hear the pitch
- match the pitch with the voice
- sing with energy
- sing with an open, relaxed jaw
- hear one part in harmony with another.

The first task is to develop the head voice. This is particularly true of young children. Most adults sing too low for children, and it is wise to use melody bells or a pitch pipe to give the starting note. This is especially true when teaching a rote song.

The following activities have been effective in helping young children sing in tune with a pure head tone.

1. Imitate a siren.
2. Question/answer patterns

Where is John? I'm here.

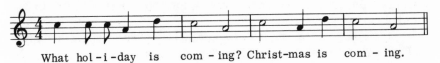

What hol - i -day is   com - ing? Christ-mas is   com - ing.

3. Let's pretend there's a little elf on top of your head, and you have to help it sing way up there.
4. Movement involving motions from low to high

I am down low.   Now I'm up   high.

5. Toss a large ball into an imaginary basket. Children sing *oo* to match the arc of the ball.
6. For those who have difficulty hearing their own voice: Cup one hand behind your ear and place the other hand in front of your mouth, thus making an echo chamber. Call *oo* into your hand.

7. Teach children to sing with energy.
   - Sing as if you are blowing out all the birthday candles on a cake.
   - Sing with enough energy to push my hand away. *(Hold hands in front of children.)*
   - For staccato: Sing as if you are saying, "Hot! Hot! Hot!" and you don't want to get burned.
   - For legato: Sing as if you are pulling taffy at an amusement park. Pull, pull, pull.

Improving tone quality. Here are some guidelines:
1. Emphasize singing lightly and never shouting or using the "playground voice."
2. Vocalize the children on exercises like the following. Be sure the vocalise does not become a routine activity, without meaning or direction.

Vee-vay-vah _____   Vee-vay-vah _____   etc.

Dalcroze   Without rhythm there would not be art. Rhythm is all about us: in nature—day and night, the seasons, the ebb and flow of the tides; in our physical systems—heartbeat, respiratory and digestive systems; in everyday activities—throwing a ball, jogging, playing tennis; and in memory—the patterns of faces, sounds, and buildings we store in our minds.

It was Émile Jaques-Dalcroze, a great Swiss music educator, who first realized that musical rhythm depended on a motor consciousness to be fully expressive. He evolved a system of rhythmic movement designed to develop mastery of musical rhythm. This system is known as eurhythmics. It begins with the simplest of rhythmic responses and proceeds, step by step, to complicated rhythmic problems. Eurhythmics, through the medium of the body, develops rhythmic potential. Elsa Findlay, for many years a teacher of eurhythmics at Cleveland Institute of Music, identified the following important objectives:

1. The use of the whole body, involving the larger muscle groups, assures a more vivid realization of rhythmic experience than does the more customary use of the extremities, such as the hands in clapping and the feet in tapping.
2. The physical coordinations developed in the well-directed rhythm class give the individual power to control [his/her] movements in related activities. This is especially true in regard to instrumental skills, where coordinations are difficult and specialized.

108

3. Bodily movement acts as a reference for the interpretation of rhythm symbols, which become truly significant when learned as the result of a vital rhythmic experience.

4. Habits of "listening" are developed by the child in the process of identifying what [he/she] *hears* with what [he/she] *does*.

5. Body, mind, and emotion are integrated in rhythmic expression.

6. The freedom of expression, which is a cardinal principle in eurhythmics, stimulates the creative impulse in every department of musical learning.

7. Finally, learning becomes joyous and meaningful when it evolves from human needs. The child who has danced [his/her] way to music will never turn a deaf ear to the greatest of all the arts.[5]

It is important for the church musician wishing to utilize eurhythmics in a choir program to choose music and texts which encompass the best in sacred music, although it is recognized that some activities may involve secular music.

Primary-age children should be taught fundamental movements, e.g., walking, running, skipping, and galloping, and should be guided in relating these movements to music.

Walking	♩ ♩ ♩ ♩ $\frac{2}{4}$ $\frac{4}{4}$ O God, Our Help in Ages Past
	Good King Wenceslas
	All Hail the Power of Jesus' Name
Marching	♩ ♩ ♩ ♩ $\frac{2}{4}$ $\frac{4}{4}$ For All the Saints (Sine Nomine)
	Onward, Christian Soldiers
	Lift High the Cross
Tiptoe, lightly	♪ ♪ ♪ ♪ $\frac{2}{4}$ $\frac{4}{4}$ Joy to the World
	From Shepherding of Stars[6]
Skipping	♪. ♪ ♪. ♪ $\frac{6}{8}$ $\frac{2}{4}$ IN DULCI JUBILO
Galloping	♫ ♩ ♫ ♩ $\frac{6}{8}$ We Sing Our Praise[7]
	Among the Lads of Nazareth[8]
Swinging, Swaying, Rowing	♩ ♩ ♩ ♩ ♩ $\frac{6}{8}$ $\frac{3}{4}$ Earth and All Stars
	Prepare the Royal Highway[9]
	The Bells of Christmas[10]

---

[5]Elsa Findlay, *Rhythm and Movement* (Evanston, Ill.: Summy-Birchard, 1971), p. 2. Copyright © 1971 by Summy-Birchard Company, SUMCO 5902, Printed in U.S.A. 6-71, All rights reserved. Used by permission.

[6]*Lutheran Book of Worship* (Minneapolis: Augsburg Publishing House, 1978), #63.

[7]*Hymns for Junior Worship* (Philadelphia: Westminster Press, 1940), #4.

[8]Ibid., #45.

[9]*Lutheran Book of Worship*, op. cit., #26.

[10]Ibid., #62.

Dramatic activities expressing a musical idea are particularly effective and are appealing to young children.

Concept: Crescendo/diminuendo
  1. Form a circle—Expand the circle on

     Come into the center for

  2. Pretend you are a tiny snowflake that grows into a large ball and finally into a snowman. Then the sun comes out and you gradually melt away.

Concept: Accelerando/ritard
     Bounce ball faster or slower.

Concept: Tempo—change of rhythm
  1. Move to the rhythm, making a change where appropriate

Walking

Running

Skipping

  2. Listen to the accents played on the drum. Change the way you walk every time you hear an accent
     walk on tiptoe
     walk on heels
     walk sideways
     walk backward

Use passages from scripture to teach rhythm patterns and movement. Gather children into a circle. (With young children, it is often best to sit in a circle on the floor. There is greater intimacy this way, and you, as an adult, become part of their visible world.) Create movement or motions to express the following passages of scripture. Add a companion rhythm pattern on a percussion instrument.

1 Corinthians 8:1	"Knowledge" puffs up, but love builds up.
1 Corinthians 13:4	Love is patient and kind.
Galatians 5:14	You should love your neighbor as yourself.
Psalm 100:1	Make a joyful noise to the Lord.

Acts 17:28   In [God] we live and move and [are,
              Hallelujah!]
Psalm 147:12 Praise the Lord, O Jerusalem!

Walking

Knowl - edge puffs   up,   but   love builds up.
(Create motions, dynamics, and articulations expressive of text.)

Praise the   Lord,   O   Je - ru - sa - lem!

Ostinato (wood block)

Je - ru - sa - lem,   Je - ru - sa - lem,   Je

Running

In God we live and move and are, Hal - le - lu- jah, Hal - le - lu-jah.
(Add wood block)

Marching

In   God we live and move and are,   Hal - le - lu - jah.
(Add drum)

Swaying

In God   we live and move and are,   Hal - le-lu - jah.
(Add triangle)

Skipping

In   God   we live and move and are,   Hal - le-lu - jah.

111

Using any of these rhythms, create a song to a pentatonic melody; try adding a call response pattern to extend the musical ideas; improvise rhythm and melodic patterns as interludes.

Orff   What is the Orff approach?

The basic tenet of Carl Orff's approach to teaching music begins with the premise that feeling precedes intellectual understanding. The young child experiences sensations of touch, taste, verbalizing, walking, running, long before dealing with the ideas or learning to read or write about them.

Orff believes this is especially true of music, that feeling must precede understanding. Therefore, he devised an approach to music education that starts with the basic element which comes most naturally to a child: *rhythm*. It is through the rhythm of a child's speech and movement that we, as teachers, can best encourage the exploration of music. Orff's approach includes specific objectives, and contains many unique devices that have been identified by Lawrence Wheeler and Lois Raebeck in their book *Orff and Kodaly Adapted for the Elementary School.*

Basic objectives.

1. To use the speech and movement natural to the child as the springboard for musical experiences.

2. To give an immediacy of enjoyment and meaning to the child through active participation in all experiences.

3. To encourage the feeling that speech, movement, play, and song are one.

4. To give a completely physical, nonintellectual background in rhythm and melody, thus laying the foundation of experience so necessary to a later understanding of music and musical notation.

5. To give experience in the component parts of the basic elements of music: in rhythmic experiences, by beginning with the rhythmic pattern of a word, then two words, gradually building in complexity into the phrase and period; in melodic experiences, by beginning with the natural chant of childhood (the falling minor third), gradually adding other tones of the pentatonic scale, tones of other modes, and finally the major and minor scales.

6. To cultivate the musical imagination—both rhythmic and melodic— and thus to develop the ability to improvise.

7. To cultivate individual creativity, as well as a feeling for and the ability to participate in ensemble activities.

Unique devices.

1. Use of speech patterns, proverbs, and children's rhymes and jingles as the basis for developing a feeling for basic note values, meter, phrase, and clarification of rhythmic problems, as well as to develop the ability to use the

voice over a wide range of pitch and dynamics (and thus help children find their singing voices).

2. Use of the rhythmic and melodic ostinati—from the very simple to the extremely complex—as an accompaniment to moving, singing, and playing.

3. Use of the natural chant of childhood as the basis for developing melodic feeling and understanding (starting with the falling minor third—sol-mi or 5-3—and gradually adding other notes of the pentatonic scale.

4. Use of unique Orff-designed instruments, along with rhythm instruments and records, to provide children with another immediate way of making music while cultivating a deeper response to rhythm and melody.

5. Use of the pentatonic scale (especially in beginning experiences) for song material and accompaniment.[11]

Choose examples from hymns or anthems. Children echo the following patterns from notation[12]:
1. Tempo:

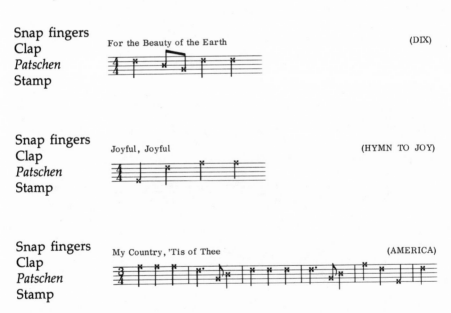

Snap fingers
Clap
Patschen
Stamp

For the Beauty of the Earth   (DIX)

Snap fingers
Clap
Patschen
Stamp

Joyful, Joyful   (HYMN TO JOY)

Snap fingers
Clap
Patschen
Stamp

My Country, 'Tis of Thee   (AMERICA)

---

[11]Lawrence Wheeler and Lois Raebeck, *Orff and Kodaly Adapted for the Elementary School,* 2d ed. (Dubuque, IA: W.C. Brown, 1977), pp. ix-xx. Used by permission.

[12]Each line indicates a physical response to rhythm, e.g., line 1—snap fingers, line 2—clap hands, line 3—left hand slaps thigh, line 4—right hand slaps thigh (lines 3-4 called *patschen*), and line 5—stamp feet.

2. Dynamics:

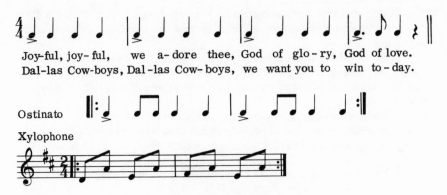

Joy-ful, joy-ful, we a-dore thee, God of glo-ry, God of love.
Dal-las Cow-boys, Dal-las Cow-boys, we want you to win to-day.

Ostinato

Xylophone

Expand the experience with a body rhythm accompaniment.

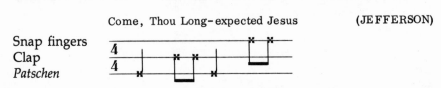

Come, Thou Long-expected Jesus   (JEFFERSON)

Snap fingers
Clap
Patschen

(Add xylophone, metallophone, or glockenspiel.)

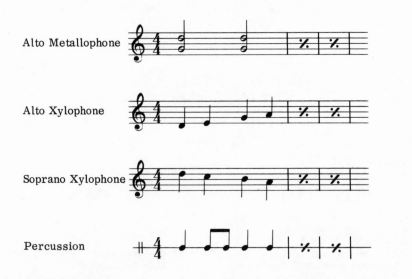

Compose a short interlude between verses and a brief instrumental introduction.

Add harmony and play it on the autoharp.

114

Teaching an Anthem   When teaching an anthem the director should use creative, effective, and interesting strategies. Children neither learn nor are excited by the "I sing, you sing" approach or by going over the anthem "one more time," which only reinforces errors. It is important that a director *teach* music to children, and to do this, the director must know the music. The first step in conducting an effective rehearsal is to study the score. This involves an in-depth analysis, followed by the development of appropriate teaching strategies.

Example: "Let All the World in Every Corner Sing"[13]

Preparation:
1. Analyze the structure and determine the form.
   A B A
2. Identify the melodic and rhythmic motifs.

Rhythm patterns:

---

[13]Music by Walter Watson. Used by permission of Ludwig Music Publishing Co., Cleveland, Ohio.

3. Identify syncopation.
4. Identify alto melodic pattern—1 2 3 2 or d r m r
5. Anticipate problems with diction.
   sin *k* for sin *g*
   A—le—lu—ia for *Ah*—le—lu—ia
   w *o* R*rld* for w*huld*

Strategies:
1. Play anthem through. Children follow words and music.
2. Discuss the mood expressed by the text.
3. Rehearse dynamics, changes.
   Alleluia—first time *forte*
                   second time *piano*
4. Rehearse the rhythmic problems.

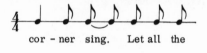

   cor - ner sing.   Let all   the

   Tap out      pattern for entire measure. Put
   together.

5. Sing variation of first phrase.

   to   our King. Let all the   world___ in ev-'ry   cor - ner sing,   let all the

6. Listen to the anthem all the way through.
7. Decide which groups of children will be from the desert, the mountains, the ocean shore, the grassy plains. Assign verses to various groups, and sing from different parts of the room. Let children decide if all should sing the *alleluia* response.

8. Use figures □ ○□ to represent the A B A sections. Select a child to be the conducting assistant who points to the figure at appropriate times.
9. Add handbells to the alleluias.
10. Sing entire anthem through, with accompaniment.

HOW TO HAVE A SUCCESSFUL CHILDREN'S/YOUTH CHOIR REHEARSAL

1. Begin and end on time. Lateness is a habit and shows disregard for other people's time. Avoid waiting for latecomers and urge those

who do come late to refrain from entering the rehearsal until there is a pause.

2. Have a written plan for each rehearsal. Know what you are going to do ahead of time. Prepare the musical score. Avoid learning the music with the children.
3. Insist on 100 percent attention at all times. Begin this way and do not conduct the rehearsal when there are distractions (from children or parents).
4. Avoid repeating, just to repeat. Create multiple ways of teaching the same thing.
5. Use visual aids to teach. One picture is still worth a thousand words.
6. Inject the unexpected into words or actions to sustain interest.
7. Don't talk the choristers into boredom. They are there to sing and participate in activities. (Tape a rehearsal and count the number of minutes you talk.)
8. Don't waste any time.
9. Make each person feel wanted and needed. Constantly bring out the talent and hidden capabilities that are there.
10. Compliment freely during a rehearsal.
11. Avoid embarrassing anyone through direct criticism.
12. Use other directors (teachers, choral directors) as models, but don't try to copy their methods and techniques. Be yourself.

Developing Choir Discipline

1. Each child/youth (and parent) must agree to assume responsibility for his/her own behavior. A church choir cannot function as a remedial situation for behavior disorders.
2. Set parameters for behavior. Never bluff! If you threaten to take a particular action, be sure that (1) you can actually do what you say you can, and that (2) you have the support of the minister and/or parents. Never threaten a disciplinary action which you cannot enforce.
3. Become aware of *everything* that is going on around you.
4. Don't hide behind the piano. Be within touching distance of the choristers. If you can't play the accompaniments and see everyone in the room at the same time, get an accompanist to help you.
5. Plan the rehearsal so that there is more to do than you can accomplish in the time. Busy children/youth have little time for mischief.
6. Plan the rehearsal carefully. Provide for variety and interesting approaches to learning the music. Visuals can be extremely helpful in teaching rhythms, dynamics, etc. Many choral directors could

cut their rehearsal time in half by using visuals to solve musical problems.

7. Keep all choristers busy. If one section is rehearsing, give the other section something to listen for, and ask questions to follow up your assignment. Children/youth should be trained to listen to music and not have it pour over them like a shower.

8. Keep your sense of humor. Funny things happen, and a good laugh is good for the director as well as for the choristers.

9. Sense the mood of the day, and be prepared to sing "quiet music" when choristers are in an extra noisy or exuberant mood.

10. Never lose your temper or self-control, although you certainly can indicate your displeasure. Avoid sarcasm.

11. Be clear on what you want the choristers to do. "Please pass your music to the right" or "Please hold your folders so that you can see me." It is often your tone of voice and the way you say something rather than what you say that causes choristers to respect you. Even though you are nervous, if you speak in a calm, positive way, you will inspire confidence and give the choristers a sense of security.

12. Establish a routine opening to the rehearsal, e.g., warm-up, chorale, anthems. The pattern may be the same, but provide a variety of warm-ups, chorales, and anthems.

13. Pace the rehearsal so there are no dead spots.

14. Always provide a goal toward which (1) the entire choir is working and (2) individuals may aspire.

Seating the Choir   Depending on the physical situation—e.g., size of room, size of choir, lighting, etc.—rehearsal seating must be planned so that there is the best possible eye contact between the director and the choir. There is no *one* way to seat a choir. Use your ears, and experiment until you get the best possible sound in the room.

1. Arrange seating so that the light comes from the side or back of the room. Avoid having choristers face the light.

2. Avoid facing the light yourself, since it blinds you to the faces of the choristers.

3. Arrange choristers so they can hear other sections.

4. Place the weaker singers in front, so you may help them and so they will hear the stronger singers.

5. Avoid surrounding one strong singer with weaker singers. It is better to have three strong singers together and two weak singers together than to frustrate the singing of the more talented.

6. If you are the accompanist, place the piano so that you can see the

choristers. If you have an accompanist, place the piano far enough away that you can hear the singers. Too often the piano drowns out whatever might be a good choral sound.

7. Use chairs for the choristers. Sitting on the floor is not conducive to good posture, breathing, or singing.

8. Assign seats but change singers around frequently. Always keep a core of strong singers together.

WHAT TO INCLUDE IN A CHOIR PROGRAM FOR CHILDREN

As in any successful endeavor, planning is of utmost importance. The more detailed your plans for the year, the easier and more exciting the program, for you are freed from the pressure of "What am I going to do next week?" Several steps are essential in this planning.

1. Compose a statement of purpose for the children's choir in your church.
2. Identify your goals for the year. (Remember, "a goal not set is a goal not met.")

   - The children will gain an understanding of the meaning of Christian faith and how it has been expressed through music.
   - The children will increase their appreciation of sacred music through singing, playing instruments, listening, moving, and creating.
   - The children will learn the meaning of worship through prayer, hymn study, and Bible study.

3. Choose a theme for the year and develop activities around it.
   Let Us Sing Joyfully
   Music of the Seasons
   Celebration
   We Believe in God
   Sing a Psalm and a Song
   Sharing God's Message
4. Create a detailed series of plans for the year, beginning with September. Allow flexibility for changes and new ideas. Try to follow the same basic plan for a full month. (Children respond to the security of continuity.)

Theme: *Let Us Sing Joyfully*
Rehearsal Plan
Junior Choir (Grades 4-6)

September

A. Get-acquainted game
Tune: "If You're Happy and You Know It, Clap Your Hands"

> *Leader:* I'm thinking of a person that is you,
> I'm thinking of a person that is you,
> I'm thinking of a person that will sing an answer to me,
> I'm thinking of a person that is you.
> *(Leader points to child.)*

> *Child:* My name is _____, yes I am,
> My name is _____, yes I am,
> My name is _____, and I'm singing you an answer,
> My name is _____, yes I am.
> *(Leader and another child repeat sequence.)*

B. Getting the body ready to sing
Stretching exercises
Vocalises
Pitch/intonation
Range
Following the director

C. Introduce: "Let All the World in Every Corner Sing."
Rhythms
Dynamics
Creating a handbell accompaniment
Phrasing (use flash cards/charts)

D. Study settings of similar texts, and see how they are the same and how they are different. Compare the music. Listen to the setting of "Let All the World" from *Five Mystical Songs* by Ralph Vaughan Williams.

Let All the World in Every Corner Sing
Robert G. McCutchan
(Hymns for Junior Worship, Westminster Press, 1940, p. 7)
Let All the World in Every Corner Sing
William Mathias, 1967
(The Hymnal of the United Church of Christ, United Church Press, 1974, #303)
Let All the World in Every Corner Sing
Martin Shaw
(Songs of Praise, Oxford University Press, 1948, #556)

E. Use charts/flash cards for study of rhythms, notation, dynamics.

F. Other anthems of praise

A Joyous Psalm (Butler, CG A-74)
Make a Joyful Noise to the Lord (Sindlinger, CG A-47)
Sing a Song of Praise (Pote, CG A-182)

G. Begin making a banner for a Choir Dedication Sunday or for Reformation Sunday. Text: "Let All the World in Every Corner Sing."

H. Discuss the meaning of a worship service: role of leadership by the choirs.

Opening of worship
Prelude
Introit
Processional hymn
Call to worship
Collect
Gloria Patri
(Continue the service next week.)

I. Sing a favorite anthem.

J. Closing prayer and group response
(Write an original tune.)

Keep your heart a-singing.
Let others hear the song.
Make your cheerful music,
Help the world along.

5. Make use of choir notebooks. Such notebooks help the child develop a personal resource of choir materials and also provide something tangible at the conclusion of the choir experience. Materials that might be included are:

Rehearsal schedules
Hymn study guides
Articles
Choir quizzes/games
Christian symbolism
Poetry
Bible study guides
Music games
Service music
Study guides for
The Organ
The Piano
The Harpsichord
Music Forms
Oratorio
Cantata
Chorale

6. Carefully plan vocal training to achieve:
   Pure tone quality
   Good intonation
   Rhythmic accuracy
   Harmonic awareness
7. Utilize melodic, harmonic, and percussion accompanying instruments.
8. Develop a large repertory of anthems and hymns.
9. Provide training in the role of a leader in worship, e.g., corporate prayers, musical responses, behavior expectations.

CREATING STUDY GUIDES: HYMNS/WORSHIP/MUSICAL INSTRUMENTS

Hymn study is a major function of a youth or children's choir. Appropriate materials should be designed for varying maturation levels. Older children may be involved in a great deal more writing than younger children. Intermediate-age children (grades 4, 5, and 6) are particularly responsive to hymn study and may create their own study guides.

1. Resource material may be found in the many hymnal "companions" published by most denominations, e.g., *Guide to the Pilgrim Hymnal*, United Church Press.

2. Always have the children read the biblical source, e.g., Psalms, scripture, or if possible, the original poem.

3. Ask questions that will help the children extract from their reading the words or ideas which are used in the hymn.

4. Create activities or guide a discussion that relates the words of the hymn to the children's lives.

5. Analyze the musical components of the hymn—e.g., repetition of melodic phrases, range of melody, rhythmic patterns, meter—and illustrate through visual aids, e.g., charts, transparencies, chalkboard.

6. Provide an incentive to memorize the verses of the hymn. (Remember that the hymns children learn remain with them for life.)

7. Explain why the tune name may be different from the title of the hymn, what the numbers 8.8.4.4. mean (meter of poem), what a translation or paraphrase is, and where to find the names of the composer of the music and the writer of the words.

Hymn Study[14]

All Creatures of Our God and King
Tune: LASST UNS ERFREUEN

---

[14]Used by permission of Choristers Guild, Dallas, TX.

The words of this hymn, written by a quiet, gentle person named Saint Francis of Assisi, became the first genuine religious poem in the Italian language. St. Francis gave up his fortune, his friends and his home to help the poor and the sick. He loved nature and valued all living things.

Inspired by Psalm 148, this wonderful hymn, "All Creatures of Our God and King," also called the "Sun Hymn," was written in 1225, when Saint Francis was almost blind, and so sick that he could hardly sit up. It is said that, upon his death, even the little birds were sad. The people from his little home town of Assisi, Italy, later built a church in his honor. Perhaps you will visit it someday.

The name of the tune is LASST UNS ERFREUEN, which is German. It means "Let us be glad" and was written for Easter. It is a very old tune that was printed in German hymn books about the time the Pilgrims were coming to America. The tune expresses the joyousness of the words "Alleluia."

Read Psalm 148. Make a list of things which praise the Lord.

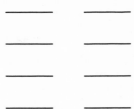

Compare this list with the things of nature mentioned in the hymn.

How many are the same? How many are different?

How many times does the word "praise" appear in the hymn?

What is a refrain?

There are only four musical phrases in this tune. Which one of the following does *not* belong in the tune?

Saint Francis believed that animals, and stars, flowers and clouds all praised God. How does he express this in the hymn?

You can praise God, too. How?

Worship Study Guide
OUR WORSHIP SERVICE

Organ Prelude: A time for preparation to worship in God's house

Collect: A prayer we all say together

Responsive Readings: Scripture from the Old and the New Testaments

*Gloria Patri: Glory be to the Father

> Glory be to the Father, and to the Son, and to the Holy Ghost; as it was in the beginning, is now, and ever shall be, world without end. Amen.

*Affirmation of Faith [The worship material used should correspond to that used in the particular church.]

> We believe in God, infinite in wisdom, power and love, whose mercy is over all divine works, and whose will is ever directed to our good:
>
> We believe in Jesus Christ, Son of God, the gift of God's unfailing grace, the ground of our hope and the promise of our deliverance from sin and death;
>
> We believe in the Holy Spirit as the Divine Presence in our lives, whereby we are kept in perpetual remembrance of the truth of Christ, and find strength and help in time of need;
>
> We believe that this faith should manifest itself in the service of love as set forth in the example of Jesus Christ to the end that the kingdom of God may come upon the earth.

Scripture and Sermon: We hear the Word of God proclaimed

Offering: We gladly give back to God part of all we own

*Doxology: A short hymn of praise

> Praise God from whom all blessings flow;
> Praise him, all creatures here below;
> Praise him above, ye heavenly host:
> Praise Father, Son, and Holy Ghost.

---

*To be memorized by all choristers

124

Prayers: We talk with God
Benediction: Ask God's blessing on us

Liturgical Year Study Guide
(EASTER)

What is the origin of the word Easter?
For how many years have people celebrated Easter?
Why do people wear new clothes on Easter?
Is there a reason for the custom of coloring eggs?
How is the date of Easter Sunday determined?
Why does the date we celebrate Easter change every year?
Do other people besides Christians celebrate Easter?
Read the article entitled "Easter" in the Encyclopædia Britannica *for the answers.*

Study Guide
Keyboard Instruments: Organ, Piano, Harpsichord

Organ. Children enjoy learning about the instrument you play with your feet. Explain how the various sounds are made and why the organ has a pedal board and more than one manual. Invite each child to play a loud sound and a soft sound. Ask if the touch is different from a piano. If possible, take the choir on a tour of a local organ factory.

AUDIOVISUAL MEDIA:
The Organ and Music of Early America. Columbia MS 6161.
The Organ in Sight and Sound. Columbia KS 7263.
The Pipe Organ. Two filmstrips and record. Educational Audio Media, Pleasantville, NY 10570.
The Austin Organ Story. Austin Organ Company, 156 Woodland St., Hartford, CT 06105.

Organ Study Guide

Color in a pipe for each rehearsal you attend.

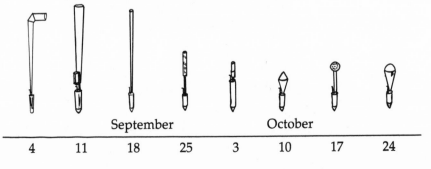

	September				October		
4	11	18	25	3	10	17	24

What is the keyboard called?
What is the keyboard called that is played by the feet?
What are stops?
Name the stops on the organ (in your church).
How many keyboards does it have?
What are their names?
What is a piston?
How can you make an organ play loudly or softly?
What are the four families of stops found on the organ?
Name three parts of an organ pipe.
What is one row of organ pipes called?
What does the length of a pipe have to do with its pitch?
What does the size (diameter) of a pipe have to do with its sound?
What kind of metal is used to make organ pipes?

Piano. Explore the many tonal possibilities of the piano. Borrow a demonstration "action" from a local piano dealer, and show the children how the hammer strikes the strings. Explore the use of the damper and una corda and sostenuto pedals. Discover the difference in sound between a spinet and a grand piano.

AUDIOVISUAL MEDIA:

Musical Instruments of the Baroque and Early Classical Eras (50 slides and cassette). Photographic Services, Smithsonian Institution, Washington, DC 20560.

An Introduction to the Smithsonian's Collection of Pianos (slide set). Photographic Services, Smithsonian Institution, Washington, DC 20560.

The Piano (16 mm. color). World-Mirror Realist: Film Associates (1967).

Piano Study Guide

1. How many keys are there?
2. How is the sound made?
3. How can the sound be made to last a long time?
4. How can the sound be made to stop almost at once?
5. Describe the size of the strings that make low sounds.
6. Describe the size of the strings that make high sounds.
7. Why is the piano's real name *pianoforte?*
8. What is the difference between a grand piano and an upright piano?
9. Name the Polish musician who composed a great deal of music for the piano.

Harpsichord. Listen to recordings of *Two-Part Invention in F* by J.S. Bach played on a piano, a synthesizer *(Switched on Bach),* and a harpsichord.

Discuss the difference in sound. Talk with musicians in the community, and try to arrange a visit with one who owns a harpsichord. Invite the children to play it, and discuss similarities and differences in keyboard size and method of creating the sound (plucking rather than striking).

AUDIOVISUAL MEDIA:

Musical Instruments of the Baroque and Early Classical Eras (50 slides and cassette). Photographic Services, Smithsonian Institution, Washington, DC 20560.

Harpsichord Study Guide

1. How is the sound created?
2. What is the name of the little "pick"?
3. What are stops?
4. What sound does a 4' stop make?
5. How does a "buff" stop change the sound?
6. How are the keys different from those of a piano?
7. How is the touch different from the touch of a piano?
8. Name two baroque composers who wrote music for the harpsichord. (J.S. Bach and George Frederick Handel)

CHOIR GAMES

Musical Olympic Relay. Create a large track and small figures of runners. Make up questions and write them on a set of cards to be drawn. Include symbols of the Christian Year, terms for the Christian Year, rhythm patterns, and mystery tunes.

There are two teams of two to four players. Each team draws a card, and if a member of the team can answer the question on the card, the runner is advanced on the track. Failure to answer correctly means that the turn goes to the other team. The first team to have a player cross the finish line is the winner.

Start	→1	2	3	4	5
					6
Finish	←11	10	9	8	7

Pick a Psalm. On a large chart list items for the game, e.g., psalms, hymns, composers. Spin the bottle. The chorister must identify or quote the item at which the bottle points. Number of points given varies with difficulty; e.g., 5 points for the first line of a psalm, 10 points for four lines,

25 points for the entire psalm. The first team to total 100 points wins the game.

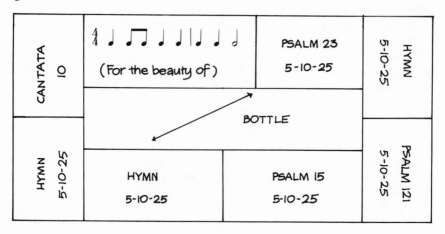

Chorister Shuffle. 24 pairs of cards (one card a picture of a chorister). Material is selected from an anthem. It may be rhythm, melodic phrases, text, dynamic markings, etc. Shuffle the cards and place them in front. Players draw cards and match up by twos. When all the cards are gone, each player may draw a card from the player on his/her left. When all the cards have been played, the person holding the Chorister wins the game.

Music Upset. Prepare 3 × 5 cards of musical symbols or patterns and attach a string to each one. Place one around the neck of each child. The leader then identifies or performs two cards. Choristers must change seats, while the leader tries to take one of their chairs. Whoever is left becomes It. Subjects for the cards might include rhythm, biblical personalities, books of the Bible, first lines of psalms, or tempo/dynamic markings.

Music Chip Toss. Two large staffs are drawn on the floor or on a large chart. A red poker chip is given to each child. Two groups form teams. A child tosses the poker chip onto the staff and must say whether the chip has landed on a line or space and then name that line or space. Failure to answer correctly gives the turn to the other team. The first team to use all their chips wins.

Confused Carols. Scramble the letters of fifteen familiar Christmas carols and write them on cards. Number each card. Place the cards around room. Each chorister has a list of numbers. As the word is unscrambled, it is placed opposite its number. Set a time limit. The winner receives a candy cane.

CHOIR AWARDS

The use of awards for youth and/or children's choirs can be a highly motivational device, if controlled properly. The criteria for the choir awards must be clearly communicated to both the children/youth and their parents. This should be in the form of a letter or other written communication. Generally, an award system is based on the accumulation of a predetermined number of points. These points may be earned in any number of ways: attendance, promptness, proper dress, memorization of hymns, notebook study projects, individual study projects, and participation in extra services.

In establishing a series of awards—e.g., first year, second year, third year, etc.—the first-year award should be the same, regardless of the chorister's age. For instance, if a pin is given as a first-year award, it might be given to a fourth-, fifth-, or sixth-grade child. Children who enter the program during the second or third year of the sequence are only eligible for the first- or second-year awards.

There are many types of awards that may be given. Choir pins with pearls to be added may be purchased from the Choristers Guild. Some churches prefer such awards as a church hymnal with the name of the recipient embossed on the cover, crosses of various types and sizes, a Bible, or books about hymns or church music. Denominational supply houses can provide additional ideas.

When an award system is used, there are always those who almost (but not quite) meet the criteria for an award. To bend the rules for these children is unfair to those who have made sacrifices to qualify. Therefore, an honorable mention card may be presented during the awards ceremony as an alternative to leaving out a chorister. Such a ceremony, which also should include recognition and appreciation of the adult choir, may take place during a special service or, preferably, during the morning worship service, which may be designated as Choir Sunday—a time when the congregation may share in the recognition of the choristers' service during the year.

CHAPTER 7

Other Musical Activities

INTERPRETATIVE MOVEMENT

An activity that is becoming increasingly popular in churches is interpretative movement. Sometimes called interpretative or liturgical dance, the term is used to describe the use of the body in a physical expression of some aspect of the worship experience. In this book the term interpretative movement describes bodily expression that involves little or no training in dance. The field of interpretative dance and/or liturgical dance invites the development of materials which may assist church musicians interested in pursuing further this genre of religious expression.

Interpretative movement is not new. We read of dance and worship in Psalm 150: "Praise [God] with timbrel and with dance." Interpretative movement in worship should provide an opportunity for the entire congregation to participate; however, many churches prefer to use small select groups. It is important to keep the movements simple and to use a familiar text and music, such as a favorite hymn. To be successful in worship, the expressiveness of the movements must be easily grasped by the congregation. Consider the following suggestions when you decide to use interpretative movement in worship, whether utilizing children or adults.

1. Be sensitive to your congregation, and choose movements that will be acceptable. Avoid those which might be rejected.

2. Remember that movement, as well as music, must always focus on the worship experience and must never become a show.

3. Interpretative movement may range from a simple expression by a child to complex, highly coordinated expressions by an adult.

4. Costuming is most important. For young children, a white surplice is often sufficient; for teenagers and adults, long flowing garments are more appropriate. Unless you have a very liberal congregation, avoid leotards, tights, and short skirts.

5. Choose nonliturgical portions of the service for expression through movement. Avoid interpreting the Lord's Prayer, at least at first, when you introduce movement to the congregation.

6. In churches where bare feet are not acceptable, the use of soft ballet slippers is recommended.

7. Movements must be graceful, proceed smoothly from one position to another, and inspire worship in participants and congregation alike.

8. Be careful of improvisation; it is better to use structured choreography rather than take the chance of offending a congregation.

9. Chart the movements with stick figures and captions that give specific directions, along with the text of the hymn or anthem (if there is one). Each movement must be learned thoroughly and executed well; full concentration must be on the interpretation and not on " What do I do next?"

10. Take courage and use interpretative movement to bring a new dimension to worship.

Interpretative Movement
"For the Beauty of the Earth"
(Tune: DIX)

Folliott S. Pierpoint,
1864, alt.

Abridged from a chorale
by Conrad Kocher, 1838

"For the beauty of the *earth*,"
Three steps toward congregation, hands down at sides. On earth *hands forward, palms up.*

"For the beauty of the *skies*,"
Turn to left, left arm up, right hand down—three steps. On skies *stop, both hands up.*

"For the love which from our *birth*"
Face congregation, cross arms over
chest. On birth *lower arms parallel*
with floor.

"Over and around us *lies*."
Curve arms outward, and lower toward
floor on lies.

"Lord *of all, to* thee *we* raise,"
On Lord *step toward congregation, left*
arm raised, right hand at side.
On all *step forward and motion toward*
congregation.
On thee *stop, touch fingers together.*
On raise *lift both arms upward.*

"*This* our *hymn of grateful praise.*"
This—*touch lips with hands.*
hymn—*both hands outstretched,*
palms up.
grateful—*arms circle upward, out-*
ward, and around.
praise—*both hands upraised.*

SUMMER CHOIR SCHOOL

One of the exciting ways of creating interest in the choir program is the summer *Choir School* or *Choir Camp*. This activity may involve a number of churches of different denominations, or several churches of a single denomination may join together.

There are wonderful advantages to the choir school or camp concept, not the least of which is the absence of pressures usually found in the church and family winter schedule. Because it is an elective activity, choristers are generally highly motivated and eager for the variety of opportunities available in such a program. Letters of invitation outlining activities, dates, location, leadership, requirements, and cost should be sent early in the spring. Registration forms need to be provided and a variety of publicity devices used, e.g., posters, articles in the church paper, notices in local newspapers, etc. A name like Young Music Makers or Junior Choir School, for example, gives the program a personality, and makes it more attractive. Most programs of this type are offered only during the morning, since so many children are involved in recreational activities, such as swimming or tennis, in the afternoon.

This is a typical schedule for such a summer program:

Junior Choir School

Monday	9:00—9:15	Get Acquainted
	9:15—10:00	Singing Is Fun (developing singing skills)
	10:00—10:30	Visit to the Organ
	10:30—10:45	Recreation (games)
	10:45—11:30	Singing Is Fun (using guitar and auto-harp)
Tuesday	9:00—9:10	Worship
	9:10—10:00	Singing Is Fun (developing singing skills)
	10:00—10:15	Recreation
	10:15—11:15	Singing Is Fun (using melody instruments: bells/recorder)
	11:15—11:30	Reports and Assignments
Wednesday	9:00—9:10	Worship
	9:10—9:30	Film: *The Guitar*
	9:30—9:45	Review, Reports, Assignments
	9:45—10:30	Singing Is Fun (developing singing skills)
	10:30—10:45	Recreation
	10:45—11:30	Singing Is Fun (Using instruments)
Thursday	9:00—9:10	Worship
	9:10—9:45	Singing Is Fun (developing singing skills)
	9:45—11:30	Field Trip to Orthodox Church
Friday	9:00—9:10	Worship
	9:10—9:30	Review of Field Trip (reports)
	9:30—10:30	Singing Is Fun (creating our own music)
	10:30—10:45	Recreation
	10:45—11:30	Singing Is Fun (music of the psalms)

* * * * *

Monday	9:00—9:10	Worship
	9:10—10:15	Singing Is Fun (preparing for worship)
	10:15—10:30	Recreation
	10:30—11:30	Singing Is Fun (developing singing skills)
Tuesday	9:00—9:10	Worship
	9:10—9:30	Singing Is Fun (preparation for Festival Service)

	9:30—11:30	Field Trip to Jewish Temple/Synagogue
Wednesday	9:00—11:30	Trip to Museum with Musical Instruments, Organ Factory, or Other Activity
Thursday	9:00—9:10	Worship
	9:10—9:30	Review: "What Have We Learned?"
	9:30—10:30	Singing Is Fun (preparation for Festival Service)
	10:30—10:45	Recreation
	10:45—11:30	Singing Is Fun (preparation for Festival Service)
Friday	9:00—9:15	Review and Questions
	9:15—10:00	Evaluation of Learning Experiences
	10:00—10:15	Recreation
	10:15—11:30	Dress Rehearsal for Festival Service
	11:30—12:30	Picnic
	7:30—8:30	Festival Service and Awarding of Recognition Certificates[1]

The Choir School should culminate in an open house and program in which the children share their musical study and experiences with their parents and the community.

SPECIAL PROGRAMS

In addition to planning and directing the music for regular Sunday services of worship, many church musicians are also expected to play organ recitals or initiate occasional musical vespers. Most musicians are familiar with a traditional organ recital, often consisting of selected works by J.S. Bach, several pieces by French, German, or American composers representative of different periods and styles, and featuring a closing brilliant toccata. While such a program may be most acceptable, two other interesting ways to plan a recital include (1) building the program around a theme, e.g., a form of worship (liturgy), the Church Year, a season, and (2) enlisting other musical talent in the church to share in the program, e.g., instrumentalists, vocalists, youth groups (church or community).

CHILDREN'S/ADULT CHORAL FESTIVALS

One of the most exciting events in the life of a church is participating in a choral festival with other singers. The discussion that follows focuses on

[1]These are available from Choristers Guild or many denominational publishing houses.

a Children's Choir Festival, although many procedures are the same or similar to those used for organizing an Adult Choir Festival.

The first step is to meet with several interested directors in the area. If there is sufficient interest, these directors will form a committee and choose a general chairperson for the festival. Decide on a date (plan at least a year ahead) and a place for the festival, recognizing that there is great need for space and an adequate organ. Contact all the children's choir directors in the area, and ask them to respond by a given date if they are interested in participating.

The second step involves deciding on a theme for the service and forming a subcommittee to examine and select music. Care should be taken to select music that will be appealing to children and that will provide variety in the service. Brass, woodwinds, strings, percussion, and handbells contribute significantly to a festival; however, Orff instruments have too delicate a sound for a group of 200 or 300 children and usually cannot be heard.

Many festivals feature a guest director. Such a person should not only have excellent music and conducting skills, but should also be able to relate to children and have a lot of patience. A Children's Choir Festival is not the place for a prima donna musician. The guest conductor should be familiar with the way the music has been rehearsed by the directors. His/her major challenge is to get a large number of children to (1) sing together, (2) sing in tune, (3) sing with good diction, and (4) sing with enthusiasm and excitement.

The key to a successful festival is the degree to which the children have learned the music. By planning a year in advance, directors may teach and use many of the choral selections in their regular choir program, thus negating a crash-learn approach.

All music should be memorized. Children do not function well when they are shuffling music and hymn sheets. A reading session for directors is essential to determine tempo, phrasing, and dynamics before the music is taught to the choirs. Once these habits are formed, no guest conductor can change them.

After the music is selected, and the date, time, and place determined, a general letter should be sent to all participating directors.

sample letter

Dear _____

We are delighted that the choir from _____ [*church*] is going to participate in the Children's Choir Festival to be held on _____ [*date*] at _____ [*time*] in _____ [*name of church*].

The following information will be helpful to you in your planning.

135

Date: Sunday
Time: 2:15 Rehearsal
     3:30 Festival
Place: Name of church
     Address
     Phone
     Host director
     Host minister

Initial Rehearsal

Date:

Time: (*Allow a minimum of two hours for choristers.*)

Place: (*It is imperative that the rehearsal be held in the same church as the festival.*)

Churches are responsible for ordering music for their singers. Remember, it is against the copyright law to make multiple copies.

Proposed Repertory

Let All the World in Every Corner Sing
     Walter Watson (C-1177 Ludwig Music)

A Lenten Prayer   Robert Powell (A-159 Choristers Guild)

Praise to the Lord   Arr. Jean Pasquet (362-0324 Elkan Vogel)

Wise Men Traveled Far   Robert Leaf (11-0343 Augsburg)

Praise Ye the Lord, Ye Children
     Richard Proulx (11-0322 Augsburg)

Keep a Joyful Song Ringing in Your Heart
     Hal Hopson (A-136 Choristers Guild)

Sing a Song of Praise   Allen Pote (A-182 Choristers Guild)

Hymns

Included is a copy of the hymn texts to be used for the festival, recognizing that words may vary from hymnal to hymnal.

     Praise to the Lord

     All Glory, Laud, and Honor

     For the Beauty of the Earth

     Old Hundredth for the Doxology

The children will not use hymnals during the festival. The congregation will sing from the hymnal.

     Please call me if you have any questions.

Sincerely,

_____

Festival Chairperson

The committee should assemble all the worship components into a proposed Order of Service, which should be enclosed with the letter to the directors, along with the general information.

Proposed Order of Service[2]
Theme: Children's Praise

Preparation for Worship
  Hymns on the Carillon
  Chorale Fantasy on "Christ the Lord Has Risen" Flor Peeters
  "Jesu, Joy of Man's Desiring" (handbells)
Processional Hymn: "Praise to the Lord"   Arr. Jean Pasquet
Invocation
Greetings
Scripture—Psalm 148
Anthems
  Praise Ye the Lord, Ye Children   Richard Proulx
  Sing a Song of Praise   Allen Pote
  Wise Men Traveled Far   Robert Leaf
Litany
Hymn: "All Glory, Laud, and Honor"
Offering
Anthems
  A Lenten Prayer   Robert Powell
  Keep a Joyful Song Ringing in Your Heart   Hal Hopson
  Let All the World in Every Corner Sing   Walter Watson
Recessional Hymn: "For the Beauty of the Earth"
Benediction
Postlude

General Information

Banners—Each participating choir is asked to make a banner to be hung in the host church for the festival.
    Theme—(example) "Children's Praise"
    Size—3' × 6'
All banners should be equipped with a wooden rod and roping.

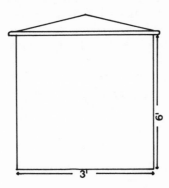

[2]Children's Choir Festival, Northern Ohio Chapter of the Choristers Guild, Canton Chapter American Guild of Organists, November 18, 1979, Church of the Savior United Methodist Church in Canton, Ohio.

137

Please bring your banner to the rehearsal. This will give the host church time to hang the banners prior to the festival. *There's Room for More*—If you know of other churches that might be interested in participating, please have them contact _____.

(chairperson)

Refreshments—The rehearsal will include a punch-and-cookie break. We are asking each church to provide two cookies per child.

Tape—A rehearsal tape is available from the reading session with the directors. However, major questions regarding the music should be addressed to the chairperson.

Postfestival Dinner/Evaluation—We are planning to have a postfestival dinner for the purpose of evaluating the festival, and we hope you will join us.

Guest Conductor—(*name of guest conductor and brief biographical sketch*)

Rehearsal Tips
1. Begin and end the rehearsal on time.
2. Assign rooms (or other appropriate area) for wraps and robes.
3. Give each director written directions for
   a. parking
   b. assigned space for wraps and robes
   c. order of the processional (which choir is first, second, etc.)
   d. place of assembly for processional
   e. general rules regarding use of music, chewing of gum
   f. location of lavatories
   g. Schedule of the rehearsal, e.g., placing of children in chancel, rehearsal of anthems, processional/liturgy/recessional
   h. Emergency procedures
4. Insist that instrumentalists be *thoroughly rehearsed*. Many a festival has been less than successful because the instrumentalists are brought in at the last minute, and musical uncertainties (even disasters) result. *It is imperative that these players attend the massed choir rehearsal.* Allow time for a complete run-through with the organist and guest conductor the day of the festival.
5. Double-check every little detail. Assume nothing!
6. Throughout all the hectic preparations, do not lose sight of the fact that the festival is a worship service and that each participant is giving his/her talent in praise of God.

HYMN FESTIVALS

Perhaps one of the most useful and flexible of special musical programs that can involve the choirs is a hymn festival. A hymn festival is a service of worship in which the gospel is proclaimed and celebrated chiefly

138

through sensitivity to the vast repertoire of Christian hymnody, and hearty singing of hymns is encouraged. While the primary emphasis should be upon congregational participation, significant involvement of the choirs makes the occasion more festive and provides an opportunity for the choirs to be part of a special program.

To create the feeling that a hymn festival is a very special musical event, it is often best to plan such a program around a specific event, e.g., the publication or introduction of a new hymnal, a specific church holiday or anniversary, a national or ecumenical festival or commemoration. Combined choirs, drawn from many churches and joined by instrumental ensembles, can add to the festiveness of the occasion. The joining of these musical forces, so typical at a hymn festival, demonstrates that such gatherings are often one of the most successful of ecumenical events, for the heritage of hymnody transcends any denominational boundaries.

In preparing for a hymn festival one must first decide upon the resources to be utilized. Is the festival to be prepared by a single church or is it to involve many churches? Will there be adult choirs only, or will children's choirs and perhaps bell choirs be involved? Will a brass ensemble or other instruments be utilized in the hymn accompaniments? Will a guest director be secured whose name and reputation will lend dignity and stature to the festival? If the event involves more than one church, where will it be held? Are the acoustics conducive to congregational singing? Is there a good organ and adequate space for the choral organizations? Perhaps the most important question to be answered is who will be the organist. Since a hymn festival should be primarily the occasion for the singing of hymns, someone who has a reputation for excellence in playing hymns should be invited to play the service. A different organist could play the prelude (perhaps prelude recital) and/or postlude.

Of course, if the festival is to be the project of a single congregation, some of these questions may not be relevant. They are offered, however, to demonstrate the potential of such a basically simple idea as gathering together to sing hymns. Additionally, the questions serve as a reminder of the importance of planning for such an event, large or small. When many choirs, especially from several churches, are involved, one must be sure that all practice from the same versions of texts and tunes. A combined rehearsal (often immediately before the service) must be scheduled. Instrumentalists need to be secured, and music must be provided and rehearsed. A planning committee to attend to such details, as well as to prepare advance publicity is often a good idea. The guest organist and/or director may wish to offer suggestions for hymns to be sung and format to be used.

After the basic decision has been made concerning the musical resources for the festival, decisions about the format or structure of the service and its contents need to be finalized. Often it is helpful to employ the regular order of service utilized by a congregation. A simple worship order (for example, prelude, opening hymn, scriptural sentences and prayer, group of hymns, offering, prayers and benediction, closing hymn, postlude) may be designed specifically for the occasion. Each part of the service should be carefully timed, for the length of the festival (excluding prelude and postlude) should not exceed 60 to 75 minutes.

In planning a hymn festival, it is well to focus on a theme and choose hymns that follow one another in a logical sequence. There are many ways to organize the hymns to be sung. For instance, a specific topical structure can be utilized—"Our New Hymnal," "American Hymnody," "Folk Hymns," "Hymns from the Reformation," "Hymns from the Psalms." A thematic structure—"Hymns from the Liturgical Year," "We All Believe in One God," "In Everything Give Thanks"—is also possible. When selecting the hymns to be sung, it is important to plan for variety in mood and treatment. Always consider balancing familiar and unfamiliar hymns and creating contrast through alternating choir and congregational singing. To explore the tonal possibilities, consider having some stanzas sung by trebles, others by basses and tenors. Use instrumental color creatively but sparingly. The experience of singing hymns a cappella can often be a high point of a festival experience. Successful hymn festivals require that there be a good, unified design, with exciting and innovative treatment.

In preparing the festival, consider the place of the spoken word. Sometimes a brief commentary, or short readings from scripture or from a major church document, e.g., The Augsburg Confession, provide a stimulating counterpoint to the hymns sung. Many times a few short meditations can effectively mark the subdivisions of a festival service. These meditations might provide background material for the hymns to be sung—origin and purpose of text and tune. Some could provide a spiritual commentary that explains the choice of hymns while others might serve to exhort the people to sing and address their role in the music of worship. Such meditations must be brief and are usually best prepared in consultation with the person or persons who designed the festival. Once prepared, the narrations must be given by an excellent speaker if their effectiveness is to be assured.

Perhaps the best way to sense how hymn festivals are organized and function is to experience them. Local chapters of the American Guild of Organists(AGO)and of The Hymn Society of America often sponsor such events. The three sample programs that follow may serve as stimuli for your own creative implementation of what is one of the most useful and rewarding of special musical events in the church—the hymn festival.

The first example uses the *Lutheran Book of Worship* as its hymn material source. The service was prepared as a special event introducing the new

Lutheran Book of Worship to the Minneapolis-St. Paul area. Thus, it involved musicians from various local institutions as well as area church leaders, each of whom was asked to address one specific dimension of the hymnal.

Hymn Festival Service
Central Lutheran Church
Minneapolis, Minnesota

Prelude   The St. Olaf Brass Choir
Processional Hymn 543   Praise to the Lord, the Almighty
                                              Setting: Paul Manz
                                          Tune: LOBE DEN HERREN
stanza 1: *All sing,* stanza 2: *choirs,* stanza 3: *all,* stanza 4: *choirs,* stanza 5, *all*
Dialogue   LBW, page 126
Prayer of the Day
   Liturgist: The Lord be with you.   People: And also with you.
Scripture: Psalm 98
Sermon: "The Hymnal Is . . .
Hymn 377   Lift High the Cross (*Congregation and Choir stand*)
                                            Tune: CRUCIFER
each refrain: *All sing,* stanza 1: *choirs,* stanza 2: *women,* stanza 3: *all,*
stanza 4: *men,* stanza 5: *all*

          . . . Handbook for Worship"   Rev. Mons Teig
Hymn 242   Let the Whole Creation Cry   Tune: SALZBURG
           stanza 1: *all,* stanza 2: *choirs,* stanza 3: *all in unison*
           . . . Resource in Christian Education"   Mr. Ronald A.
           Nelson
Hymn 463   God, Who Stretched the Spangled Heavens
                                            Tune: HOLY MANNA
           stanza 1: *women,* stanza 2: *men,* stanza 3: *all*
           . . . Ecumenical Songbook"   Dr. Louis H. Gunnemann
Hymn 508   Come Down, O Love Divine   Tune: DOWN AMPNEY
           stanza 1: *all in harmony,* stanza 2: *men,* stanza 3: *women,*
           stanza 4: *all, unison*
           . . . Book of Devotions"Mrs. Ivar (Maybelle) Sivertsen
Hymn 444   With the Lord Begin Your Task   Tune: FANG DEIN WERK
           stanza 1: *all,*   stanza 2: *women, men join at "Save you from
           . . . . "*
           stanza 3: *men, women join at "Who in wisdom. . . . "*   stanza
           4: *all*
           . . . Musical Treasure Chest"   Mr. Jerry Evenrud
Hymn 534   Now Thank We All Our God
                                          Tune: NUN DANKET ALLE GOTT
           stanza 1: *all,*   stanza 2: *brass and organ,*   stanza 3: *all*

141

Offering
Anthem   O How Amiable Are Thy Dwellings   Ralph Vaughan
           Williams

                                    text: Psalm 84
                                          Psalm 90 paraphrased
                                          by Isaac Watts

Liturgist: Hear my prayer, O Lord.
People: Listen to my cry.
Liturgist: Keep me as the apple of your eye,
People: Hide me in the shadow of your wings.
Liturgist: In righteousness I shall see you;
People: When I awake, your presence will give me joy.
Evening Prayers and The Lord's Prayer
Benediction
Recessional: 278 All Praise to Thee, My God, This Night

TALLIS' CANON

stanza 1: *all*,   stanza 2: *all in harmony*,   stanzas 3, 4,: *in
canon; men begin with organ, women follow one measure
later*,   stanza 5: *all in unison*

Participants:

Musicians: Paul Manz, organist—Cantor, Mount Olive Lutheran Church;
Miles Johnson, conductor, St. Olaf College Brass Choir; John
Ferguson, conductor—Music Director and Organist, Central
Lutheran Church; Senior Choirs of Mount Olive and Central
Lutheran Churches

Liturgists: Hoover T. Grimsby—Senior Pastor, Central Lutheran Church
Alton Wedel—Pastor, Mount Olive Lutheran Church

Homilists: Mons Teig—Director for Parish Worship and Celebration, The
American Lutheran Church; Ronald A. Nelson—Director of
Music, Westwood Lutheran Church; Louis H. Gunne-
mann—Dean (retired), United Theological Seminary of the
Twin Cities and Chairperson, Commission on Worship,
United Church of Christ; Maybelle Sivertsen—Member,
Central Lutheran Church; Jerry Evenrud—Director for Parish
Music and the Arts, The American Lutheran Church

The second service is planned as an event for a single congregation
which has a fine adult choir. It makes use of *The Hymnal of the United
Church of Christ.* Accompaniments can be enriched by modest use of
handbells and Orff instruments. A brief narration should be provided for
each of the seven sections.

A Hymn Festival

We Sing the Year Round

Opening Hymn of Praise 12   O Be Joyful in the Lord   ROCK OF AGES
Scripture Reading: Psalm 98—No. 410

for Advent

Hymn 86   O Come, O Come, Emmanuel   VENI EMMANUEL
        stanza 1—choir
        stanza 2—trebles
        stanza 3—men
        stanza 4—all

for Christmas

Hymns 90   Angels We Have Heard on High   GLORIA
     128   Ah, Holy Jesus   HERZLIEBSTER JESU
The congregation will sing hymn 90 in alternation with
the choir singing hymn 128 as follows:
        Hymn 90, stanza 1—all
        Hymn 128, stanzas 1 and 2—choir
        Hymn 90, stanza 2—all
        Hymn 128, stanzas 3 and 4—choir
        Hymn 90, stanza 3—all

for Epiphany

Hymn 115   What Star Is This   PUER NOBIS NASCITUR
        stanza 1—all   stanza 3—trebles
        stanza 2—choir   stanza 4—all

for Lent

Hymns 263/264   A Mighty Fortress Is Our God   EIN' FESTE BURG
        stanza 1—all at 263, in harmony
        stanza 2—choir at 264
        stanza 3—organ at 264
        stanza 4—all at 263, in harmony

for Easter

Hymn 131   Alleluia! The Strife Is O'er   VICTORY
     stanza 1—all, in unison   stanza 3—all, in harmony
     stanza 2—all, in harmony   stanza 4—all, in unison

for Pentecost
    Hymn 147 Come Down, O Love Divine   DOWN AMPNEY
                  stanza 1—choir
                  stanza 2—all, in harmony
                  stanza 3—all, in unison

and throughout the year
    Hymn 224 I Bind unto Myself Today   ST. PATRICK
                  stanza 1—choir
                  stanzas 2 and 3—all
                  stanza 4—choir
                  stanza 5—all
    Hymn 358 Praise God from Whom All Blessings Flow
                                                  Tamil Melody
                  sung twice, first by choir, then all

Closing Prayers
    Hymn 238 All Praise to Thee, My God   TALLIS' CANON
                  sung in canon, trebles first

The third service utilized the Presbyterian *Worshipbook* and was planned as a cooperative venture by the Cleveland Chapter, AGO, the Hymn Society of America, and Fairmount Presbyterian Church. Choral leadership was provided by the Fairmount Presbyterian Church Choir of Cleveland Heights, Ohio under the direction of Dr. H. Wells Near. The Metropolitan Brass Quartet of Cleveland assisted. A special feature of this festival was the close relationship of scripture and hymns.

A Hymn Festival Celebrating Our Unity in Faith

Prelude for Organ
    Partita on JESU, MEINE FREUDE   Johann Gottfried Walther

**Processional Hymn (supplement)   **Congregation stands
    Lift High the Cross   CRUCIFER
      (The verses in stanzas 1 and 2 are sung by choirs alone. The congregation sings the refrain each time, and verses 3, 4, 5.) Descants by Donald Busarow. The banners carried in the procession represent (1) the Nicene Creed and (2) the Apostles' Creed.

**The Nicene Creed (first article)
We believe in one God, the Father Almighty, Maker of heaven and earth, and of all things visible and invisible.

Homily   W. Thomas Smith

Scripture   Malachi 2:10; Ephesians 2:10; Psalm 104:24

Hymn 594   The Man Who Once Has Found Abode   TALLIS' CANON
1. Congregation in unison
2. Choir in harmony
3. In canon: women beginning, men following
4. In canon: pulpit side, followed by lectern side
5. In canon, sung twice: (a) women, pulpit side; (b) women, lectern side; (c) men, pulpit side; (d) men, lectern side

Scripture   1 John 3:1-2

Hymn (supplement)   When in Our Music   ENGELBERG
1. All;   2. Women;   3. All;   4. Men;   5. All

Scripture   Psalm 103:19-22

Hymn (supplement)   Before the Lord Jehovah's Throne   DE TAR
1. Choir;   2. All;   3. Women;   4. Men;   5. All

The Recognition and Installation
of officers of The Cleveland Chapter,
American Guild of Organists

Congregational Response
There are different gifts,
But it is the same Spirit who gives them.
There are different ways of serving God,
But it is the same Lord who is served.
God works through different people in different ways,
But it is the same God whose purpose is achieved through them all.
Each one is given a gift by the Spirit,
To use it for the common good.
Together we are the body of Christ,
And individually members of Him.

**Hymn (supplement)   You Are the King   MARGARET
1. Men;   2. Women;   3. All;   and on each refrain

**The Nicene Creed (second article)
We believe in one Lord Jesus Christ, the only-begotten Son of God, begotten of the Father before all worlds: God of God, Light of Light, Very God of Very God, begotten, not made, being of one substance with the Father by whom all things were made; who for us, and for our salvation, came down from heaven, and was incarnate by the Holy Spirit of the Virgin Mary, and became human.
He was crucified also for us under Pontius Pilate. He suffered and was buried, and the third day He rose again according to the Scriptures, and ascended into heaven, and sitteth on the right hand of the Father.
And He shall come again with glory to judge both the quick and the dead, whose kingdom shall have no end.

Scripture   John 1:1-5; Luke 2:10b-12

Hymn 534   Of the Father's Love   DIVINUM MYSTERIUM
1. Men;   2. Women;   3. All. Descant by Donald Shelhorn.

Scripture   John 10:11-18

Hymn (supplement)   The King of Love   KING DAVID

Scripture   Isaiah 53:5-6

Hymn 280   Ah, Holy Jesus   HERZLIEBSTER JESU
1. All, unison;   2. In canon: pulpit side begin; lectern side begin one
measure later;   3. Choir;   4. All, unison

Scripture   Matthew 28:5b-7

**Hymn 328   Christ Is Risen   CHRIST IST ERSTANDEN
1. Choir;   2. All;   3. All. Introduction by Flor Peeters.

Scripture   Acts 1:8-11

Hymn (supplement)   Rejoice, Ye Pure in Heart   VINEYARD HAVEN
1. Choir;   2. Men;   3. Women;   4. All

**The Nicene Creed (third article)
We believe in the Holy Spirit, the Lord and Giver of Life, who
proceedeth from the Father and the Son, who with the Father and the
Son together is worshiped and glorified, who spoke by the prophets.
And we believe one Holy catholic and apostolic church. We
acknowledge one baptism for the remission of sins. And we look for the
resurrection of the dead, and the life of the world to come. Amen.

Scripture   Acts 2:1-4

Hymn 334   Come Down, O Love Divine   DOWN AMPNEY
1. Choir;   2. Choir;   3. All.
                              Stanza 2 and descant by Donald Busarow.

Scripture   Acts 2:29-33, 36

Hymn (supplement)   Earth's Scattered Isles   DOMINUS REGNAVIT
1. Choir;   2. Men;   3. Women;   4. All

Scripture   Revelation 7:9-10, 13-17

**Hymn 369   For All the Saints   SINE NOMINE
1. All;   2. All;   3. Women;   4. Choir;   5. Men;   6. All.
              Introduction by Paul Manz; descant by Donald Busarow.

The Benediction

Organ Postlude   on CWM RHONDDA   Paul Manz

146

FINE ARTS FESTIVALS

Religious fine arts festivals have flourished in many parts of the country, and preparing and presenting such a festival can be a rewarding experience for both the church musician and members of the congregation. There are many opportunities for discovering artistic talent previously unknown, and the many ways of expression—such as painting, sculpture, drama, dance, etc.—bring a new dimension to the worship of God.

Preparations for a fine arts festival must begin many months in advance; a year is not too far ahead. Assemble a small group of people who are interested in the arts, and discuss the idea of such a festival. Consider possibilities of using a theme, e.g., a celebration from the Christian Year (Reformation, Pentecost), an event in the life of the church (anniversary, dedication), and determine possible dates. At this initial meeting, consideration should be given to the weekend (Saturday-Sunday) festival, the week-long festival, or some other viable alternative. Identify those members of the congregation who might serve as committee chairpersons in such areas as visual art, drama, music, dance, publicity, coordinator. Set up a calendar for accomplishing the various steps in preparation, and plan meetings around these progress points. Early, detailed planning pays dividends in a smooth-running festival. Keep your standards high. It is an arts festival and not a crafts show, therefore it is necessary to have a committee (use at least one outside "expert") to judge those items/activities that will be included in the festival.

Prepare a program of activities and publicize well in advance. Use all the church media, e.g., bulletins and weekly papers, as well as local newspaper publicity. Pictures of artists and their work, as well as scenes from plays, and rehearsals, are particularly attractive to newspapers. Involve as many people as possible, and the generated interest may well continue on in other areas of the church's life and throughout the year.

CHAPTER 8

Using Instruments in Worship

Recorders, handbells, guitars, autoharps, melody bells, Orff instruments, as well as orchestral instruments can often enhance worship, adding new color and excitement to the singing of hymns and anthems. Choirs respond to the added variety of instrumental color. There are a great many anthems, especially for children's choirs, that incorporate a flute, recorder, or violin descant. Larger choral works, e.g., cantatas, oratorios, masses, are traditionally written for orchestral ensembles, although the church musician on a limited budget frequently must utilize a keyboard reduction of the score. Sometimes the addition of one or two instruments can transform a piece. For example, the addition of a harpsichord to Handel's *Thanks Be to God* adds an interesting orchestral tonal color. Another example is the use of a violin descant on Mozart's "Laudate Dominum" (*Vesperae Solennes de Confessore* K. 339). Many organists add two trombones when performing Charles Marie Widor's "Toccata" from the *Fifth Organ Symphony*, and a harp adds shimmering beauty to a performance of Saint-Saën's *Christmas Oratorio* or Fauré's *Requiem*. Using instrumentalists from the congregation is a wonderful way to develop interest in the music program.

This chapter focuses on a brief discussion of the recorder, handbells, autoharp, and guitar—functional instruments in the church music program. For an in-depth study of the recorder and guitar, refer to the many fine pedagogical works that have been published.

RECORDERS

The use of recorders, particularly with children's voices, has increased dramatically in recent years. The recorder has a clear, pure tone that is most effective with young voices. It is even more effective than the traditional flute stop on the organ, and many composers have written children's choir music employing this lovely instrument. Of particular interest are small recorder ensembles, consisting of both soprano and alto recorders. Older children and adults who have studied orchestral instruments find playing recorders in such groups an especially rewarding experience.

Use a consort of recorders SATB or SATT as an extension of the organ. They are most effective to introduce a hymn, to play a single stanza, or to provide an interlude. Each year more and more anthems are published in which one or more recorders are specified. Actually, any two-part anthem may be used as a potential recorder piece, since the singers may perform one voice part and the recorder, another. Recorders may also be utilized on descants to hymns, as well as with any anthem that calls for a flute.

A useful technique is to double the vocal line of a children's anthem with recorder or flute in order to provide more body for the vocal tone and to give clear pitch definition. Such a technique is especially valuable if the

organ pipes are placed at a great distance from the singers, who feel little support from the organ.

Use an alto recorder whenever possible. It has a pure mellow tone and blends well with children's voices. If you are performing a Bach cantata, these instruments may be used instead of the modern flute; Bach cantatas BWV 13, 18, 25, 39, 103, 122, 142, 180, and 189 specifically call for recorders.

Try using recorders to accompany an a cappella anthem. During the Renaissance, instruments were interchanged with voices. Recorders—either single, e.g., soprano, tenor, or in consort SATB—can add gentle support to the vocal lines without being obtrusive. Use a solo sonata for recorder. Perhaps you can borrow a harpsichord for the accompaniment, and add an exciting new dimension to worship. The organ may be used as accompaniment, but the heavy sound of a piano should be avoided. Recorders are relatively inexpensive, and establishing a small consort can be an attractive and stimulating addition to a choral program.

A selected list of music for recorder solos, duets, trios, and quartets will be found in Appendix C.

HANDBELLS

In America the popularization of ringing handbells began in 1937, when Margaret H. Shurcliff organized the New England Guild of Handbell Ringers. Within the following 2 years, six groups were formed—all members were adults. During the 1940s handbells were introduced into such churches as Brick Presbyterian Church, of New York City, and College Hill Presbyterian Church, of Easton, Pennsylvania. The movement has continued to grow until now there are thousands of handbell groups—children, young people, and adults—in schools, churches, and hospitals throughout the country. The American Guild of English Handbell Ringers (AGEHR) is a national organization devoted to the art of bellringing.[1]

One challenge for a handbell choir is to develop the necessary skill to ring accurately and musically. Many choirs settle for playing the correct notes and rhythms, and pay little or no attention to dynamics, phrasing, or articulation. To be successful, a handbell choir must adhere to the following rules:

1. A handbell choir must have regular rehearsals of at least an hour, preferably 2 hours, per week.
2. Players must have minimal skill in reading music notation and an excellent sense of rhythm.

---

[1] AGHER, Inc., P.O. Box 10123, Winston-Salem, NC 27108.

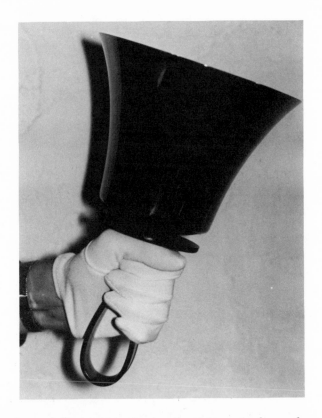

3. Players must be dependable and regular in attendance at rehearsals and performances. Each ringer is truly indispensable.
4. Members of a handbell choir must have confidence in one another; each is dependent on another for a musical performance.

All fine handbells are cast of pure bronze in approximate proportions of 80 percent copper and 20 percent tin. The two most prominent tones are the fundamental and the twelfth. The twelfth is the most important partial, and is the one with which the tuner is most concerned. Pitches sound one octave higher than they appear on the staff, thus the pitch

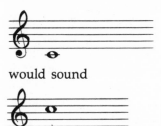

would sound

151

Questions always arise: (1) What kind of bells should be bought? (2) How much should be spent? (3) How many bells should be purchased? (4) What kinds of music stands/tables are needed?

As with any purchase, it is wise to read the literature of each company carefully, for there are major differences in design and sound. If at all possible, ask for a demonstration by a sales representative, and analyze the bells according to your particular needs. Visit churches/schools that have sets of handbells, and examine their equipment, methods of teaching, and organization. As in the choice of any musical instrument, the final judgment must be made by your ears, while considering the flexibility and durability of the product. Four leading manufacturers of handbells are:

Whitechapel Bell Foundry
34 Whitechapel Road
London E.1, England

Schulmerich, Inc.
Carillon Hill
Sellersville, PA 18960

Malmark, Inc.
21 Bell Lane
New Britain, PA 18901

I.T. Verdin
221 Eastern Avenue
Cincinnati, OH 45202

Selection of a set of bells (25-, 37-, 49-, or 61-note chromatic range) is frequently determined by the funds available, but you will find a 37-bell set somewhat standard. A set of 25 bells imposes severe limitations on music that can be played, while 49- and/or 61-note sets should only be considered where there is an extensive program of bellringing involving concertizing. The average church with one or two handbell choirs will find the 37-bell set adequate.

Bell tables are essential, and the director is wise who selects small aluminum tables (the kind that fit into a trunk or on a luggage rack). The only other necessary piece of equipment is a foam rubber pad on which to lay the bells. A useful adjunct to the table is a heavy three-ring binder, in which each ringer's music may be placed. Some binders are constructed in a special manner that enables their use as a music stand. In addition, many directors have individual lamps for each ringer.

Techniques

Holding the Bell: Grasp the handle firmly, with knuckles against the collar of bell. Line the clapper up with your shoulder. When not ringing, hold the bell near your body, just above the waist.

Ringing the Bell:
1. Move your arm straight back toward your shoulder, and cock your wrist.
2. Move the handbell in a downward arc, snapping your wrist and creating a clear single tone.
3. Continue in an upward arc to the starting position.

Damping: Damping is the term used for stopping the tone of the bell. It is usually accomplished by holding the bell against your shoulder, to stop the vibration. Damping assures clarity of melody and is effective on changing harmonies.

Muting: Hold your thumb against the bell while ringing.

Thumping: Place the bell on the table, and snap the clapper against the lip of the bell. This is used for special effects and broken chords.

Trill: Ring the bell in a fast forward-backward motion, letting the clapper strike both sides of the bell. This motion is used to sustain a pitch, create harmonic effects, and add variation.

Swing: After ringing the bell in the usual way, bring your arm downward and back in an arc, returning the bell to the starting position. The swing is used to sustain chords and alter the sound.

Gyro   : After striking the bell, swing your arms up and around in a circle—keeping the bell upright throughout. Return to the starting position. This is used to sustain chords and create special visual-acoustical effects.

Preparing Music/Assigning Bells   Bells should be placed on the tables as a keyboard. (Page 154.) If this method is followed, the bells will always be in the same place, and the risk of errors from having to remember the location of a particular bell is minimized. Of course, this means that every bell must be returned to its keyboard position after it is rung.

In a beginning group it is wise to start with familiar melodies, and to assign no more than one or two bells per player. Always assign the players with the most coordination and musical technique to the most

153

active bells. Some directors mark the music for each player, but this frequently leads to a dependence on the marking rather than the musical notation, thus it is not recommended. Directions placed in the music in regard to anticipating a change, e.g., playing a C#, are helpful, however. A position at the bell stand should be established for each player, although these positions may change for various musical compositions. It is better, however, to change bell assignments rather than positions; thus, the ringer in fifth position always remains there and rarely moves to sixth or seventh position.

In most published handbell music, the number of bells required is identified at the top of the music. Each of the following examples is designed to utilize ten players, the average number needed to play a 37-bell set. (Page 155, top.) You will notice that each of the ten players has a musical responsibility. It is important that all ringers be given an opportunity to play as much as possible; disinterest develops when one sits around waiting for a turn.

After ringers feel comfortable ringing one or two bells and can sense the melodic line of the music through ringing, chords may be introduced. The ringing technique called the swing ↓ ↑ may also be introduced at this time. Chord patterns can be created for many traditional folk songs and spirituals, but players must always be aware of the melodic line and not let the chords dominate. (Pages 155, bottom, and 156.)

Of the Father's Love   (DIVINUM MYSTERIUM)

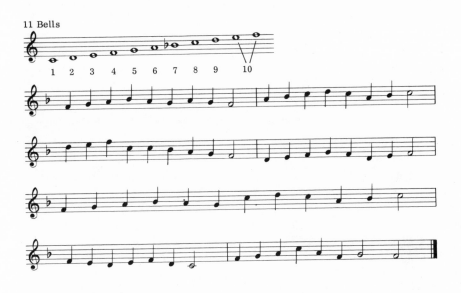

Go Tell It on the Mountain   (GO TELL IT)

155

How Brightly Shines the Morning Star (WIE SCHON LEUCHTET)

After ringers learn to play a melody with a chordal accompaniment, they may proceed to chorales. These may be selected from any hymnal and are easy to arrange; generally, the first phrase is played as a single melody, the second phrase in two parts, and the rest of the chorale in four or more parts. (Above.)

Many times a tremolo and/or swing may be added to provide variety in the playing of a hymn. (Page 157.)

As the ringers' skill increases, it is desirable for each ringer to be responsible for playing more than two bells. The decision of how many extra bells to add depends on the complexity of the music. The director should study the score, and determine who will have hands free to play extra bells on either side of a position; thus, a ringer responsible for C-D may also play C#, D#, or B, E. Sometimes ringers may even reach across a fourth, such as C-F-G. Any such changes must occur precisely in rhythm, and it would be helpful for the player to mark these in the music. On occasion, when there are few ringers, an extra accidental can be placed on a cord around a ringer's neck, so that it is available for that one note needed in the composition. Some ringers have developed complex ringing techniques, in which they play two bells at a time, by crossing the handles and alternating the direction in which the clapper strikes the bell.

Handbells may be combined with other instruments, such as recorder, flute, guitar, autoharp and Orff instruments, to produce interesting and unusual effects. Although handbells and other instruments are used for accompaniment in many children's anthems, the creative director can easily enrich hymns and folk songs by using them for pitch reinforcement on a processional or an a cappella anthem, or by introducing a peal-like figure to set tonality or creating a quasi-fanfare for festive occasions.

For example, the hymn "O Come, O Come, Emmanuel" is most effective when sung in unison, a cappella, with a simple figure of two notes (if in E minor—E# B), moving at the same speed as the notes of the tune, and rung at the beginning of each stanza and at all subsequent cadences. A unison psalm tune may be enhanced by ringing tonic bells between each verse, thus assuring pitch stability for the choir. In lieu of handbell choirs some directors employ bells only as cited above, preferring them to be adjunct to the singing choirs. If this is the case, it is well to train a few people in each choir to play the bells, so that confusion over ringing techniques does not delay the choir rehearsal.

AUTOHARP/GUITAR

Accompanying instruments like the autoharp and/or guitar are especially useful with children's voices as well as in ensembles for popular music. Many times such instruments, along with melody bells, are far more effective than a piano, and children's voices—especially those of very young children—can easily be heard, even in a large room.

The autoharp is small, easy to carry, and relatively inexpensive, and may be used to play harmonic accompaniments or even melody and harmony. There are three basic positions in which this instrument may be played, depending on the situation: (1) table position, (2) lap position, and (3) upright position (used for Appalachian style of playing). (Page 159.) Finger picks or other types of materials may be used to create a variety of tonal colors. A plastic or metal pick, a coin, or a credit card creates bright sounds: the soft part of the thumb or an eraser creates more subdued, darker sounds. Placing the autoharp on top of an open wastebasket amplifies the sound considerably, and may be especially effective with a large group or in a large room.

Instruments vary in size from 6 chords to 21, although a 15-bar autoharp usually provides adequate versatility for the average choir. To strum a chord, simply depress one of the chord bars, e.g., C, and strum from bottom to top of the autoharp. For diversity, divide the autoharp "keyboard" in two parts, and strum the lower strings on the strong beats and the upper strings on the weak beats. Another technique is to strum the lower strings on the strong beat and to use a down-up strum on the weak beat.

Playing the strings in different registers, strumming close to or far away from tuning pegs, also introduces different tonal colors. The above techniques may be used with the autoharp in any of the three positions mentioned earlier. For the upright position, however, you will need a

plastic or metal thumb pick and two picks for your right hand. Interesting effects can be created by "pinching" the strings; that is, the thumb and middle fingers pluck the strings toward each other, the thumb on the bass and the third on a melody string. Since depressing the chord bar stops all strings from sounding, except those in the chord, it becomes a relatively simple matter to play a melody. The player is cautioned not to strum the chord higher than the melody tone.

Making mistakes sound musical is a unique feature of the autoharp. So take courage, and experiment with the many tonal possibilities this instrument has to offer.[2]

The guitar has achieved great popularity in our society and its use in the church is encouraged, particularly its potential as an accompanying instrument for children's and youth choirs. The director who does not play guitar usually can find someone within the choirs or the congregation who does and would be happy to assist. Many people feel that they can easily learn the guitar, and many do teach themselves. However, the busy director who would like to play guitar is advised to find a good teacher for a few basic lessons. By learning only five chords and four strumming techniques, directors (and choristers) may experience immediate success, leading to a new dimension of musical expression and awareness.

[2]Gustav Wachaus and Terry Lee Kuhn, *Fundamental Classroom Music Skills* (New York: Holt, Rinehart & Winston, 1979), pp. 191–92.

CHAPTER 9

Designing, Purchasing, and Maintaining the Organ

After the building itself, the most significant capital investment is, for most churches, the organ. It is fair to say that while possession of an organ is not a requirement for good music in worship, it is especially useful for the musical leadership of a large assembly. The organ, which is no more religious or secular than any other instrument, is quite flexible tonally. When playing an organ, one musician can produce a large volume of sound with a reasonable variety of tonal colors. A brief discussion of the organ, considerations involved in the selection of one, and its maintenance is appropriate.

Simply stated, the organ is a large collection of whistles. Each whistle or pipe is made to play (voiced) and is adjusted (finished) to sound its best in its eventual location. The pipes are arranged in rows (ranks) of like-sounding pipes, and each rank is activated by a control called a stop. Normally, each stop has one pipe per manual key or pedal key. In early organs all the pipes controlled by a key sounded simultaneously when that key was depressed. An early improvement was the stop, which silenced or stopped selected pipes. Various stops are usually identified by pitch length, e.g., 16', 8', 4', 2'. The pitch designation in feet refers to the approximate length required for an open pipe to sound the lowest pitch on the manual or pedal keyboard. For instance, when using an 8' stop and playing middle C on the organ, the pitch is the same as middle C on the piano keyboard; the 4' stop sounds one octave higher and the 2' stop, two octaves higher. Conversely, the 16' stop sounds one octave below middle C.

The size of an organ may be calculated by counting either the number of ranks or stops in an instrument. Since it is possible in some techniques of organ-building to utilize one rank of pipes for more than one stop—a process called unification (usually not the most desirable practice)—it is best to determine the number of ranks in an instrument to ascertain its size. Such an approach is better than counting the number of keyboards (manuals), since a small number of ranks can be distributed over many keyboards. For example, the many keyboards of the old theater organ controlled an instrument of very few ranks.

Various mechanical systems are used to supply organ pipes with the wind required to activate their speech, all resulting in the opening and closing of valves under the pipes. The oldest and still the best system involves a direct mechanical linkage from keyboard to pipes; it is called mechanical, or more commonly "tracker" action. Other systems use electricity or a combination of electric and pneumatic action. ("Electric" actions should not be confused with instruments whose sound source is electric; these will be discussed later.)

There are advantages to both systems of pipe organ actions. Those involving electricity offer the greatest flexibility for placement of the console in relation to the pipes and choir, and thus provide the best opportunity for the organist to monitor the sound. Electric and electropneumatic actions tend to be less expensive than mechanical actions by about 10 to 30 percent. However, the "flexibility" of electricity has often led to unfortunate installations, where pipes are placed in closets, attics, or even basements, and therefore rarely sound at their best in the room. Such a physical arrangement presents an impossible situation, since the organist cannot control the musical results.

In a completely mechanical action organ both the key action and the stop action controls are connected directly and mechanically with the pipe mechanism. The stop action is cumbersome enough so that a detached console is impractical. Thus, the console is integrated into the base of the organ itself, where it becomes part of the organ case. Some builders and organists consider this approach ideal, because it provides for mechanical simplicity and ultimate intimacy between musician and instrument. Such an arrangement does present a problem in those churches where the organist is also the choir director, for it is difficult to conduct a choir when facing the organ. However, it must be added that such situations do exist in some churches where well-trained musicians produce excellent music.

An alternative to the completely mechanical action organ is to combine mechanical key action with electric stop action. This arrangement allows the console to be separated from the pipework (console rigidly in place, rectilinearly in relation to the pipe chests and from 8 to 12 feet removed). It then becomes possible to place the choir between the organ proper and the console. Mechanical action, or "tracker" organs have much to commend them. They are simple and troublefree, if built well initially, and have no leathers to deteriorate as do electropneumatic action instruments. Above all, mechanical action does provide a direct link between the key and the pipe, so that the player opens and closes the valves, causing the pipes to speak. There can be no doubt that this direct sense of control leads to better playing, and while one could discuss the musical implications of mechanical action in greater detail, it is enough to observe that the best music is made when musician and instrument are intimate, which is the case with most mechanical action organs. The nature of mechanical action fosters compactness in all aspects of organ design.

As can be deduced from this brief discussion, the organ is a complicated device. Its size and complexity have encouraged many enthusiasts, who take great pleasure in extolling the virtues of various instruments. At any large gathering of organists, one sees groups gathered around consoles, enthralled by the number of stop knobs or the kind of wood used for the keys; others are arguing over the merits of certain ratios of lead to tin in pipe metal. Recently, some organists have endorsed the idea of copying certain historically important instruments, blithely forgetting that an organ and the room in which it is placed are so much one, that a copy of an instrument without a copy of its acoustical environment is no copy at all. On aesthetic grounds, many people question the practice of making reproductions of instruments or portions of instruments, especially for parish churches. They ask if such copies are creative or honest, thus undermining the integrity of the art of organ-building. A healthy church should not be a museum where religious rites are reenacted to preserve them as a cultural treasure, but rather a living, changing organism requiring a more eclectic approach to music than that implied in copying a specific organ from another place in an earlier century.

Through all the heat generated by the many discussions about organ-building, from styles of action to kinds of stop lists, one of the most important things to remember is that organ-building did go to extremes in the late nineteenth and early twentieth centuries. Builders attempted to imitate orchestral sounds—something neither possible nor desirable—and organists, as well as congregations, became obsessed with size, as if size were a measure of quality. As organs grew larger, they were placed all over buildings in spaces called chambers (tombs would be a more apt term), with resultant soft and distant tones that encouraged a style of playing that emphasized dreamy sentimentality.

Builders, in attempting to recover the clarity and "presence" of sound that has been the organ's long-time character, often referred to the baroque organ as an ideal. In the late thirties, the terms baroque, classic, and/or romantic entered the vocabulary of organists, builders, and enthusiasts. While helpful, these labels have done much to confuse some who assume that baroque means shrill or harsh, and that romantic means beautiful or rich. The only way to judge organs is to listen, not to read stop lists or go by any set of labels that are arbitrary at best and often misleading. An unforced, clear, and blended sound is ideal. Such sounds are pleasant in themselves; they encourage and indeed invite participation in congregational singing.

But what of the electronic organ? About 1930, certain devices utilizing various electrical and electromechanical processes produced tones that, because of their steady state, sounded more like an organ than they did anything else. These instruments offered portability and seemingly great reliability. To the casual listener, they sounded enough like an organ for the name organ to seem appropriate. The early electronics were especially popular in taverns, where their vibrato-filled sounds reminded many of the throbbing theater organs just beginning to disappear because of the introduction of sound motion pictures.

From early on the "improvement" of nonpipe organs has been a history of introducing imperfections to a too-perfect sound. Because the pipe organ is a wind instrument, it is subtly imperfect. No matter how hard one tries to achieve perfection, the organ is never perfectly in tune. Since each pipe contributes to the overall ensemble, the sounds of even a small pipe organ come from many locations (some say the pipe organ is the ultimate stereo). In contrast, the very perfection of the electronic system of tone production, combined with the utilization of banks of speakers reproducing many pitches, results in a sterile or lifeless sound.

The virtues and liabilities of pipe versus electronic organs could be discussed indefinitely. However, the most important comment to make here is that there are good and bad pipe organs, and better and poorer electronic organs. The church organist, on undertaking a position, must accept (while not overlooking possibilities for improvement or replacement) the instrument provided, and must make the best music possible. One does not need to love an instrument, but one would be most unprofessional not to respect it.

ACOUSTICS AND PLACEMENT OF THE ORGAN

Critical factors influencing the success of the organ are its location in and the acoustics of the room. The instrument (pipes and console) should be placed within the room in which it is to sound. Chambers, sound ducts, etc. always impair the direct, unforced presence of the organ within the room. Ideally, the instrument should be located high and on the main axis of the room, preferably away from windows and heating or air-conditioning grilles, with the console and choir arranged so that all are close to one another for best visual and aural communication. In this regard, note that a string quartet plays in a kind of huddle, not dispersed all over a room, while an orchestra or a concert choir performs in a semicircle, a modified huddle. Unfortunately, this principle of arrangement is still overlooked by church architects who propose placing choirs in inflexible pews, usually in long straight lines, with the organ console off in the corner or down in a pit. It is wise to place the organ all in one place; after all, it is one instrument. This proviso rules out the divided chancel arrangement, so popular and so detrimental to good organ-building. A signficant benefit of properly locating an instrument is that it stays in tune better, since all the pipes are in one place and not in various locations, where temperature variance can become a problem.

For best results, it is essential for the room to be resonant. All music, especially organ music, takes on a warmth when sounding in a room that has some resonance. Congregational singing is always better in such rooms, where the individual becomes less self-conscious and is freed to participate, encouraged by the resonant sound of other singers and the organ. Even the spoken word sounds better with resonance to enliven it, provided, as with music, the resonance is about the same for high-, medium-, and low-pitched sounds.

A complete discussion of acoustics is beyond the scope of this book, or the competence of the authors for that matter, but a few general comments may be made. The practice of acoustical engineers might better be called the practice of acoustical artisans, in that acoustics is an inexact "science" at best (witness the expensive redoing of "acoustically ideal" concert halls, built and rebuilt, sometimes many times, during the past twenty years). A major reason for this inexactness is that "good acoustics" are measured, for better or worse, rather subjectively by each listener. Yet it is generally accepted that resonance is essential for congregational singing, and for organ and choir music. It is also important to remember that anyone with a bit of practice usually needs no amplification in a room seating under 500 persons, and that amplifying systems are not the sure cure for acoustical problems. Whenever a voice is filtered through an electronic system, there is a loss of the personal quality inherent in human communication. In most situations, carpeting and other sound-absorbing materials (pew pads, draperies, acoustical tile) should be avoided, because such soft surfaces absorb sound and thus reduce resonance. If questions about acoustics arise, it would be best to consult with a responsible organ-builder. Then, with the advice of the organ-builder, an acoustical consultant could be engaged, if needed.

165

SELECTION OF A NEW ORGAN

At some time in their lives, many church musicians find themselves involved in the selection of new organs. Such selections have been made in almost as many ways as there are churches. While no one way is effective for all, the following suggestions should prove helpful. They are organized in a three-stage process.

Stage One   The first step is to appoint a small committee comprised of musicians and nonmusicians. Included on this committee should be the organist, the choir director, and the minister. The most important requirements for membership are (1) a willingness to devote substantial amounts of time to study and discussion, and (2) an open mind. Since choosing and purchasing an organ is *not* like trading cars (as many assume), and since most people have had little previous experience with such a task, it is essential to allow sufficient time for a learning process to occur. In discussing organs, one soon discovers that issues of aesthetic quality are as important as issues of functional need.

As soon as the committee is selected and organized, it should seek direction from the major governing body of the congregation. At this time the process of communication between the committee and the congregation it serves needs to be established. Such communication is necessary to the development of an environment of trust, without which the project is doomed.

At this preliminary stage the committee should read more extensive discussions of organs and organ-building than provided here.[1] Also at this stage the committee, with its church musicians, should decide if a consultant is needed.

The consultant is someone, usually reasonably close geographically, who can act as an interpreter for the committee and the congregation in sharing ideas with organ-builders and vice versa. The consultant can assist in evolving an appropriate design philosophy for the specific situation through asking questions, helping the committee to perceive the church's needs, and sharing technical knowledge about the art of organ-building. In some situations the consultant may serve as architect or engineer in supervising the actual construction and installation of the organ. The consultant should not make decisions that are properly the responsibility of the committee and the congregation, nor attempt to impose specific, personal ideas on others. Often the consultant can assist the organ committee in communicating ideas to the congregation, since the consultant may be accepted as a more neutral party than the organ-builder.

---

[1]See Bibliography for references on organs/organ-building.

Early in the selection process the committee should hear many instruments and become familiar with the work of various builders. The committee should develop a language that can be used by the members in describing the sounds heard (coarse, rich, warm, sharp)—any terminology all can agree on that facilitates making comparisons among instruments. If possible, listen to the instruments without the sales representatives being present. The organist of the church may or may not be the best person to demonstrate the organ. For consistency, the same organist should play each instrument and utilize at least some of the same repertoire each time. Or if the church is willing to make the investment, the consultant could be engaged to visit instruments with the committee and play each one.

After listening to a variety of instruments, the committee should agree on one or two builders. If the issue of electronic vs. pipe organ is being considered, this should be resolved. The conclusion of Stage One is to write a report of the committee's findings, and seek the endorsement of the appropriate boards and/or congregation. The report should include a statement such as the following: "Your organ committee recommends that the church enter into negotiations for the design of a pipe organ from firms A and B. We have examined the work of (number) builders, both pipe and electronic, and believe that a pipe organ by firm A or B will best meet this congregation's needs. . . ." Endorsement by the appropriate boards and/or congregation is important, because it tends to diminish potential problems that might occur at a later date, when someone raises a question about work previously approved. For example, "Mr. Jones, that question was answered by the committee at our January meeting, and the answer was affirmed by the congregation when it voted to proceed. Therefore, your question, while helpful in refreshing our memories, is somewhat out of order, since the congregation has already acted in that regard." A congregation that is informed and involved throughout the entire selection process is more likely to support the committee's recommendations and provide financial support.

Notice that in the above process there is no mention of competitive bidding. A pipe organ is a work of art whose value depends not only on measurable features, like a stop list, but also on hard-to-identify qualities, such as a builder's skill and integrity as an artisan. Often a single stop list circulated among builders for bids results in widely differing prices, not just because of quality, but because some builders can construct certain types of organs more economically than others. Competitive bidding is impossible with nonpipe instruments, since each company's product is so varied.

A better procedure in each situation is to deal in dollar amounts—but very cautiously. Early in the study it is best to avoid being too specific about dollar figures. During the usual 1- to 3-year process of deliberations of the organ committee, prices and ideas can change considerably. Likewise, a congregation's perception of its needs often changes, and many a committee has found its credibility questioned because a final recommendation involves a dollar amount considerably higher than that mentioned early in the study. Of course, one needs to have a notion of the range in which to work. Honest answers to such questions as the following can assist in determining that range:

1. Is music important to the congregation?
2. Is congregational singing important?
3. Do we hope to have excellent musical leadership?
4. Is the parish in debt?
5. Does the program envision choir concerts and organ recitals?

A great deal is contingent on local circumstances, which, of course, will influence the ultimate decisions.

In all situations, investment in an organ should be considered as a capital investment to be prorated over many years, even if paid for reasonably quickly. It is in this regard that the proven longevity of the pipe organ becomes significant. While initially more costly than the electronic, its longevity is such that from the perspective of 25 to 100 years (life expectancy for a pipe organ depends on style and quality of construction, and consistency of maintenance), the pipe organ is often more economical.

Because the decision regarding a pipe or nonpipe organ should be made at this stage, a few additional comments seem in order. The following statement by Edward Sovik, respected architect and consultant in church design, is helpful.

> From what has been said earlier about the virtues of integrity, it should be clear that the electronic church organ ought to be avoided. One can say good things about the bar room electronic; it is cheap, it is loud enough, it produces a sound which is distinctively its own. No one will mistake it for a pipe organ. But the electronic imitation of the pipe organ, which is sometimes so good an imitation that a [layperson] can't distinguish it from the real thing, is another matter. The better the imitation, the more reprehensible it is. That it is the product of ingenuity and great skill and that it is somewhat less expensive than a pipe organ make it attractive, but these attractions don't change the fact that it is a phony imitation.[2]

Sovik's thesis is an interesting one. The inherent dishonesty in a copy (mostly poor copies at that) is, for him, morally abhorrent, especially in the church, where integrity and honesty are of great importance. This,

---

[2]E.A. Sovik, *Architecture for Worship* (Minneapolis: Augsburg Publishing House, 1973), p. 97.

and other arguments notwithstanding, does not alter the fact that many churches feel compelled to select an electronic instrument, if only because of financial considerations.

Today, churches considering an investment of between $20,000 and $40,000 should examine both options. Pipe organs (albeit small and rather limited) are being built in this price range by reputable firms. These instruments can meet the needs of worship leadership where the demands are relatively modest. An electronic instrument in the same price range provides more flexibility of tone color and a wider range of apparent loudness, although with less musical quality. When one begins to think in terms of over $25,000, it becomes harder to justify investment in an electronic organ. Although there are electronics made that are priced as high as $100,000, the tonal results are usually little better than smaller versions; all one gets is a large console, which looks impressive, and more speakers. But if a congregation (and organist) chooses to listen more with eyes than ears, the huge electronic is an acceptable, if unfortunate, choice.

The major question remains one of sound. The committee must listen, listen, and then listen again. Do not be confused by claims for numbers of stops, or manuals, or speakers; let your ears tell you what you need to know. Do not be misled by claims of endorsements by prominent artists, or by prestigious installations. Although some claims may be honest, others may involve financial arrangements with companies, ranging from "commissions" to loans of instruments at little or no cost.

The best way to listen is in other church sanctuaries that are much like yours. Each dealer has a special, favorite installation. Listen to one of these, but listen elsewhere as well. Having your organist or consultant, in addition to salespeople, play each instrument provides a kind of consistency from one instrument to another. Listen to the "full organ" sound, often used in playing hymns. Remember that the organ's most important function is leading the hymn-singing, rather than providing background music to cover the sounds of a congregation gathering or a minister walking.

After this intensive listening, and when the choice is narrowed to one or two electronics, a visit to worship in a church using an electronic instrument about the size you envision might be helpful. Organ salespeople often are hesitant to encourage such unannounced visits, because they have no control over the quality of music that is played. They have a valid point, yet a visit for worship can still be enlightening for the committee as it deliberates its final choice of brand and size of instrument.

At this point the decision is made to place a contract for an electronic or to proceed with securing a pipe organ. If the choice is electronic, the second and third stages discussed below are not needed, although certain information might be useful. Before going on, one other possibility should be mentioned. If the budget is limited but the congregation is musically sensitive, the purchase of a good grand piano might be considered. The piano has the advantage of being musically honest, and its sound is capable of filling large spaces adequately. For some it might be more desirable than a small electronic instrument.

Stage Two Stage Two begins after the initial decisions (pipe or nonpipe and selection of one or two builders) have been endorsed by appropriate boards and/or the congregation. It is now fitting for the builder and consultant, if any, to assist in responding to the felt needs of the congregation, as perceived by the organ committee, and to propose designs suitable to the specific situation. Working with one or two builders at this point avoids much of the confusion of too many varied proposals.

During this stage the specific needs of the church, size of the building, dimensions of the music program, and hopes for the future should be considered in order to determine appropriate parameters for the design. The building should be examined for proper location of the instrument. Often in existing buildings, a good builder proposes that the new organ not be placed where the old one was. Take such advice seriously! In buildings not yet constructed early collaboration between architect and organ-builder is essential to assure the optimum location for the organ. Experience suggests that final decisions about the tonal design of the organ in a yet-to-be-constructed building might wait until the building is completed. Even though this could mean a year without the organ, no architect or acoustical engineer can be exactly sure how a new space will function acoustically. There is nothing like making and experiencing music in a given space before finalizing specific details for an instrument.

When Stage Two is completed a second report to official boards and perhaps the congregation should include specific recommendations as to builder and approximate size of the organ. Then, upon endorsement of the appropriate boards, final planning can begin between one builder and the committee with its consultant. Fund-raising may also begin at this stage.

Stage Three During the third and final stage, firm decisions about visual and tonal design are made. The impact, if any, of other remodeling or installation costs is assessed, and bids are obtained. When completed, the work of Stage Three results in a firm proposal submitted for final approval to the boards and the congregation. As the building of the organ begins, the church may wish to retain the services of its consultant, to watch over the final installation of the instrument in the church.

Three specific points should be noted in this three-stage program for organ selection. First, the congregation is informed as plans progress, thus assisting in generating support for the project and assuring that measure of trust essential to the work of the committee. Second, the congregation may endorse, influence, and even abort the project at stages along the way, but it is discouraged from attempting to do (or more usually to undo in an hour or two) the many hours of work put in by the organ committee. Third, a single builder is selected relatively early in the process. The pipe organ is too complex and individual in its design parameters to involve many competing builders for long. A builder who knows he/she is one of many being considered will not (and should not be expected to) expend as much time in the detailed planning for design and installation as should be done *before* final decisions are made and contracts executed. The pipe organ is a work of art, and one must select the artisan early and then enter into a trusting relationship that will result in a satisfied congregation and a happy builder.

MAINTENANCE OF THE ORGAN

Perhaps the most important observation about the maintenance of the organ is *do take care of it*. One continues to marvel at the large number of churches willing to make substantial investments in organs but unwilling to budget the minimal amounts needed to provide for yearly care.

All organs need some maintenance. For some nonpipe instruments the care required is minimal. On purchasing an instrument or assuming a position in a church with an electronic unfamiliar to the organist, it would be wise to check with the local representative to learn what attention is recommended. If dealing with an existing instrument, attempt to ascertain the model and the year manufactured, as this information may influence the representative's recommendations. Take the data to the appropriate board, and solicit approval for the approximate amount required to implement the program recommended. Most boards are happy to have someone who cares, and will respond positively to such a request.

The pipe organ is a bit more complicated. Since the initial investment is usually higher than with an electronic, it becomes even more important to protect that investment by proper care. Again, a wise tactic would be to propose a program for regular maintenance, after consulting with the organ-builder or tuner. There are two major factors to consider in pipe organ maintenance: mechanical care and tuning.

The best way to assure that the organ works reliably is to use it. The complex mechanical components remain free and quick in their movement if the organ is used more than to meet the worship and practice requirements of the incumbent organist. Therefore, the church should encourage *free* access to the instrument for practice by responsible students, always with the stipulation that the worship and musical requirements of the congregation take precedence over any scheduled practice time. It costs very little to operate the average pipe organ. (For example, one large church recently discovered that its four-manual organ cost only 20 cents an hour to operate.) Assuming that a student does not expect the temperature to be raised or lowered to 70 degrees for comfort while practicing, few churches have any excuse for denying the use of their instruments, especially since such use is not detrimental to the longevity of the instrument.

The few regular mechanical maintenance problems of an instrument should be part of a yearly check by the organ tuner. If the blower is not permanently lubricated, it should be periodically checked and lubricated, as required. The organist should keep a record of any malfunctions and report them to the tuner. Even if a problem is sporadic, it should be reported, since it may be a harbinger of greater trouble.

Tuning is the major maintenance requirement of the pipe organ. A yearly tuning that includes attention to mechanical problems has worked well for many churches. This process is *not* a 1-hour touch-up of a few notes, but a complete tuning of most of the instrument. Such a procedure requires about one day for a 15- to 25-rank organ, depending on age and condition. The organist should be present for at least part of this time to communicate concerns with the tuner and hear from the tuner about any problems discovered during the work. This dialogue between tuner and organist can materially assist in assuring the best possible care of the instrument. If the church desires, minor touch-ups of a few ranks may be scheduled for other times in the year, perhaps before major holidays. For extremely large instruments, more attention to tuning may be required, with monthly touch-ups.

The major enemy of the well-tuned pipe organ is temperature instability. In this energy-conscious age there are few churches interested in maintaining a stable temperature in the sanctuary for the benefit of the organ. Actually, such a policy is not needed if one is careful and plans properly. The important factor is to have the *same* temperature any time the instrument is to be used in worship. For example, 65 degrees for Sunday and 55 to 60 degrees for the rest of the week should work well, if adequate time is provided for stabilization of the 65-degree temperature. The thermostat should be advanced to 65 degrees at least 24 hours before the instrument is to be used in a service or concert.

Interestingly, most energy engineers also recommend at least 24 hours for warm-up and stabilization of space, so that the fabric of a room, especially floor and furniture, will feel warm to the touch. A stable room at 65 degrees with furniture at that temperature feels warmer than an instable room where the air is at 70 degrees but the furniture still feels cold. Of course, when the organ is tuned, this same temperature must be maintained well in advance of the organ technician's arrival. One strategy is to schedule the major tuning late in the fall, after the heat has been turned on, so that a stable temperature in the room can be achieved. Obviously, for air-conditioned buildings the procedure is reversed.

A major factor to consider in securing temperature stability for the organ is the free circulation of air from the sanctuary around and through the instrument (again, the chambered organ is at a disadvantage). Most builders discourage direct heat sources in the organ, because the resulting extremely dry air is detrimental to the wood in the instrument. Some churches should consider providing adequate moisture content for the sanctuary to prevent extreme dryness in the organ. Again, a conference with the organ-builder or tuner may be in order to determine what is necessary in each situation. Such a discussion might identify ways to provide better circulation of air in the organ, thus enhancing stability of tuning.

Some organists are competent to repair an occasional cipher (a pipe that sounds constantly) and do minor tuning. Such operations should be done with extreme care, and for many organists *not at all*. Essentially a simple machine in principle, the organ, because of its size, quickly becomes complex and should be treated with respect. A conversation (and perhaps a lesson or two) with the builder or tuner should serve to establish the limits as to one's ability to do minor emergency repairs. After all, another "Silent Night" might be preferable to a damaged organ because of a misguided attempt to effect emergency repairs.

Selecting and designing an organ is a demanding but rewarding undertaking, involving countless hours by committee and builder, and yet when completed, few can find anything but joy as the new instrument fills the sanctuary with its glorious sound. Although less exciting, the mundane work of caring for a good organ is also satisfying. The end result of all this labor is the enriching of worship through the music played on the organ—"the king of instruments."

CHAPTER 10

Expectations and Remuneration of the Church Musician

DEVELOPING A PHILOSOPHY OF SACRED MUSIC

At some point in each church musician's life there must be an effort to formulate and articulate what is believed to be important about music in the church. The importance of a philosophy of sacred music cannot be overemphasized or underestimated, since it usually influences one's choice of position, all the music one chooses to perform, and the quality of each performance. Developing a philosophy is difficult but rewarding, for only then can one articulate and perceive goals and their importance.

The first step in developing a philosophy involves the question "What is music?" What is it that sets music apart from other disciplines? What can music do for people that other arts cannot?

The second step must focus on worship. What role has music played in the history of worship? In what ways has music proved meaningful in the lives of worshipers?

The third step is to identify general functions of music in the Christian church. Four such functions are (1) theological, (2) aesthetic, (3) social, and (4) educational.

The fourth step involves assessing all the above concepts and considering how these ideas influence and determine the quality of the music selected and the performance expectations.

As you ponder and reflect upon these questions, you will clarify what it is you wish to share with a church and how you will go about the task. It is important to remember that there is no one answer to these questions, and that any individual's concept and philosophy of sacred music may well be in a state of flux throughout life. An example of a statement of philosophy follows:

A Philosophy of Sacred Music

Music is an integral part of a person's expressive being. Through music, one expresses a depth of feeling that often transcends words or other experiences with the arts. Music often appeals to the senses in an emotional way and, throughout history, has stirred minds and souls to acts of courage and valor, love and compassion. Music is personal. It is something each can express and experience in his/her own way. No two performances of a musical composition will ever be quite the same, nor are listeners ever the same upon hearing performances of music.

Music has been part of the worship experience since before any written records were kept. The book of Psalms stands as a monument to the power of music. Few Christians fail to be stirred by the words of these immortal psalms:

> Psalm 121: "I lift up my eyes to the hills."
> Psalm 23: "The Lord is my shepherd."
> Psalm 100: "Make a joyful noise to the Lord."

Music serves at least four general functions in the Christian church: (1) theological/didactic, (2) aesthetic, (3) social, and (4) educational. Music is an expressive art form, and in its theological and aesthetic functions expresses feelings of praise, reflection, meditation, inspiration, and challenge. As a social function, music (1) attracts new members to the church, (2) provides an opportunity for the church to reach out and bring the community into the church, (3) offers opportunities for personal fulfillment, and (4) offers opportunities for interpersonal relationships and building group spirit. The educational function of music in the church is fulfilled through study and experiences with the heritage of sacred music, both by congregation and choir, and the development of music skills and appreciations by individual participants.

To achieve these goals, only quality music must be selected for worship, and it should be presented with the highest performance expectations possible, for the worship experience should raise each of us into God's presence. While standards in performance of music and perceptions of quality in music vary greatly, it can be observed that the same standards which govern such judgments in other musical situations are valid when applied to the practice of sacred music.

ASSESSING YOUR POTENTIAL AS A CHURCH MUSICIAN

After you have formulated a philosophy of church music and what it is you wish to share with others, you are ready to look for a position that will provide you with this opportunity. One of the first steps is to determine what skills you have and the degree of their development. Challenge is important for every individual, but being overwhelmed because of insufficient musical skill only leads to frustration for both you and the church. Examine your musical strengths, and begin to build on these, remembering that there is a great variety of talent-mix possibilities for church musicians.

Although titles often indicate specific duties and have individual job descriptions, each church tends to evolve its own meaning for these titles. Essentially, there are three roles for the church musician: conductor, organist, and administrator. Here are some typical job descriptions for various combinations:

The *Organist-Choir Director* generally is responsible for all the music in the morning worship service, as well as for special seasonal services and musical events. He/she has skill in service-playing and in conducting from the console, as well as a broad knowledge of organ and choral repertory suitable for the church. The organist-choir director is seldom responsible for the children's, youth, or handbell choir.

The *Organist-Director of Music* is responsible for the total music program of the church, including all services, special events, and music in the church school. He/she may direct the children's, youth, or handbell choir or may supervise an assistant. Extensive education in sacred music is required for this position, which is generally considered full time or at least half time (20 hours or more per week).

The *Organist* is responsible for playing the organ at all services in the church, and for a separate fee plays most, if not all, weddings and funerals. He/she has a broad repertory of organ music suitable for worship services, and possesses skill in hymn-playing, accompanying, and improvisation. Other responsibilities include seeing that the organs/pianos are maintained and choosing appropriate organ music for services of worship. The organist accompanies all choir rehearsals and is responsible to the choir director.

The *Choir Director* is responsible for the adult choir. He/she has extensive knowledge of choral repertory, an understanding of rehearsal techniques and the human voice, and is sensitive to people. The choir director works cooperatively with the minister and the organist in planning services of worship.

The *Director of Music* usually has a choral background, and is responsible for all facets of music in the church, including music in the

176

church school, special services, and events. He/she works closely with the organist and ministerial staff in planning and performing music in worship services.

The *Minister of Music* is a title generally reserved for a full-time ordained minister whose responsibilities, in addition to pastoral duties, include administering and directing the music program. Such a person may or may not be the organist. However, a part-time minister of music is frequently the organist as well, and generally serves the same function as the organist-director of music.

The *Director of the Children's/Youth Choirs* exhibits knowledge of both the child and adolescent voice, and has developed skill in effective rehearsal techniques. He/she cooperates with and is responsible to the director of music in planning and selecting music suitable for worship.

The *Director of the Handbell Choir* is responsible to the director of music, and works closely with the director of youth choirs and the ministerial staff. He/she generally possesses a knowledge of instrumentation and skill in teaching instrumental music. The ability to arrange music for handbells is considered essential.

APPLYING FOR A POSITION

When you are ready to apply for a position, a first step might be to contact the president (dean) of the local chapter of the American Guild of Organists and/or Choristers Guild and express your interest in finding a church position. Tell your friends and professional colleagues what you are looking for. Call organ and/or voice teachers in the community, and ask for any leads they might have. Join a music club, such as the Music Teachers Association (if you are a teacher), and let your interest be known. Friends from your college music sorority/fraternity might also help. Perhaps the best time for job openings is in the spring, following Easter, since many transfers and professional changes are made during the spring and summer months. Most churches want a complete staff as they move into the fall programming, and will want to interview candidates as early in the summer as possible.

When you hear of a position that is open (and it is unethical to apply for one that is not), obtain the name of the person chairing the search committee by contacting the church. The chairperson may be a layperson, minister, or the director of music. Call and express your interest in the position, and ask what procedure you should follow to apply. Either you will be asked to submit a formal letter of application with supporting credentials, following which you may be invited for an interview/audition; or you may be invited to meet with the committee and to bring your credentials with you.

The matter of credentials, or vita, is relatively new to the musician looking for a part-time church position, but it is an increasingly important part of the application process, as it has long been in business and professional career opportunities. There are two forms of such a document. One, the short resume, is usually two or three pages in length, and should comprise (1) a statement of your philosophy of sacred music, (2) your education, (3) your full-time professional experience, and (4) your professional experience in music, with any experience as a church musician cited first. Always begin with the current year, and list information in reverse chronological order. A list of persons who would serve as professional references is usually included as well.

The second document is a complete vita. This is much longer and is placed in a notebook, with a table of contents and supportive data. In addition to such resume data as above, such a notebook may contain copies of programs you have given; letters of commendation received from parents, professional colleagues, and administrators; pictures of musical activities, etc. It should be neat and attractive, with colored dividers and clearly marked indexes, and the materials should be cellophane-covered. Even though this latter requirement may make the book a little more bulky, it enables the reader to see your work clearly and with ease. It is also a good indication of how meticulous you are, for it truly represents your "life."

THE INTERVIEW/AUDITION

After you have been invited to interview/audition for the position, there are important preparations to be made. The committee and minister will ask many questions designed to examine your qualifications and personality. It is at this point that your philosophy becomes very significant. As you talk with the committee, you need to understand the committee's philosophy, for to be happy and effective in any church, your philosophy of sacred music and the church's philosophy of sacred music must be compatible.

Don't talk yourself out of the job. Focus on the needs of the church and on how you may serve, rather than on family problems or on the problems of churches previously served. You should have thought about salary before entering into negotiations. There are still churches whose members expect the musician to work for the "glory of the Lord" rather than for money, but as professional musicians, no matter how dedicated we are, we must respect ourselves and our musicianship enough to negotiate a salary commensurate with our professional status.

Your most important preparation is musical. If you are applying for an organ position, you should be prepared to play (1) an organ prelude, (2) an organ postlude, (3) a hymn of your choice, (4) a hymn of the committee's choice, (5) a modulation from any key to the Doxology, (6) an anthem or solo accompaniment, and (7) a short improvisation. If possible, ascertain in advance what will be asked of you at the audition, and arrange to practice on the instrument that you will play for the audition. A choir director interviewed by the search committee may be expected to conduct a "demonstration" rehearsal of the church choir or a group of singers gathered especially for the interview. It is important to know before meeting with the committee what will be expected so that you may be prepared. Some committees may ask you to rehearse a hymn; others may want you to work on an anthem or two. In doing these things you should attempt to demonstrate your knowledge of voices and rehearsal techniques, sensitivity to the volunteer singer, and creativity in planning choral music for worship. Interviews/auditions for other directing positions (children's choir, handbell choir) are often conducted in the same manner.

If at all possible, you, as the candidate, should insist on playing, singing, or conducting music during the Sunday morning worship service. This is the best way for the musician to get the "feel" for the church, and also for the church to determine the musical skill of the musician. If not, do attempt to work with the choir and/or accompany the committee in hymn-singing. While not ideal, these experiences provide some insights into the church. An unannounced visit to a Sunday worship service also may be of value.

ACCEPTING A POSITION

If offered a position, consider your credentials and the scope of the position when negotiating salary. The American Guild of Organists has published an excellent booklet to help you determine your "worth," based on your training, experience and number of hours expected.[1] Don't sell yourself short, but be realistic in terms of the musical skills and insights you bring to church music. An applicant with extensive study in sacred music has more to offer initially than the musician who has had no study of sacred music, even though he/she may be a fine performing musician.

There are a number of questions that must be answered before you can enter into a contract and a meaningful relationship with a church. Categories include philosophy; physical plant; time requirements; professional needs/obligations; policies for extra services, weddings, and

---

[1]American Guild of Organists, *Compensation of the Church and Synagogue Musician* (New York: American Guild of Organists, 1978).

179

funerals; budget; other music personnel; ministerial/music planning. Satisfactory answers to these questions will assure you of a rewarding and happy tenure.

Philosophy/Job Description

1. What is the philosophy of music held by the minister, music committee, congregation?
2. Does the church provide a job description?

Physical Plant

1. What kind of organ is in the church? (Will you be musically satisfied playing the instrument?)
2. What policies does the church follow concerning maintenance of the organ/pianos? Are funds budgeted for these needs?
3. Who determines the use of the organ?
4. Is the church heated during the week?
5. Is there a rehearsal room? Does it have adequate ventilation? lighting? heat? acoustics?
6. Does the church provide you with office space?

Time Requirements

1. How many services are there on Sundays?
2. How many extra services are there during the year? (Do you receive extra remuneration for these or are they included in the annual contract?)
3. Are you expected to meet with the ministers on a regular basis for planning?
4. How many hours does the church expect of you in order to fulfill the job description?
5. Are you expected to attend social functions, music committee/board meetings, church school classes?
6. Are you expected to join the church? (Some musicians hold the view that it is better *not* to become a member of the congregation one serves professionally. Others believe just the opposite.)

Professional Needs

1. Does the church have a sick-leave policy? (Even organists and choir directors are subject to human ills.)
2. Does the church provide vacation time with pay? (Four weeks is essential.)
3. Are there funds for continuing education? (e.g., conferences, conventions, etc.)

Policies for Weddings/Funerals/Extra Services

1. You should expect to play for weddings/funerals.
2. If there is a conflict with your regular full-time position, who plays for these?
3. Are you the person who sets the fees for weddings? (Remember, weddings are not included in the salary of your contract; they are extra duties. It takes thought and preparation for such activities, and it is not just "playing for 15 minutes before the wedding," as many people think. Conferences with the bride, practice, rehearsing with soloists, the wedding rehearsal—all should be considered in determining the fee.)
4. Are you the person who sets the fees for funerals? (Remember, as a part-time musician your salary is based on regular services of worship and rehearsals. While some organists feel that playing for funerals is part of their ministry, it is important to remember that you should expect a fee, and that an understanding about the fee must be made while negotiating the details of the position.
5. All churches have certain extra services. The most common are Christmas Eve, Ash Wednesday, Maundy Thursday and/or Good Friday, and special services on Easter. Certain traditions (Lutheran, Roman Catholic, Episcopal) may include many additional services, especially during Lent. There may also be extra services on Thanksgiving Day, Christmas Day, and New Year's Eve. Be sure you are clear that the offered salary is commensurate with the extra professional services required.

Budget

1. How much money is provided for the purchase of new choral music?
2. Are there any funds for instrumentalists, e.g., brass players for Easter?
3. Is robe-cleaning included in the budget?
4. Are adequate funds provided for tuning the organ and pianos?
5. Is there provision for funding of publicity for special musical programs?

Personnel

1. Are there paid singers?
2. Who is responsible for their selection and quality of performance?

Ministerial/Music Planning

1. To whom are you responsible? minister? chairperson of music? personnel committee? other?

2. Are there regular meetings with appropriate committees to share your ideas and problems?
3. Does the minister take time to plan services far enough in advance for you to rehearse the choral/organ music suitable for the occasion?
4. Who chooses the hymns? Are you consulted?

Evaluation/Contract

1. Is there an evaluation procedure each year in which the activities and performance of the church musicians are reviewed?
2. Does the church provide a written contract? (This is strongly recommended.)

The following is a sample contract for use by church musicians and churches, and should be adapted to individual situations. It is suggested as a guide, and includes important areas of interest for organist, choir director, singer, and any other musician considered for employment.

sample contract

Date

Name

Title of Position

Name of Institution

Committee Responsible for Hiring

Name of Chairperson

Name of Minister

Name of Musician

have hereby entered into an agreement herein provided beginning _____[date] and terminating_____[date] at a salary of $_____per year, payable_____.

The salary will be reviewed annually, and when the budget for the ensuing year is considered, performance and qualifications of _____ [musician] as _____ [title] will be evaluated and negotiations entered into for determining cost of living and/or merit increases for the following year.

1. The above-named person shall be accountable to_____
   and is responsible for the following:
   a. Select and perform organ/choral music for all scheduled Sunday services.
   b. Select and perform organ/choral music for additional services of worship, e.g., Christmas Eve, Maundy Thursday, lenten midweek, etc.
   c. Serve as director of the following choirs:_____
   _____ .
   d. Rehearse weekly with all choirs and such additional rehearsal time as necessary to achieve the musical goals of both the musician and the church.
   e. Plan regularly with the ministerial staff and lay leadership to integrate music into the life of the church.
   f. Purchase all music supplies within the budget of $_____ allocated for _____ [year].
   g. Select assisting soloists/instrumentalists within the budget of $_____allocated for_____[year].
   h. Consult with the proper committees regarding the maintenance needs of organ/pianos. The church will provide adequate funds for continued maintenance.
   i. Play for all weddings/funerals as time permits, or provide a competent substitute. The fee for such services is determined by the organist in consultation with the minister.
2. _____ [name of musician] may use organ/piano facilities without cost for practice/private teaching. Lessons scheduled and practice time allotted to students must not interfere with regularly scheduled church activities. Use of organ/piano practice facilities will be supervised.
3. A vacation of_____ weeks with full salary will be granted annually. The church musician will assist in finding a competent substitute.
4. The church musician will be granted _____ Sundays (or days) sick leave per year, which may accumulate to _____.
5. The church shall provide the following fringe benefits: social security, other _____.
6. The church shall provide $_____ annually for continuing education, e.g., conferences, conventions, workshops, etc.
7. The church musician shall give notice of his/her termination of employment at least (60) days in advance. The church should likewise give (60) days notice in the event it wishes to terminate the contract.

_____   _____
(Signature of Responsible Party)   (Signature of Musician)

Date_____   Date_____

After all your conferences with the representatives of the church, ask yourself, "Will I be happy in this situation, and do I think the church will be happy with me?" No amount of money can take the place of satisfaction, and since working in the church often involves expressing our deepest emotions, it is important that the relationship between the musician and the church be thought through carefully, before a commitment is made by either the church or the musician. When you find yourself in "harmony" with the church, throw yourself with abandon into an enthusiastic and exciting experience that is one of the most rewarding in the world: serving God through music.

The Copyright Law and the Church Musician

As the convenience and availability of modern copy machines increases, as the price of music escalates, and as money for music is reduced, the church musician may succumb to the temptation of copying a piece of music (choral, vocal, organ) for performance. However, no longer can the musician hide behind ignorance and say, "Oh, I didn't know that was illegal," for there are a multitude of publications, both from publishers and the government, that define parameters in making copies of a work.

The first reason for obeying the copyright law is a moral one. It is *wrong* to deny an author or composer a justified monetary return for his/her talent and time investment. It is also wrong for anyone employed by the church, which teaches "thou shalt not steal," to engage in such copying.

A second reason is that making copies, except under the conditions specified by the law, is illegal, and subject to heavy fines and/or imprisonment. Numerous schools and churches throughout the country have been surprised by investigators who have appeared armed with search warrants to examine the contents of choral libraries. Most of these "visits" have resulted in heavy fines for the offending institution.

Church musicians need accurate information concerning the entire issue. Several music publishers, selected at random, were contacted for suggestions that would clarify the matter of copyright. Some of the responses are excerpted below.

Robert Mabley, executive secretary of Galaxy Music Corporation of New York wrote: "Our position on the copyright situation in the U.S. is essentially that taken by the Music Publishers Association, i.e., that the duplication and use of copyrighted music without the express permission of the copyright owner is not only contrary to the U.S. Copyright Law, but is morally wrong."

W. Thomas Smith, executive director of The Hymn Society of America, sent the following statement:

Copyright Policy
The Hymn Society of America, Inc.

1. There is no charge made for use in denominational hymnals, although a donation or membership will be accepted.
2. There is no charge for use in individual congregations for bulletins, or hymn collections made by individual congregations for non-commercial use, although a donation will be accepted and active membership in The Hymn Society is encouraged.
3. There is a $25 charge for each hymn copyrighted by The Hymn Society and used in a publication sold by subscription or for educational publications by denominational publishers. Active membership in The Hymn Society is encouraged.
4. There is a charge of half of the royalties (5%) for use of any copyrighted text for a commercial venture such as octavo form publications, anthems, etc.

One copy of the hymnal, church bulletin, hymn collection or other publication should be mailed to the Hymn Society of America, National Headquarters, Wittenberg University, Springfield, Ohio 45501.

Joyce Horn of Oxford University Press, London, added an international dimension:

With regard to the reprinting of copyright hymns for local use, in general we grant permission for churches, schools, etc., to reprint items from hymn books provided that they apply to us in good time and let us know the type of collection and the proposed printing number. We charge a small fee for the use of our material in supplements and collections to be put into continuing use, but we generally grant free permission where the item is to be used on one occasion only. In all cases we require the inclusion of the author/composer's name and dates, together with an acknowledgement to ourselves, and to the source book (if appropriate).

Our main problem with overseas requests is insufficient information. It is quite common for us to be given the first line of a text, with or without a source book, in a request for a hymn tune only, and we frequently cannot trace the hymn tune without its name because we do not sing it to the particular text quoted, which is not our copyright! Almost all hymn tunes have names, and we do need to know them in order to trace which material is being asked for. We do not always have copies of the non-UK hymn books from which enquirers are quoting and thus cannot refer to them. This is why we prefer people always to apply to us *first*, so that at that stage we can correct any misinformation and can redirect requests where necessary.

Arnold Broido, president of Theodore Presser Company, Bryn Mawr, Pennsylvania enclosed with his response a copy of *The United States Copyright Law: A Guide for Church Musicians*, noting that it had not been copyrighted and could therefore be reprinted:

**Guidelines for the Use of
Copyrighted Music Material**

PRELUDE

On October 19, 1976, President Gerald R. Ford signed into law—Public Law 94-553—setting forth the law of the land in regard to copyrights. This new law became effective January 1, 1978.

No copyright is claimed in this booklet. You are encouraged to reproduce it in order to assure the widest possible circulation.

GUIDELINES FOR THE USE OF COPYRIGHTED MUSIC MATERIAL

The organizations listed on [page 194-95] have participated in the preparation of this booklet to inform church musicians, ministers, and the laity of the provisions in this new statute which have particular application to the use of music in their respective ministries.

This guide does *NOT* presume to be a comprehensive summary of the Copyright Act of 1976. It does *NOT* attempt to deal with all the issues covered by the legislation, nor does it provide answers to many of the legal questions.

It is intended, however, to be a guide to understanding the nature of copyright by the users of church music to improve their ministries, to maintain proper standards of ethics, and to help protect themselves and their churches from incurring liability or subjecting themselves to the possibility of being sued.

A complete copy of the Copyright Law of 1976 and further information may be obtained by writing: The Copyright Office, Library of Congress, Washington, DC 20559.

THE COPYRIGHT LAW

A. Why a Copyright Law?

1. United States copyright laws stem from Article I, Section 8 of the Constitution. Our founding fathers determined that it was in the public interest that the creation of a person's mind and spirit, should, under law, belong for a limited time to that person and/or, if deceased, to the family of that person.

2. The law is designed to encourage the development of the arts and sciences by protecting the work of the creative individuals in our society.

B. What Is a Copyright?

A copyright is a statutory grant of certain rights for limited times.

C. What May Be Copyrighted?

Original works of authorship which are fixed in a copy or a phonorecord. The law provides 7 classes:

- literary works
- musical works, including any accompanying words
- dramatic works, including any accompanying music
- pantomimes and choreographic works
- pictorial, graphic, and sculptural works
- motion pictures and other audiovisual works
- sound recordings

D. When Is a Work Copyrighted?

A work is protected from the moment of creation, fixed in a copy or phonorecord. Copyright Registration is another step in the process and while it is not mandatory for protection to register a copyright, it is advisable to do so for additional protection in cases of infringement.

E. Who Owns a Copyright?

The composer and lyricist or the duly authorized agent (Publisher) to whom they have transferred ownership.

188

RIGHTS OF COPYRIGHT OWNERS

F. What Are the Exclusive Rights of Copyright Owners?

1. To reproduce the copyrighted work in copies or phonorecords.
2. To prepare derivative works based upon the copyrighted work.
3. To distribute copies or phonorecords of the copyrighted work to the public by sale or other transfer of ownership, or by rental, lease, or lending.
4. In the case of literary, musical, dramatic, and choreographic works, pantomimes, and motion pictures and other audiovisual works, to perform the copyrighted work publicly.
5. In the case of literary, musical, dramatic, and choreographic works, pantomimes, and pictorial, graphic or sculptural works, including the individual images of a motion picture or other audiovisual work, to display the copyrighted work publicly.

DURATION OF A COPYRIGHT

G. What Is the Duration of a Copyright?

A major change in the law has to do with the length of the protection provided to copyright owners.

1. Works created after January 1, 1978 will be protected for the life of the composer (author) plus 50 years.
2. Works copyright prior to January 1, 1978, if renewed will be protected for 75 years from the date copyright was originally secured.

GUIDELINES FOR THE 1976 COPYRIGHT LAW

A limitation on the exclusive right of copyright owners to reproduce a copyrighted work is dealt with in Section 107 of the law under the title "Fair Use" which reads in its entirety:

"Notwithstanding the provisions of section 106, the fair use of a copyrighted work, including such use by reproduction in copies or phonorecords or by any other means specified by that section, for purposes such as criticism, comment, news reporting, teaching (including multiple copies for classroom use), scholarship, or research, is not an infringement of copyright. In determining whether the use made of a work in any particular case is a fair use the factors to be considered shall include: (1) the purpose and character of the use, including whether such use is of a commercial nature or is for nonprofit educational purposes; (2) the nature of the copyrighted work; (3) the amount and substantiality of the portion used in relation to the copyrighted work as a whole; and (4) the effect of the use upon the potential market for or value of the copyrighted work."

As active participants in the shaping of the new law, music publishers and music educators have developed Guidelines for Educational Uses of Music, in both graphic and recorded form, that set forth specific uses which are permissible and those which are prohibited. These Guidelines are published in the official Report on the Copyright Law of 1976, which supplements and amplifies the meaning of the Law itself.

Although developed for inclusion in and now contained in the Report on the new law, to clarify Fair Use as it applies to music education, the following Guidelines should be useful as a guide to all users of music.

A. Guidelines for Educational Uses of Music

The purpose of the following guidelines is to state the minimum and not the maximum standards of educational fair use under Section 107 of HR.2223. The parties agree that the conditions determining the extent of permissible copying for educational purposes may change in the future; that certain types of copying permitted under these guidelines may not be permissible in the future; and conversely that in the future other types of copying not permitted under these guidelines may be permissible under revised guidelines.

Moreover, the following statement of guidelines is not intended to limit the types of copying permitted under the standards of fair use under judicial decision and which are stated in Section 107 of the Copyright Revision Bill. There may be instances in which copying which does not fall within the guidelines stated below may nonetheless be permitted under the criteria of fair use.

1. Permissible Uses

a. Emergency copying to replace purchased copies which for any reason are not available for an imminent performance provided purchased replacement copies shall be substituted in due course.

b. For academic purposes, other than performance, single or multiple copies of excerpts of works may be made, provided that the excerpts do not comprise a part of the whole which would constitute a performable unit such as a section, movement or aria, but in no case more than ten percent (10%) of the whole work. The number of copies shall not exceed one copy per pupil.

c. Printed copies which have been purchased may be edited or simplified provided that the fundamental character of the work is not distorted or the lyrics, if any, altered or lyrics added if none exist.

d. A single copy of recordings of performances by students may be

190

made for evaluation or rehearsal purposes and may be retained by the educational institution or individual teacher.

e. A single copy of a sound recording (such as a tape, disc or cassette) of copyrighted music may be made from sound recordings owned by an educational institution or an individual teacher for the purpose of constructing aural exercises or examinations and may be retained by the educational institution or individual teacher. (This pertains only to the copyright of the music itself and not to any copyright which may exist in the sound recording.)

2. *Prohibitions*

a. Copying to create or replace or substitute for anthologies, compilations or collective works.

b. Copying of or from works intended to be "consumable" in the course of study or of teaching such as workbooks, exercises, standardized tests and answer sheets and like material.

c. Copying for the purpose of performance, except as in 1a above.

d. Copying for the purpose of substituting for the purchase of music, except as in 1a and 1b above.

e. Copying without inclusion of copyright notice which appears on the printed copy.

B. Additional Information

YOU MAY NOT: —make copies of a recorded performance for distribution without securing the permission of the copyright owner and paying the royalty provided of 2¾¢ per selection or ½¢ per minute of playing time, whichever is greater.

The copyright owner cannot deny this permission if the work has been previously recorded by himself or with his consent. You may procure this permission from the copyright proprietor, or contact the Harry Fox Agency which handles recording rights for most music publishers. The Harry Fox Agency, 110 East 59th St., New York, NY 10022 (212) 751-1930.

C. Performance

Performance is one of the copyright owner's exclusive rights. The new law provides that:

YOU MAY:—perform non-dramatic musical works or dramatic-musical works of a religious nature, in the course of services at places of worship or at a religious assembly.

—perform a non-dramatic musical work if there is no purpose of

direct or indirect commercial advantage, no fee or compensation paid to the performers, promoters or organizers, and no admission charge; if there is an admission charge, all of the proceeds must be used only for educational or charitable purposes. The performance may not take place if the copyright owner objects in writing seven days before the performance.
—perform a non-dramatic musical work on closed circuit television to other classrooms or to disabled persons for teaching purposes, only if the transmission is part of the systematic activities of the church, and only if the performance is directly related and of material assistance to the teaching content of the program.

Complete information concerning licensing of performances of copyrighted non-dramatic musical works may be obtained from ASCAP, BMI, or SESAC.

Broadcast Music, Inc.
40 West 57th Street
New York, NY 10019

SESAC Inc.
10 Columbus Circle
New York, NY 10019

American Society of Composers, Authors and Publishers
ASCAP Building
One Lincoln Plaza
New York, NY 10023

PENALTIES FOR INFRINGEMENT

The remedies provided by the law to a copyright owner could mean that churches found making illegal copies, or otherwise infringing, could face:

1. Payment of from $250 to $10,000 (statutory damages) and if the court finds willfulness, up to $50,000 per infringement;
2. If willful infringement for commercial advantage and private financial gain is proved, fines of up to $50,000 and/or two years' imprisonment, or both.

The nature of the remedies provided by the law indicates that copyright infringement is something serious and needs to be viewed with concern.

Church musicians need to understand "fair use" and make the most of the privileges it grants, but they must also abide by its very definite limitations.

USEFUL INFORMATION

1. How to Tell If a Work Is Copyrighted

All copyrighted works bear a copyright notice in which the date of copyright is included. Under the old law, the term of copyright was 28 years with the possible renewal of an additional 28 years. However, during the legislative process leading to the new law, all copyrights from September 19, 1906 which had been renewed but which would otherwise have expired were extended so that they did not fall into public domain. Thus, all subsisting copyrights, if renewed, will have, under the new law, a term of copyright of 75 years from the date copyright was originally secured. Therefore, to be safe, a church musician should assume that any publication which bears a copyright notice of 1906 or later is protected. Absence of copyright notice does not necessarily mean it is free.

2. Out-of-print Works

When copyrighted works are out of print it may be, occasionally, that church musicians would like to procure a copy or copies for specific purposes. You must write to the copyright owner to inquire of their policies for procuring copies or for permission to reproduce. You may write to the Music Publishers Association (MPA) or National Music Publishers Association (NMPA) for a simple form relative to the procurement of out-of-print works.

3. Copyright Owners Action

Copyright owners are fully prepared to prosecute for infringements under the new law in order to protect their rights. Be advised that there are innumerable ways of discovering infringements and that damages resulting therefrom are clearly defined.

4. Addresses of Publishers

Sometimes, a church musician who wishes to secure a permission, to make an arrangement, or for some other copyright inquiry, may have difficulty in locating the copyright proprietor. The name, of course, may appear with the copyright notice on the title page or elsewhere in the publication. Sometimes, however, the publishing company has been absorbed by another; changed its name and address, or for some other reason is difficult to locate. The following organizations will undertake to supply that information. While this may not always be possible, the information available to those organizations makes them the best source to assist all those who have difficulty in locating a music publisher.

Church Music Publishers Association (CMPA)
P. O. Box 4329
Washington, DC 20012

Music Publishers Association of the United States (MPA)
Third Floor
130 West 57th Street
New York, NY 10019
(212) 582-1122

National Music Publishers Association, Inc. (NMPA)
110 East 59th Street
New York, NY 10022
(212) 751-1930

POSTLUDE

The 1976 Copyright Law is an honest attempt to balance the rights of the copyright proprietor with the needs of a democratic public and certain of its members such as church musicians.

Many church musicians realize that they depend upon the creative efforts of composers for success in their ministry and are, above all others, arbiters of integrity and honesty in support of obeying the law. These church musicians are setting a splendid example for they realize that there is no justification for breaking the law for "Religious Service."

Obedience to the new copyright law can establish a new day for encouragement of the creative process by composers and authors.

The new law provides a good opportunity for a new resolve to uphold the law. Encourage your church to provide an adequate budget in order to avoid a temptation to break the law. Explain to ministers and governing boards the facts of the law and the possible damages for infringements.

In no way does the intent of the new law inhibit the encouragement or practice of the creative arts. Rather, it defines and establishes a climate in which the creative process can mature and thrive with equal protection for all.

Only you, the church musician, can assure its success.

This brochure is produced by The Church Music Publishers Association and issued jointly by the following organizations:

American Guild of Organists
American Lutheran Church, Parish Music and the Arts
Association of Disciple Musicians
Choristers Guild

Fellowship In The Arts—United Church of Christ
Fellowship of American Baptist Musicians
Hymn Society of America
Lutheran Church in America
Music Publishers Association
National Association of Pastoral Musicians (Roman Catholic)
National Church Music Fellowship
National Music Publishers Association
Presbyterian Association of Musicians
Southern Baptist Church Music Conference
Standing Commission on Church Music of the Episcopal Church

Vignettes on the Role of Music in Major Worship Traditions

EASTERN ORTHODOX

Historical and Theological Background   The oldest established church in Christendom is the Eastern Orthodox, which began in the Holy Land before there were any Christians in Rome. Orthodoxy (from the Greek *orthos* and *doxa*, "true belief") comprised the one, holy, catholic, and apostolic church for Christianity's first thousand years. Differences in doctrine and discipline, e.g., clerical celibacy, use of unleavened bread for Holy Communion, and Christ's role as the second person in the Trinity, led to the Great Schism of 1054, which resulted in the excommunication of the Pope and the establishment of the Church of Rome.

Orthodox worship is permeated by a sense of awe and mystery. The most sacred things and actions are veiled, not declared; signifying rather than representing. Here the focus is not so much on the suffering of Christ on the cross, but the majestic figure of the risen Christ as represented in the great creations of Byzantine art.

The growth of liturgy brought a change in the architecture of Orthodox churches, which became known as Byzantine style. The Greek temple, which was meant to be viewed from the outside, was replaced by the Christian basilica, in which the focus was on the inside, with its interior colonnades and painted or mosaic embellishments on the walls and semidome apse. In keeping with the emphasis on the mystical and inner self, these basilicas had no windows through which to view the outside world, for those of the clerestory were too high and too deeply set to allow even a glimpse of the sky. In this atmosphere, lit by flickering candles, an inner radiance of the spirit rather than natural light was sought.[1]

Form of Worship   The Liturgy of St. Basil—later shortened to the Liturgy of St. Chrysostom—used today in Greek Orthodox churches, was the first to become fixed and also the first in which Lent, Christmas, and Epiphany were observed. Later changes that took place included (1) development of a service of prothesis: a private preparation of the clergy, including prayers and preparation of the oblation; (2) use of prayers and singing to prepare worshipers for the reading of the Holy Scriptures, which were invariable and prescribed; (3) addition of a spoken creed; and (4) increased mystical significance expressed through a more elaborate ceremony.

A dramatic change was the development of a sanctuary screen decorated with pictures called *icons*, and subsequently called an *iconostasis*. In the iconostasis (which remains in use today) there were three doors. The center one, opposite the Holy Table, was called the Royal Door; through this door the bread and wine were brought in for the celebration of the Eucharist. At this point in the liturgy the Cherubic Hymn was sung, along with the anthems of the Mystic Supper. Both these musical forms were highly florid and contained a great deal of repetition.

At first there were only one or two cantors (singers); later choirs were formed that came to represent the people, voicing most of the responses in the liturgy. Cymbals and bells were used, but there is little record of the use of other instruments in Greek Orthodox worship. Choirs today continue this tradition of a cappella singing.

Heritage and Practice of Music   Hymns of the Byzantine Church are Eastern Christianity's most distinctive contribution to music and poetry. These originated from the short responses known as *troparia*, which were inserted between the reading of the verses of the psalms. Byzantine chant was monodic, and its rhythm was free, e.g., no regular metric division. Chants, consisting of melodic passages illustrating the meaning of the words, were organized by a series of short motives, rather than a scale, which were put together by the performer.

A large repertory of music sprang up in the late nineteenth century, when such composers as Rachmaninoff, Gretchaninov, and Ippolitov-

---

[1]William Fleming, *Arts and Ideas* (New York: Holt, Rinehart & Winston, 1974), p. 81.

Ivanof created anthems with rich textures, e.g., Rachmaninoff, *Vespers*; Gretchaninov, *Salvation Is Created*; and Ippolitov-Ivanof, *Carol of the Bells*. Each of these compositions features divisi of parts (up to 16) and places emphasis on low bass sounds. These deep resonant sounds remain one of the chief characteristics of music in Orthodox churches.

ROMAN CATHOLIC

Theological/Historical Background   The Roman Catholic Church became an entity when the Great Schism (separation from the Orthodox Church) took place in 1054, a time when the Pope and the Patriarch of Constantinople anathematized each other. The distinction between these two halves of Christendom ran deep, and the Roman Church grew as the Latin West increased in wealth, power, culture, and self-confidence.

Historically, the Roman Catholic Church has been apostolic, that is, it was founded on the apostles St. Peter and St. Paul. This view is reiterated in the Nicene Creed, said each week: "We believe in one holy, apostolic Church." Historically, the Roman Catholic Church views itself as universal in character, the one true Christian church. The Roman Catholic Church is a sacramental church, that is, it observes the following as sacraments: baptism, confirmation, Eucharist, penance, marriage, holy orders (ordination of priests, deacons, bishops), and anointing of the sick. The Roman Catholic believes that the real presence of Christ is embodied in the Eucharist.

Historically, two of the impressive features of a Roman Catholic church are the exterior and the interior of the building, where great attention is given to adornment. Expressed is a philosophy that nothing on this earth is too good or beautiful to reflect the love of God. The Roman Catholic believes that, just as we celebrate special occasions by putting on our most festive clothes and setting our tables with flowers and candles and fine linens, so the Church seeks to vest priests in beautiful robes, and provide flowers and lights on the altar to show love for Christ. Each garment, each object and ornament has a traditional meaning and purpose. To express the varying moods of the days and seasons of the Christian Year, the Church has long used vestments and hangings of different colors: white or gold, signifying joy for Christmas and Easter, as well as for other feasts, such as weddings; violet for penitence during the solemn seasons of Advent and Lent, and on all penitential days; green for immortality during the long Trinity season, as well as for Epiphany. Red is used for Pentecost—signifying the tongues of fire—and also for the blood of martyrs on the feasts of saints who died martyrs' deaths; black is used for mourning at funerals and on Good Friday.

During the Mass the congregation takes an active physical part—

kneeling, standing, and sitting. Kneeling expresses adoration, penitence, gratitude, helplessness, and humility. A Catholic also believes that kneeling helps to quiet the worshiper and to prepare him/her for God's response to prayer. The worshiper stands to praise and pour forth joy and exultation in hymns and psalms. For instruction the worshiper is seated, because it is believed that one is more relaxed and better able to concentrate on the sermon or meditation. In the Roman tradition, each person who faces or passes an altar where there is a light burning, either on the altar or in a hanging lamp above it, genuflects, i.e., bends the right knee until it touches the ground. The genuflection is a gesture of adoration for Christ, who is present there. Around the walls hang 14 plaques or paintings, called the Stations of the Cross, that depict the principal events of the day of Christ's crucifixion. For many centuries Christians have made pilgrimages to the Holy Land and have followed the steps of Christ on his way to Calvary. The stations provide an opportunity for such a pilgrimage, either through private devotions or through corporate worship in a special service. Paintings and statues of saints provide a visible reminder that through the doctrine of the Communion of Saints, all faithful Christians—living and dead—have an intimate relationship which death does not interrupt; that they are in communion with one another and can help one another.

The tabernacle candle burns in churches to remind the worshiper of the real presence of Christ. In some churches the flickering candles that burn day and night before the statues of Christ and the saints are symbols of love. They are lit in hopefulness, in gratitude, and as small memorials. Just as prayers enter into eternity and into the sight of God, so the candles burn on in a quiet church long after the worshiper has returned to the world.

Form of Worship   The Roman Catholic liturgy, called the Mass, consists of the following:

Proper (Spoken)	*Proper* (Musical)	*Ordinary* (Musical)
Collects	Introit	Kyrie
Epistle	Gradual	Gloria
Gospel	Alleluia	Credo
Preface	Tract	Sanctus
	Offertory	Agnus Dei
	Communion	Benedictus

Since 1962, the liturgy has been divided into the Liturgy of the Word and the Liturgy of the Eucharist. The Liturgy of the Word follows a prescribed order:

Greeting and Prayer
Old Testament Lectionary
  Responsorial (Music)
New Testament Epistle
  Alleluia (Music)
Gospel
Sermon
Creed
Prayer Petitions

Variables include the Penitential rite, and the saying/singing of the Kyrie and/or Gloria in Excelsis.
 The Liturgy of the Eucharist consists of three parts:

   I. Canon
        Preface
        Holy, Holy, Holy (Sanctus)
        Prayer of Thanksgiving
        Memorial Acclamation
        Great Amen
  II. Communion Service
        Lord's Prayer
        O Lamb of God (Agnus Dei)
        Receiving of Communion by Faithful
 III. Dismissal

Heritage and Practice of Music   In the early church the practice of chanting was generally used in the musical portions of the Mass, which was sung in Latin. With increased congregational participation and use of the vernacular, there has been a decline in the singing of Gregorian chant. It will be helpful, however, to review some of the most important characteristics of this beautiful music.
 There are three types of chant:
 1. Syllabic, in which melodies are quite simple and each syllable of text is set to one note.

Vic - ti - mae pa - scha - li   lau - des   im - mo - lent Chri -sti - a - ni

 2. Neumatic, in which some syllables have two or three notes.

Be - a - ta vi - sce - ra Ma - ri - a vir - gi - nis

200

3. Florid (melismatic), in which there are many notes for one syllable.

Ky - ri - e _____ e - - le - i-son.

The rise and fall of chant melodies was built on grammatical accents of the liturgical text. Intervals seldom exceeded a fifth, whether ascending or descending, leaps of a sixth were extremely rare, and an octave was found only in sequences or proses. The finality of a chant was often emphasized by a melodic extension of the final syllable, much like a delayed cadence.

A most dramatic event in the twentieth century for the Roman Catholic Church, as well as for all Christendom, was the Twenty-first Ecumenical Council (Vatican II), convened on October 11, 1962 by Pope John XXIII. This council was dedicated to reuniting all Christians. As the Church examined all facets of its heritage and present practice, the liturgy was examined and retained as an exercise of the priestly office of Jesus Christ. In the liturgy, worship experiences—e.g., praise, adoration, confession, absolution, and symbols—are manifested by signs perceptible to the senses. Vatican II stated that the liturgy depends solely on the authority of the Church and that sacred scripture is of paramount importance.

Worshipers are encouraged to take an active part by means of acclamations, responses, psalmody, antiphons, and songs, as well as by actions, gestures, and bodily attitudes. The new liturgy involved the people far more than the passive inactivity of the earlier liturgy. Great emphasis was placed on the use of the vernacular for the Mass, and although Latin is still considered the language of the Roman Catholic Church, English is used in American churches today.

While great emphasis had been given sacred music to serve as a means of increasing holiness and enriching the sacred rites, Vatican II also encouraged the preservation of sacred music, including Gregorian chant, but also acknowledged other forms of sacred music as well. The pipe organ remained the traditional musical instrument, but other instruments were also approved for use in divine worship, and many churches turned to folk music accompanied by guitar. Hymn-singing by Roman Catholic congregations has been encouraged, and hymnals containing words and music have been published. New choral music has been written, both on the traditional Mass texts, e.g., Kyrie, Gloria, and also on texts drawn from Holy Scripture and other liturgical sources. Vatican II required that any other texts set to music should conform to Catholic doctrine.

Summary   Music was a major part of the Greek Orthodox and the Roman Catholic worship traditions. The fixed structure of the liturgy tended to restrain musical development in the Greek Orthodox tradition, except for the rise of a large body of a cappella music, while the variable portions of the Roman Mass provided opportunities for the subsequent development of a rich musical heritage of masses and motets that sprang from the pens of composers, especially during the Renaissance.

LUTHERAN

Theological/Historical Background   Worship in the Lutheran Church has its roots in music and theology, and was an outgrowth of Roman Catholic worship at the time of the Reformation. Music, which has always been valued highly, holds a place of importance and distinction in this worship tradition. Like the Greek Orthodox and the Roman Catholic traditions, Lutheran worship is liturgical, that is, it has a fixed form of worship based on the cycles of the Church Year.

Only Martin Luther, the first of the major Reformers, welcomed music into the corporate worship of God and placed it next in importance to theology. Later Reformers, such as John Calvin, Ulrich Zwingli, and John Huss, tended to reject music—especially musical instruments—and it was not until the Moravians, and John and Charles Wesley that there was an awareness again of the importance of music in worship of the reformed tradition.

By the eighteenth century, Lutheran worship was centered in a preaching service, with occasional celebrations of the Eucharist. During this period there was a concerted effort to get rid of everything that did not contribute to instruction or morality. This spirit of purge and rejection of formal worship is revealed in the rise of many nonliturgical sects, in which most liturgical elements were rejected. Sermons were replaced by lectures, and hymns were changed at will. It was a time when the influences of the Puritan ethic and the influences of Calvinism permeated all non-Roman Catholic worship traditions. By the nineteenth century there developed a desire to return to the liturgical practice of singing chorales and chants, and thus the liturgical movement was reborn. Since then, Lutheran churches have reordered their worship around the Formula Missae of 1523 and have cultivated a great treasury of church music. The Eucharist has again become a central feature, although proclamation of the Word—written, preached, and sung—remains the center of Lutheran worship.

In 1917 the American movement to return to the liturgy of the Reformation climaxed with the publication of the *Common Service Book*. In this work the liturgy was given a musical setting, largely English in origin.

It provided a wide-ranging collection of hymns that not only included many traditional German chorales, but a large number from the Anglo-American tradition as well. During the early part of the twentieth century there was no unity among Lutheran churches other than a common heritage and the liturgy. This diversification was reflected in the divisions of the Lutheran Church—Missouri Synod, English Lutheran, Augustana Lutheran, and American Evangelical Lutheran Church, among others. Many of these churches were composed of nationality groups: i.e., the Norwegian immigrants formed the Norwegian Evangelical Lutheran Synod, the Danish formed the Danish Evangelical Lutheran Church, and the Swedish formed the Augustana Lutheran Synod.

By the middle of the twentieth century almost all Lutherans had begun to think of themselves as American and almost all were using the *Common Service Book*. In 1958, through the cooperation of eight branches of the Lutheran Church, a new hymnal, *Service Book and Hymnal of the Lutheran Church in America*, was published.[2]

Form of Worship   At the time of the Reformation, the Lutheran Church retained the Mass as a fixed form of worship. The Proper parts of the Mass that are traditionally assigned to the choir consist of the Introit, the Gradual, the Alleluia, the Tract, the Sequence, the Offertory, and the Communion. The Proper maintains a sense of unity in the liturgy, and since this must center on a particular phase of the church calendar, the service cannot become a subject of the individual wishes and preferences of the pastor.

Like Roman Catholics, Lutherans may observe "hours." These are usually Matins or Morning Prayer, and Vespers or Evening Prayer. In these services the texts vary according to the Church Year and are called the Antiphons, the Psalms, the Responsory, or Response, and the Canticles. All music selected for use in Lutheran worship must be suitable for liturgical worship and must follow the fixed form of the Church Year. In Lutheran worship the organ and other instruments that were banished by the Calvinists have always had a special place of prominence. In fact, many of these, such as brass, stringed, and percussion instruments, were much preferred to the organ.

In 1966 the Inter-Lutheran Commission on Worship was formed. One of its primary goals was to produce a new hymnal and service book for all Lutherans. The resulting *Lutheran Book of Worship* was published in 1978. The liturgy is outlined below.

---

[2]*A Handbook of Church Music*, ed. Carl Halter and Carl Schalk (St. Louis: Concordia Publishing House, 1978), p. 19.

Lutheran Book of Worship (1978)
Holy Communion

Brief Order of Confession and Forgiveness
The Entrance Hymn (or Introit Psalm)
Apostolic Greeting
Kyrie
Hymn of Praise (Gloria in Excelsis, Worthy Is Christ, or appropriate hymn)
Salutation and Prayer of the Day
First Lesson
Psalm
Second Lesson
Verse (Alleluia or Tract)
  The word alleluia is sung twice, followed by a psalm verse and a simple Alleluia. It is performed after the Second Lesson (New Testament epistle). The *Tract* replaces the Alleluia during Lent or on penitential days. It consists of several psalm verses without antiphon or response.
Gospel with Acclamations
Sermon
Hymn of the Day
  The Hymn of the Day is related to the theme or festival—e.g., Advent, Christmas—and involves the congregation and the choir.
Nicene or Apostles' Creed
The Prayers
The Peace
The Offering
The Offertory and Offertory Prayer
  Preparation of Bread and Wine
The Great Thanksgiving (includes Sanctus/Benedictus)
Prayer of Thanksgiving (concluding with Lord's Prayer)
Communion
  Agnus Dei or other hymns
  Blessing
Postcommunion (canticle or other appropriate hymn)
Blessing
Dismissal
(After the offering, if there is no communion, worship concludes as follows: the Offertory, Offertory Prayers, Lord's Prayer, and the Blessing.

Heritage and Practice of Music   Music in the Lutheran Church is a corporate activity involving choir, congregation, clergy. Gregorian chant, polyphonic choral works, and stately chorales all have contributed to a flourishing tradition of church music, but by far the most important contribution of the sixteenth-century Lutheran Church was the establishment of congregational singing. This corporate activity through song became a central feature in the Lutheran Church. Then, as now, it centered in the singing of hymns, in particular the chorale, which exerted enormous influence on later-developing worship traditions and on choral masterpieces of such composers as Dietrich Buxtehude, Johann Pachelbel, and J.S. Bach.

Melodies for these chorales were drawn from Gregorian chants, secular melodies, nonliturgical Latin songs and German songs of the pre-Reformation period, and newly composed melodies and texts. Theology centered on the basic tenets of the Christian faith, e.g., sin, salvation, praise and thanksgiving, death and resurrection. Most of the texts are rich in medieval symbolism expressed through beautiful use of figures of speech.

> A Mighty Fortress is our God,
> A sword and shield victorious;
> He breaks the cruel oppressor's rod
> And wins salvation glorious.
> The old satanic foe
> Has sworn to work us woe!
> With craft and dreadful might
> He arms himself to fight.
> On earth he has no equal.
>
> No strength of ours can match his might!
> We would be lost, rejected.
> But now a champion comes to fight,
> Whom God himself elected.
> You ask who this may be?
> The Lord of hosts is he!
> Christ Jesus, mighty Lord,
> God's only Son, adored.
> He holds the field victorious.
>
> Though hordes of devils fill the land
> All threat'ning to devour us,
> We tremble not, unmoved we stand;
> They cannot overpow'r us.
> Let this world's tyrant rage;
> In battle we'll engage!
> His might is doomed to fail;
> God's judgment must prevail!
> One little word subdues him.

God's Word forever shall abide,
No thanks to foes, who fear it;
For God himself fights by our side
With weapons of the Spirit.
Were they to take our house,
Goods, honor, child, or spouse,
Though life be wrenched away,
They cannot win the day.
The Kingdom's ours forever![3]

In these stanzas from Ein' Feste Burg the writer utilizes medieval symbolism to compare God's strength and power with a medieval fortress, well known to sixteenth-century citizenry. In many chorales this unique wedding of text and music binds worshipers together. Music, and the chorale in particular, was a vital ingredient in worship; it served as a central expression in the liturgy. In some of the later traditions a hymn was selected as an appendage to worship, rather than as a vehicle for the proclamation of the Word of God. The chorale continues to influence musical practice in Lutheran worship. Throughout all Lutheran history the utilization of music affirms a tradition of involvement that considers all music "both its creation and its re-creation, as a gift of God both useful and necessary for corporate worship."[4]

The psalms of the Old Testament provide the texts for the oldest hymns used by all worshiping traditions. Because of their poetic beauty and universality of devotional expression, they have remained in the repertoire of hymnbooks and psalters throughout the centuries. Psalms follow the structure of Hebrew parallelism, that is, each verse is coupled with another verse or half-verse which reiterates what has gone before. Here is an example from Psalm 100.

> Make a joyful noise unto the Lord
> Serve the Lord with gladness
>
> Come into his presence with thanksgiving
> And into his courts with praise.

Many congregations and choirs say/sing these psalms antiphonally, e.g., the choir sings a verse and the congregation sings the next verse; or the pastor reads a verse and the choir and congregation sing a response. The

---

[3]Text reprinted from Lutheran Book of Worship, copyright 1978, by permission of Augsburg Publishing House, representing the publishers and copyright holders.
[4]A Handbook of Church Music, op. cit., p. 19.

reading and singing of psalms is an essential element of the Lutheran liturgy.

In the Lutheran tradition the choir serves to help the congregation in the liturgy in three ways:

1. Supports and enriches the congregational singing of hymns and the liturgy
2. Brings richness and variety to congregational worship by singing the portions of the liturgy entrusted to it
3. Enriches congregational worship by presenting attendant music as appropriate and possible.[5]

Summary   The Lutheran Church follows a liturgy, an ordered form of worship consisting of (1) readings and music variable according to the Church Year, the Proper, and (2) sections that are fixed, called the Ordinary. Its rich heritage affirms the importance of music along with theology, and encourages active participation of the congregation in the service of worship. The chorale remains a unique musical contribution to all Christian worship. While retaining the spirit of Roman Catholic worship, Lutherans have adapted the liturgy to the twentieth century and, although they value the music of the past, provide opportunities to experience contemporary music as well.

THE AMERICAN PROTESTANT EPISCOPAL CHURCH

General Historical/Theological Background   The origin of the American Protestant Episcopal Church is the Church of England, established in 1532-44, during the reign of King Henry VIII, who was declared the head of the English Church. No longer did the English Church have any ties or allegiance to Rome or the Pope, for the highest obedience now was to the English Bishops, in particular the Archbishop of Canterbury.[6]

Form of Worship   The liturgy of the Church of England was closely tied to the Roman Catholic Mass, although the language used was English. In 1548, Archbishop Cranmer drew up an Order of Communion in English that consisted of the Invitation, General Confession, Absolution, and Comfortable Words as they appear in the Anglican service today. These were followed by the Prayer of Humble Access, the

---

[5]Ibid.
[6]Richard M. Spielmann, *History of Christian Worship* (New York: The Seabury Press, 1966), p. 95.

lay people's Communion, and a blessing, whereupon the service reverted to the traditional form of the Latin Mass. The English Litany of 1544 and the Order of Communion of 1548 prepared the way for the *Book of Common Prayer* in 1549. "Common Prayer" means prayers and worship services to be used in common with others, when all people are gathered together. It is a devotional manual through which the worshiper may participate directly in the services of the church.

Mary I repealed the prayer book in 1553; it was restored by Elizabeth I in 1558, and subsequently, in 1645 was again banned by the Puritans. It was not until the Restoration of Charles II, in 1660, that the prayer book was used again officially by the Church of England.

The liturgy consisted of (1) Communion, (2) Morning Prayer, and (3) Evening Prayer. Musical settings of the canticles prescribed at Communion were Kyrie, Credo, Sanctus, and Gloria in Excelsis; Morning Prayer—*Venite, Te Deum* (or *Benedicite*), *Benedictus* (or *Jubilate*); and Evening Prayer—*Magnificat* (or *Cantate Domino*) and *Nunc Dimittis* (or *Deus Misereatur*). A polyphonic setting of the communion service was called simply a Service; a service written in full polyphonic style was called a Great Service, while a service written in homophonic and syllabic style was called a Short Service. Composers wrote each movement of the service in the same key, thus there is the Morning Service in E flat, Short Service in G, or Complete Service in C. Many of these services are masterpieces of writing, both in craftsmanship and musical expression, and are still performed regularly in Episcopal churches.

Heritage and Practice of Music   Any discussion of music in the Episcopal worship tradition must draw a distinction between parish worship, and worship in cathedrals and college chapels. Some of the greatest choral music ever written springs from the English cathedral tradition, and since many American Episcopal churches follow this tradition, let us consider some of the characteristics of performance as well as music of selected composers.

Although cathedrals were often enormous, the choir was usually relatively small. Music was performed by small forces of trained singers, men and boys; e.g., 6 men (alto, tenor, bass) and 16 boys (treble). The choir was divided in half; one choir sat on the south side (decani), and the other, on the north side (cantoris). Music was not intended for congregational participation, since the congregation was usually separated from the choir by a screen.

This arrangement accounts for the restrained quality of English cathedral music. The antiphonal qualities made possible by the division of decani and cantoris was utilized to the fullest by such English composers as Thomas Tallis, William Byrd, and Orlando Gibbons.

During the Reformation the religious Reformers in England objected to organs and disliked choir music, with its repetition and polyphonic textures. This type of music was generally replaced by the more accepted form of one syllable for every note. An early example of this was John Merbecke's setting of the prayer book (1550). Here the melodies were designed for unison singing without accompaniment.

In keeping with the Reformers' attitude toward music, the earliest congregational music consisted of metrical psalm tunes. Many of these tunes appeared in psalters, and they are still sung from contemporary hymnals; OLD 100TH from *Day's Psalter*, OLD 127TH from the *Genevan Psalter* of 1558, and BRISTOL from *Ravenscroft Psalter* of 1621 are but three examples.[7]

The first Episcopal church in America was King's Chapel, Boston (1689). The name Protestant Episcopal was adopted in 1789, the term Protestant being used to distinguish it from the church of Rome, and the word Episcopal to distinguish it from the Presbyterian and Congregational traditions. The Protestant Episcopal Church was the Church of England in America, in which the *Book of Common Prayer*, with its constitution and canons was adopted. Modifications included the restoration of the Nicene Creed and replacement of prayers for King and royalty to prayers for "the President of the United States and all in civil Authority." Services used in the American Protestant Episcopal Church are (1) Holy Communion, (2) Morning Prayer, (3) Evening Prayer. Sample services for Morning Prayer and Holy Communion (Rite I) follow:

The Third Sunday of Easter
Order for Morning Prayer

Prelude
Hymn
The Opening Sentences
  General Confession
  Antiphon
  Venite
  Antiphon
  Psalm
    Glory to the Father and to the Son, and to the Holy Spirit:
    as it was in the beginning, is now, and will be for ever. Amen.
First Lesson
Magnificat
Second Lesson
Nunc Dimittis
Apostles' Creed

7Watkins Shaw, "Church Music in England" in Friedrich Blume, *Protestant Church Music* (New York: W.W. Norton, 1974), p. 701.

Anthem
  Collect of the Day
  Collects
  Prayer for All Sorts and Conditions of Men
  Prayer for the Human Family
  The General Thanksgiving
  The Grace
Hymn
Offertory
Hymn
The Sermon
Hymn
Postlude

The Octave of All Saints
The Holy Eucharist Rite I

Prelude
Hymn
  CELEBRANT: Blessed be God: Father, Son, and Holy Spirit.
  PEOPLE: *And blessed be his kingdom, now and for ever. Amen.*
Collect for Purity
Summary of the Law
Kyrie Eleison
Gloria in Excelsis
The Collect of the Day
Lesson
Epistle
The Holy Gospel
Sermon Hymn
The Sermon
The Nicene Creed
The Prayers of the People
The Confession of Sin
The Peace
  CELEBRANT: The Peace of the Lord be always with you.
  PEOPLE: And with thy spirit.
Hymn
Offertory
The Great Thanksgiving (Prayer II)
Sursum Corda
Sanctus and Benedictus
Prayer of Consecration

The Lord's Prayer
The Breaking of the Bread
    CELEBRANT: Alleluia. Christ our Passover, is sacrificed for us;
    PEOPLE: Therefore let us keep the feast. Alleluia.
Distribution
Agnus Dei
Prayer of Humble Access (celebrant and people)
Prayer of Thanksgiving
Dismissal
    DEACON OR CELEBRANT: Go in peace to love and serve the Lord.
    PEOPLE: Thanks be to God.
Hymn
Postlude

The evening service, called Evensong, is usually composed almost entirely of music and readings. At present the Episcopal Church has adopted a revision of the *Book of Common Prayer* and is planning a revision of *The Hymnal, 1940*, considered by many to be one of the finest hymnals published this century.

The retention of cathedral architecture style by Episcopal churches in America contributed to an active leadership role by choir and clergy. Churches were divided into two parts: the choir and the nave. Between these two sections was the chancel, an area kept for celebrating the Eucharist and for other services such as marriage. The nave was used for Morning Prayer, Evening Prayer, and sermons. A font, often elaborately carved, was placed near the church door and signified entrance into God's church by the ancient rite of baptism. The reading desk and pulpit were either opposite each other or on the same side of the nave. From these posts the lectionaries were read and the sermon preached.

In contrast to the English cathedrals with their chairs, early American churches utilized straight pews, usually placed in a small rectangular enclosure, with a seat on three sides and an opening on the fourth, in which occupants sat and knelt facing one another. Many wealthy parishioners purchased pews, and engraved name plates were often affixed to the entrance doors of the enclosures. These boxes were generally 4 or 5 feet high, and only the heads of the occupants could be seen over the top. Worshipers usually faced the reading desk and pulpit rather than the altar.

American architects of the late nineteenth century followed the cathedral style of design; thus, parish church choirs of men and boys dressed in surplices were seated in divided chancels. These surpliced choirs grew in number and with them was established a pseudocathedral type of choral service.

METHODISM

General Historical/Theological Background   Methodism derived its structure and form of worship directly from the Church of England through the teachings and practices of its founder, John Wesley, an Anglican priest who was educated at Oxford University. From the moment his heart "was strangely warmed," on May 24, 1738, during a prayer meeting at Aldersgate Street, London, John Wesley began preaching a social gospel of ministry to the physical, intellectual, and social needs of people. This concern with social action and justice remains a tradition with today's United Methodist Church, which continues to take positions on controversial political, social, and economic issues.

Early Methodist worship was both evangelical and sacramental. Sunday morning worship consisted of preaching the word and partaking of the Lord's Supper. A characteristic of early Methodist communion was the congregation's coming to the Table in groups, not as individuals, thus giving expression to the idea of the communion of saints. Another characteristic of the Methodist observance is that Holy Communion is closely linked to evangelical preaching, with its offer of redemption through Christ. Consequently, an open invitation is given to all worshipers to commune at the Table of the Lord, provided they love the Lord Jesus Christ "in sincerity and truth."

Methodism was especially adaptive to American life. Itinerant preachers sought out the scattered homes on the frontier and followed the movement westward, preaching the gospel and organizing societies. Methodists were strict in doctrine and discipline but were episcopal in their form of church government. They believed in the regeneration of the spirit (new birth or conversion), the possibility that human beings may be "made perfect in love," repentance of sin, universal redemption (Christ died for all), and justification by faith (the great affirmation of the Reformation).[8]

The legal document governing the Methodist Church is called *The Discipline*. This lists what a Methodist is supposed to do or not do, and while it currently reflects a more liberal attitude, at one time *The Discipline* was a systematic guide to Christian conduct, e.g., dress, recreational activities (no card-playing, dancing), and language (no profanity). The Methodist Episcopal Church was formally organized in Baltimore, in December 1784. In 1939 the Methodist Episcopal Church South and the Methodist Episcopal Church North united to form the Methodist Church, and in 1968 the merger between the Evangelical United Brethren Church and the Methodist Church took place, resulting in the United Methodist Church.

---

[8] Spielmann, *History of Christian Worship*, op. cit., pp. 727-28.

Forms of Worship   In the Methodist Church, the form of worship was guided by the New Testament. Prepared prayers were retained, along with the Apostles' Creed and festivals of the Christian Year, such as Advent, Lent, and Pentecost; however, few musical instruments, e.g., organs and pianos, were used, and paintings and sculpture were not allowed.

Originally, Methodist worship consisted of an evening meeting that included scripture, exposition, prayer, and personal testimony. It was considered a supplement to the established Anglican Morning Prayer and emphasized the personal nature of religion. A unique feature of the evening service was the close examination of the spiritual state of each member by the worship leader, followed by appropriate advice. Hymns and hymn-singing came to serve as a liturgy and exercised an incalculable influence upon religious thought and feeling. Later, gospel songs, composed of easy tunes and foot-tapping rhythms, assumed a major role in Methodist worship.

Heritage and Practice of Music   Hymnody was the greatest musical contribution of Methodism. Charles Wesley, brother of John Wesley, wrote over 6,000 hymns in which he set forth in song the whole range of evangelical faith. Every hymn, steeped in metaphor, is intense, full of color, and highly personal.[9] Such is the power of Charles Wesley's hymns that they remain an integral part of all hymnals in Christendom. The revival methods of Wesley and his followers, emphasizing the social character of religion, found expression in words that were clear and understandable, and in tunes that were frequently taken from popular songs. Congregational singing, which the Wesleys introduced, appealed to people because it was something new. John Wesley found hymn-singing to be of practical value, because it served as a means to stir religious emotion; music became one of the most effective agencies in creating an atmosphere in which conversions might occur.

John Wesley encouraged good singing. The Methodists stood to sing, and every effort was made to get everyone to sing with intelligence and heartiness. To this end, John Wesley wrote his famous "Rules for Hymnsinging."[10]

1. Learn these *tunes* before you learn any others; afterwards learn as many as you please.
2. Sing them exactly as they are printed here, without altering or mending them at all; and if you have learned to sing them otherwise, unlearn it as soon as you can.

---

[9] John Bishop, *Methodist Worship* (London: Epworth Press, 1950), p. 140.
[10] From John Wesley's preface to *Sacred Melody*, 1761.

3. Sing *all*. See that you join with the congregation as frequently as you can. Let not a slight degree of weakness or weariness hinder you. If it is a cross to you, take it up, and you will find it a blessing.
4. Sing *lustily*, and with good courage. Beware of singing as if you are half-dead or half-asleep; but lift up your voice with strength. Be no more afraid of your voice now, nor more ashamed of its being heard, than when you sing the songs of the Devil.
5. Sing *modestly*. Do not bawl, so as to be heard above or distinct from the rest of the congregation—that you may not destroy the harmony—but strive to unite your voices together so as to make one clear melodious sound.
6. Sing *in time*. Whatever time is sung, be sure to keep with it. Do not run before nor stay behind it; but attend close to the leading voices, and move therewith as exactly as you can; and take care not to sing too slow. This drawling way naturally steals on all who are lazy; and it is high time to drive it out from among us, and sing all our tunes just as quick as we did at first.
7. Above all, sing *spiritually*. Have an eye to God in every word you sing. Aim at pleasing [God] more than yourself, or any other creature. In order to do this, attend strictly to the sense of what you sing, and see that your Heart is not carried away with the sound, but offered to God continually; so shall your singing be such as the Lord would approve here, and reward you when He cometh in the clouds of heaven.

Revivals brought hymn-singing into the churches, produced hymn writers and hymnbooks, and forever enriched the hymnology of the church.

PRESBYTERIANISM

Historical/Theological Background   Like Luther, John Calvin—the great Reformer from Geneva, Switzerland—intended to bring back a general communion of the laity and to make the Eucharist central to worship. In Calvinist churches, communicants came forward, sat or stood at a table, shredded the loaf, and passed it to one another. This was followed by drinking wine from a common cup; thus in these acts the ancient symbolism of the Last Supper was restored.

Calvin believed in a church for all people; for him, the supreme religious fact was God's majesty and otherness, and the nothingness and simplicity of humanity.[11] His followers, called Calvinists, cast out all the traditional accoutrements of Catholicism: its episcopal order, its liturgy, and its symbols. No organs or choirs were permitted in the austere Calvinist churches, nor colors or ornaments. There were no ceremonial acts or gestures. Calvinists regarded the singing of psalms as the *only*

---

[11]Evelyn Underhill, *Worship* (New York: Harper, 1937), p. 286.

music suitable for public worship. Religious Reformers who followed Calvin continued this rejection of music and other art forms in worship. They, too, objected to organs and disliked choir music, with its polyphony and repeated words. Archbishop Cranmer, in his *Second Book of Homilies*, wrote "piping, singing, chanting and playing upon the organs are things which displeased God so sore, and filthily defiled his holy house."[12]

The fundamental beliefs of the Presbyterian Church, based on Calvinism are:

1. The sovereignty of God in Christ is the salvation of the individual.
2. Each believer's salvation is part of an eternal divine plan.
3. Salvation is a spiritual gift from God and is not a reward for faith.
4. Regeneration is an act of God alone.
5. Those who are once actually saved will always remain saved.[13]

Form of Worship   The austere Calvinistic form of worship subsequently was adopted by the Presbyterian Church of Scotland and of America. Scottish Reformer John Knox preached in Genevan gown, later to become the "robe" of Protestant ministers, and read fixed prayers from the liturgy. But there was also opportunity for extemporaneous and prophetic prayer, so much a part of Protestant worship. The reading of the scriptures and the recitation by the people of the Lord's Prayer and Creed, along with the singing of appropriate psalms were all part of Scottish worship. Theologically, there was an intimate connection between faith and words and the dedication of the moral life as the ultimate act of worship. Emphasis was placed on severe ethical standards and redemption from sin.

In America during the seventeenth and eighteenth centuries, free worship—that is, worship lacking liturgical organization—became the norm. Preaching of lengthy sermons based on biblical passages and long extemporaneous prayers became primary features of these services that emphasized simplicity. The following service of worship used in the Presbyterian Church in Geneva, Switzerland (1542), is followed by the service for the Lord's Day found in *The Worshipbook* of 1970.

Opening Sentence
Confession of Sins (absolution and pardon)
Psalm sung in meter
Decalogue
Prayer of Illumination

---

[12]Blume, *Protestant Church Music*, op. cit., p. 698.
[13]Stanley I. Stuber, *How We Got Our Denominations* (New York: Association Press, 1965), pp. 166-67.

Scripture
Sermon
Intercessory Prayer (pastoral prayer, concludes with Lord's Prayer)
Apostles' Creed (recited by minister)
Benediction

Service for the Lord's Day found in *The Worshipbook* of 1970:

Call to Worship
Psalm or Hymn of Praise
Confession of Sin
Declaration of Pardon
Prayer for Illumination
Old Testament Lesson
New Testament Lesson
Sermon
Creed
A Hymn May Be Sung
Concerns of the Church
The Prayers of the People
The Peace
Offering
Hymn or Doxology
Invitation to the Lord's Table
The Thanksgiving
Prayer of Thanksgiving
Lord's Prayer
Hymn
Benediction[14]

Heritage and Practice of Music   John Calvin believed that texts from the Bible were the only permissible texts to be sung. Although known for his views on music, Calvin himself edited a songbook published at Strasbourg in 1539. This edition contained 19 versified psalms with 18 melodies and, in addition, the canticle of Simeon and the Ten Commandments, also in song form.[15] The first complete *Genevan Psalter* (today the generally accepted name for the songbook authorized by Calvin in Geneva) was finished by 1562, and the resulting 63 recorded editions show with what enthusiasm it was received and undoubtedly introduced to every Calvinist family.[16] Seldom in the history of hymnody

---

[14]*The Worshipbook* (Philadelphia: Westminster Press, 1970), pp. 25-42.
[15]Blume, *Protestant Church Music*, op. cit. p. 517.
[16.]Ibid., p. 530.

has there been such a treasury of poems and songs embraced by every Protestant denomination.

Despite the strict limitations of service music to unaccompanied congregational singing of the psalms, there arose an amazing number of polyphonic arrangements. The most influential polyphonic arranger was Claude Goudimel. His French psalm compositions had a significant historical impact on church music, and the more than 70 cyclic psalm-lied arrangements that he composed are among the most important creations of Protestant church music.

Presbyterians, as well as Methodists and Baptists, embraced the revival movement during the nineteenth century, and there was a rise in folk-type music, such as Walker's *Southern Harmony*, first published in 1835, and the *Sacred Harp* collection, compiled by B.D. White and E.J. King in 1844. Such hymns as "Amazing Grace" have been restored to the *Lutheran Book of Worship* (1978) and *The Hymnal of the United Church of Christ* (1974).

The immediate instigator of the camp-meeting movement appears to have been James McGready, a Presbyterian minister. These camp meetings focused on emotional religious fervor and resulted in the creation of a large stock of popular hymnody. Gospel songs became the trademark of not only Presbyterian camp meetings, but Methodist and Baptist as well. They are characterized by simple harmonies, short easy tunes, and catchy rhythms. Many Presbyterians still list such gospel songs as "What a Friend We Have in Jesus," "Living for Jesus," and "When the Roll Is Called Up Yonder" as their favorite hymns.

In 1970 *The Worshipbook* of the United Presbyterian Church was published. One of the major purposes of *The Worshipbook* is to employ contemporary English in worship; however, the translations rest upon the foundation of the scriptures. *The Worshipbook* is a Presbyterian book, as well as an ecumenical one. While Presbyterians value variety and freedom in worship, they also value orderliness. In addition, there is a contemporary quality to the selection of hymns, since many new hymns were written, old hymns were altered—in both musical and literary structure—and many folk hymns and spirituals were added.

BAPTISTS

Historical/Theological Background   During the Reformation a group of people came to believe that the state should have no control of the church or of its believers, and that members of the church should have no part in the affairs of state, e.g., hold office, bear arms. To belong to the church a person only needed to be baptized as a believer. These early Reformers condemned infant baptism as invalid, stating instead that the

217

one real baptism in the sight of God was when a grown person stood up and declared his/her faith. Therefore, they were called Anabaptists, which meant "baptized again." Some of the English Separatists had gone to Holland, where they met the Mennonites, who were Anabaptists. Their ideas of religious freedom for every individual, no control of the church by the state, and baptism only for believers were brought to England, where those who followed this persuasion came to be called by a shorter name—Baptists.

In America the first Baptists settled in Rhode Island, descendants of those who had followed Roger Williams. Here Baptist preachers made many converts and organized congregations in other states as well. The Baptist belief that each member of the congregation should vote seemed consistent with the growing independence of religious thought. The Baptists joined the Methodists and Presbyterians in evangelizing the American frontier, conducting camp meetings and revivals wherever they went. The movement became particularly strong in the South and Southwest, where even the smallest town had a Baptist church.

Form of Worship   For the Baptist, there is no creed, nor are there any imposed statements of faith. The Order of Service is determined by each congregation. The Lord's Supper is observed quarterly as a memorial to Jesus Christ and in some churches is restricted to those who have declared their faith through baptism, which must be by immersion. Led by the laity and pastor, each church is totally independent and determines its own affairs. Baptists are an evangelical people, and have always been leaders in missionary and educational efforts throughout the world. They were the first denomination to introduce the Sunday school, later encouraged and developed by every major Protestant denomination.

Heritage and Practice of Music   Baptists, like Methodists and Presbyterians, sang a great many gospel hymns in worship. These gospel hymns, a distinctive American phenomenon, developed out of the camp meeting songs of the early nineteenth century and focused on winning souls through conversion. Many of these remain popular in Baptist churches, particularly in those parts of the country where revival meetings still take place.

DISCIPLES OF CHRIST

Historical/Theological Background   The word union might be called the chief slogan of the Disciples' Brotherhood, a movement begun in the early 1800s by Thomas Campbell and fellow Reformers who were interested in restoring pure and simple Christianity and unity to divided Christians.[17]

Since its founding, one of the chief characteristics of the Christian Church has been its emphasis on the ecumenical movement and the uniting of all Christians. To this end, the denomination has been a leading force in the ecumenical deliberations of the Faith and Order Commission of the World Council of Churches.

Form of Worship   The Disciples of Christ (Christian Church) is an autonomous group, each church believing in attending to its own affairs, not bound by liturgy, creeds, formulas, or outward forms of religious observances. The Bible occupies a central place in worship, and Disciples believe it to be divinely inspired. Each Sunday, communion is observed as a memorial feast, since it was a desire of the founders to restore practices of early Christian worship. Baptism is considered by a majority of Disciples as a sacrament; while others view it as an ordinance, it is always observed by immersion.

Heritage and Practice of Music   As a frontier church, the gospel songs of the camp meeting dominated worship services; however, singing schools were still conducted as late as 1853.

> All the singing elements, young and old, attended the singing school, each with his own copy of A.S. Mayden's "Melodeon" containing both words and music and printed with the "buckwheat" style notes. The drilling of the congregation was a wonderful help toward the church service. In those days congregational music really amounted to something because every member was trained and self-reliant.[18]

While singing was accepted by Disciples, the use of musical instruments was not. A pipe organ in a church was a serious matter and the subject of much controversy. New England churches hotly debated the issue, and in 1827, a New England "Christian" conference resolved: "We recommend to the churches and preachers that they use their influence to prevent the introduction of instrumental music into our

---

[17]Winfred Garrison and Alfred DeGroot, *The Disciples of Christ, A History* (St. Louis: Christian Board of Education, 1948), p. 21.

[18]Dorothy L. Siegling, *Our Heritage, The Story of One Hundred Years* (Cleveland Heights, Ohio: Euclid Avenue Christian Church, 1943), p. 18.

meetings and worship, and to suppress them where they have already been introduced."[19]

One of the early editors of the *American Christian Review* wrote in March 1867:

> We by no means object to a well trained choir, made up of the faithful members of the church, and specifically of the young. We do not even object to a good instrument, when it is simply used as support to the singing. But those little wheezing, grunting instruments we do most heartily oppose. . . . If the instrument must be used, place it in the choir. . . . And let the choir and the instrument be kept under the control of the Elders of the Church.[20]

By the beginning of the twentieth century, urban churches joined the trend toward a professional quartet choir. It was not until the midforties that there was a revival of the volunteer choir and greater emphasis placed on music by Disciples' congregations.

Architecture   Buildings of the early Methodist, Presbyterian, and Baptist churches usually consisted of a small frame building, with a pulpit in the center. In Methodist churches the communion table was separated from the congregation by a communion rail, while in other denominations the communion table occupied a place in front of the pulpit. There was no altar in these nonliturgical churches. Often there was a small pump organ and a few chairs for the choir, which also served as an "Amen" section to the prayers and preaching. Later, the Akron style architecture dominated many of these churches. These buildings had a central pulpit, with the choir and organ situated above and behind the minister, and the communion table in front of the pulpit. Pews in the sanctuary were usually placed in a semicircle, and there was often a balcony and a Sunday school wing that opened off the sanctuary. During the late nineteenth century, churches began to use stained glass windows. In the more wealthy churches of the urban areas, windows depicted specific events in the life of Christ. The architecture of these churches was conducive to congregational hymn-singing, and the choir and organist were usually in full view. Many times there was a song leader, especially for the Sunday school sing-along.

During the early twentieth century many Gothic cathedral-style churches were built; these utilized a divided chancel and separated the lectern and the pulpit. Contemporary architecture has sought to combine flexibility and liturgical function, often placing the pulpit in the center of the congregation and also providing for a variety of seating arrangements.

---

[19]Garrison and DeGroot, *The Disciples of Christ, A History,* op. cit., p. 343.
[20]Ibid., p. 344.

UNITED CHURCH OF CHRIST

In 1957 the Evangelical and Reformed Church and the Congregational Christian Churches united to form the United Church of Christ. Like some other Protestant denominations, the United Church of Christ (UCC) does not require affirmation or allegiance to a creed for membership, but its Statement of Faith[21] does reflect those things most commonly believed by its members:

We believe in God, the Eternal Spirit, Father of our Lord Jesus Christ and our Father, and to his deeds we testify:

He calls the worlds into being,
    creates man in his own image,
    and sets before him the ways of life and death.

He seeks in holy love to save all people from aimlessness and sin.

He judges men and nations by his righteous will declared through prophets and apostles.

In Jesus Christ, the man of Nazareth, our crucified and risen Lord,
    he has come to us
    and shared our common lot,
    conquering sin and death
    and reconciling the world to himself.

He bestows upon us his Holy Spirit,
    creating and renewing the church of Jesus Christ,
    binding in covenant faithful people of all ages, tongues, and races.

He calls us into his church
    to accept the cost and joy of discipleship,
    to be his servants in the service of men,
    to proclaim the gospel to all the world and resist the powers of evil,
    to share in Christ's baptism and eat at his table,
    to join him in his passion and victory.

He promises to all who trust him
    forgiveness of sins and fullness of grace,
    courage in the struggle for justice and peace,
    his presence in trial and rejoicing,
    and eternal life in his kingdom which has no end.

Blessing and honor, glory and power be unto him. Amen.

---

[21] Approved by the General Synod of the United Church of Christ at Oberlin, Ohio, July 5-9, 1959.

The merger of the Evangelical and Reformed Church with the Congregational Christian Churches was a joining of groups that earlier had merged: the Congregational with the Christian Churches in 1931, and the Evangelical Synod with the Reformed Church in 1934.

Form of Worship   Each of the four traditions that joined to become the United Church of Christ has contributed to the richness and diversity that characterizes worship in this denomination. Thus it is difficult to cite one specific style or order of worship. Because it is a church body within the so-called Free Church tradition, there are no fixed or rigid formularies mandated for corporate worship, and individual churches tend to follow worship practices influenced by local tradition and incumbent pastors.

The major contribution of the Congregational Churches was the spirit of the Puritan Reformation, with its rejection of fixed shapes for worship. The Puritan spirit, along with a desire for a more free and spontaneous response to the good news of the gospel, was combined with a strong concern for the furthering of the sanctification of the believers, which was reflected in an emphasis on preaching as a means of ethical instruction. American Congregationalists were influenced, as were most American denominations, by the evangelical revivalism movement of the eighteenth and nineteenth centuries, with its emphasis on the religious experience of the individual believer. The Christian Churches contributed a strong concern for rationalism, with an emphasis on the right of the individuals to interpret God's truth for themselves, with the Bible as a rule of faith and practice. The interweaving of these strands resulted in a Congregational Christian style of worship that derived primarily from Reformed church traditions.

Different but sometimes similar influences marked the shaping of worship life in the Evangelical and Reformed Church. Congregational Christian churches were predominantly Anglo-Saxon, while the Evangelical and Reformed churches were predominantly German. Thus the shaping influences in the Evangelical and Reformed tradition consistently reflect their continental, European sources. This continental influence was primarily liturgical, and little of the Puritan resistance to fixed and mandatory forms of worship can be found among these churches of German background. Yet they exhibited considerable freedom and flexibility in their modification of the different liturgies brought with them from Europe. They too were influenced by the revival movements, and as they became Americanized their strong Reformed sense of corporate worship was threatened. Yet, because of counter reactions to the revival movements, a good understanding of liturgical worship practice was never lost in the Evangelical Synod of North America or in the (German) Reformed Church in the United States.

When the United Church of Christ was formed, in 1957, these four traditions provided a rich, if potentially confusing, basis upon which to build a new worship tradition, incorporating the spirit of freedom within a framework of order and responsibility that marks the worship styles within the four bodies. A Commission on Worship was appointed, which issued *The Lord's Day Service* and *Services of Word and Sacrament*, as well as other orders of worship that are sensitive to the heritage of worship styles but yet look forward. Significant in this regard is the greater interest in a more liturgical style of worship, with more frequent celebration of Holy Communion as part of the weekly "Service of Word and Sacrament." Members of the denomination are now at work in preparation of what will be the first worshipbook for the UCC, which will include various services and appropriate music, a volume to complement *The Hymnal of the United Church of Christ*, published in 1974.

Selected Repertory Lists

We have read and compiled numerous lists of anthems, vocal solos, and organ repertory. Each list presents problems; it is too extensive, too abbreviated, obsolete, or highly subjective in judgment of difficulty.

Perhaps the only useful repertory list is that which is produced at a specific point in time to meet a single need, e.g., music for Christmas, music for Easter, etc. For these reasons extensive repertory lists have not been included in this book; however, three areas deserve special consideration: (1) vocal solo literature—an area that has received relatively little attention; (2) hymn- and chorale-based organ literature— an area that is of great interest because of the number of new hymnals being produced, as well as renewed interest in introducing greater variety into hymn-singing; and (3) recorder literature, often rather difficult to find. Where there are several publishers of a single solo, or a major work is identified, no publisher is listed.

VOCAL SOLOS

Soprano
Antes, John

And Jesus Said, It Is Finished

Boosey/Hawkes

Go Congregation, Go

Boosey/Hawkes

	Loveliest Emmanuel	Boosey/Hawkes

Bach, J.S.
Bleed and Break (*St. Matthew Passion)*
God My Shepherd Walks Beside Me
(Cantata 208: WAS MIR BEHAGT)
I Follow Thee, Also (*St. John Passion)*
Jesu, Joy of Man's Desiring
May We Complete This Year   (Cantata 41:
JESU, NUN SEI GEPREISET)
My Heart Ever Faithful (Cantata 68: ALSO HAT
GOTT DIE WELT GELIEBT)
Praise God: The Year Is Nearly Ended
(Cantata 28: GOTTLOB: NUN GEHT DAS JAHR ZU ENDE)

Barber, Samuel
Lord Jesus Christ (*Prayers of Kierkegaard)*
G. Schirmer

Baumgartner, H. Leroy
This Is the Victory   Concordia

Bax, Arnold
A Christmas Carol   Chester

Britten, Benjamin
At the Round Earth's Imagined Corners
Boosey/Hawkes

Bruckner, Anton
Jesus, Redeemer, Our Loving Saviour
Peters

Buxtehude, Dietrich
My Jesus Is My Lasting Joy (solo cantata)
H.W. Gray
Beloved Christians (*Rejoice, Beloved Christians*)   H.W. Gray
Sing to the Lord a New Song   Concordia
God Create in Me a Clean Heart
Concordia

Cherubini, Luigi
Come to the Waters   Carl Fischer

Distler, Hugo
O Rejoice in the Lord at All Times
Concordia

Dvořak, Anton
Biblical Songs, vols. I, II   Associated

Freed, Isadore
Psalm 8   Southern Music

Freudenthal, Josef
A Lamp unto My Feet   Transcontinental
Let Us Sing unto the Lord Transcontinental

Gounod, Charles
Song of Ruth: "Entreat Me Not to Leave
Thee"   G. Schirmer

Grieg, Edvard
Ich Liebe Dich   G. Schirmer

Hageman, Richard
Christmas Eve   Galaxy

Handel, G.F.
God's Tender Mercy Knows No Bounds (*Sixth Chandos Anthem*)
How Beautiful Are the Feet (*Messiah*)
I Know That My Redeemer Liveth (*Messiah*)
If God Be for Us (*Messiah*)

225

	O Magnify the Lord (*Fifth Chandos Anthem*)	
	O Magnify the Lord (*Eighth Chandos Anthem*)	
Harker, F. Flaxington	How Beautiful upon the Mountains	
		G. Schirmer
Ives, Charles	Serenity	Associated
	Shall We Gather at the River	Peer
Lekberg, Sven	I Will Lift Up Mine Eyes	M. Witmark
Liddle, Samuel	The Lord Is My Shepherd	Boosey/Hawkes
Lippé, Edouard	How Do I Love Thee (Wedding)	Boston
Lovelace, Austin	We Lift Our Hearts to Thee (Wedding)	
		G. Schirmer
Mendelssohn, Felix	Hear My Prayer	G. Schirmer
	Hear Ye Israel (*Elijah*)	
	I Will Sing of Thy Great Mercies (*St. Paul*)	
	Jerusalem that Killest the Prophets (*St. Paul*)	
Mozart, W.A.	Lord, Give Thy Blessing (*Glory, Praise and Power*)	
Pelz, Walter L.	A Wedding Blessing	Augsburg
Purcell, Henry	An Evening Hymn	Schott and Co.
Rorem, Ned	Cycle of Holy Songs	
		Southern Music (New York)
Rowley, Alex	A Cycle of Three Mystical Songs: Three Jolly Shepherds, The Prophecy, The Birthday	
		Boosey/Hawkes
Schuetz, Heinrich	Five Short Sacred Concertos	Peters
	Wedding Song	Chantry Press
Sowerby, Leo	O God of Light	H.W. Gray
	O Jesus, Lord of Mercy Great	H.W. Gray
	O Perfect Love	H.W. Gray
	Thou Art My Strength	H.W. Gray
Thiman, Eric	O for a Closer Walk with God	H.W. Gray
Vaughan Williams, Ralph	The Bird's Song (*Pilgrim's Progress*)	Oxford
Willan, Healey	O Perfect Love (Wedding)	H.W. Gray

Alto

Bach, Johann Christoph	Softly Rest Within a Manger (*The Childhood of Christ*)	J. Fischer
Bach, J.S.	All Hail Thou Gladsome Light (Cantata 61: NUN KOMM DER HEIDEN HEILAND)	
Beethoven, L. van	Come to Me	G. Schirmer
	Song of Penitence	Boston Music
Durufle, Maurice	Pie Jesu (*Requiem*)	
Gaul, A.R.	Eye Hath Not Seen (*Holy City*)	

Handel, G.F.	Courage My Soul (*St. John Passion*)
	Merseberger
	He Was Despised (*Messiah*)
	Praise Him, All Ye That in His House Attend
	(*Sixth Chandos Anthem*)
Head, Michael	Acquaint Now Thyself with Me
	Boosey/Hawkes
Helfman, Max	Hear Our Voice, O Lord Transcontinental
Lovelace, Austin	Star in the East Galaxy
Mendelssohn, Felix	But the Lord Is Mindful of His Own (*St. Paul*)
	O Rest in the Lord (*Elijah*)
Moe, Daniel	The Greatest of These Is Love (Wedding)
	Augsburg
Rorem, Ned	A Christmas Carol Elkan-Vogel
Saint-Saëns, C.	Patiently Have I Waited for the Lord (*Christmas Oratorio*) G. Schirmer
Schuetz, Heinrich	Herzlich Lieb hab' Ich Dich (*Symphonia Sacra*) Bomart
Sowerby, Leo	I Will Lift Up Mine Eyes H.W. Gray
Thiman, Eric	The God of Love My Shepherd Is Novello
Vivaldi, Antonio	Que Sedes Dexteram (*Gloria*)
Willan, Healey	Three Songs of Devotion
	Frederick Harris Co.

Tenor

Bach, J.S.	All Hail Thou Gladsome Light
	(Cantata 61: NUN KOMM DER HEIDEN HEILAND)
	Deposuit (*Magnificat*)
	Haste Ye Shepherds (*Christmas Oratorio*)
	I Know That My Redeemer Lives
	(Cantata 160: ICH WEISS DASS MEIN ERLÖSER)
	'Tis Thee I Would Be Praising (*Christmas Oratorio*)
Distler, Hugo	O Rejoice in the Lord at All Times
	Concordia
Freed, Isadore	Psalm 8 Southern (Peer)
Handel, G.F.	Every Valley Shall Be Exalted (*Messiah*)
	Forever Blessed (*Jeptha*) Boosey/Hawkes
	Jehovah! to My Words Give Ear (*Occasional Oratorio*) G. Schirmer
	O Come Let Us Worship (*Fifth Chandos Anthem*)
	Sound an Alarm (*Judas Maccabeus*)

	Thou Shalt Break Them (*Messiah*)
Haydn, F.J.	In Native Worth (*Creation*)
Mendelssohn, Felix	Be Thou Faithful unto Death (*St. Paul*)
	If with All Your Hearts Ye Truly Seek Me (*Elijah*)
	O Great Is the Depth (*St. Paul*)
Mozart, W.A.	Agnus Dei (*Mass in C Minor*)
	O Let Your Songs Be of Him (*Glory, Praise, Power*)
Rorem, Ned	Cycle of Holy Songs Southern (New York)
Vaughan Williams, Ralph	Four Hymns for Tenor Voice
	Boosey/Hawkes
Vivaldi, Antonio	Domine Deus (*Chamber Mass*)

Baritone

Bach, J.S.	Come, Healing Cross (*St. Matthew*)
	Mighty Lord and King All Glorious (*Christmas Oratorio*)
	O Lord, My Darkened Heart Enlighten (*Christmas Oratorio*)
Brahms, Johannes	Four Scriptural Songs Associated Music
Brubeck, David	When I Behold the Heavens (*Light in the Wilderness*)
	Shawnee
Buxtehude, Dietrich	Behold I Come (*Rejoice, Beloved Christians*)
	H.W. Gray
Copland, Aaron	Old American Songs, vols. I, II
	Boosey/Hawkes
Handel, G.F.	But Who May Abide (*Messiah*)
	O Praise the Lord (*Twelfth Chandos Anthem*)
	The People That Walked in Darkness (*Messiah*)
	That God Is Great (*Sixth Chandos Anthem*)
	To God, Our Strength (*Occasional Oratorio*)
	The Trumpet Shall Sound (*Messiah*)
	Vouchsafe, O Lord (*Dettingen Te Deum*)
	Why Do the Nations? (*Messiah*)
Haydn, F.J.	Now Heaven In Fullest Glory (*Creation*)
	Rolling in Foaming Billows (*Creation*)
Hovhaness, Alan	Three Odes of Solomon Peters
Mendelssohn, Felix	Is Not His Word like a Fire (*Elijah*)
	Lord, God of Abraham (*Elijah*)
	O God, Have Mercy (*Elijah*)
Pinkham, Daniel	Who Shall Separate Us Peters
Poulenc, Francis	Hymn from the Roman Breviary Salabert
Vaughan Williams, Ralph	Five Mystical Songs Galaxy

All Voices

Bach, J.S.	Be Thou with Me (BWV 508)	
Barnby, Joseph	O Perfect Love (Wedding)	Carl Fischer
Bone and Fenton	The First Psalm	Carl Fischer
Cornelius, Peter	Six Songs	Peters
Creston, Paul	Psalm 23	G. Schirmer
Freudenthal, Josef	The Earth Is the Lord's	Transcontinental
	Psalm 24	Transcontinental
Gore, Richard T.	O Sing unto the Lord a New Song	
		J. Fischer
Head, Michael	The Little Road to Bethlehem	
		Boosey/Hawkes
Holst, Gustav	The Heart Worships	Galaxy
La Montaine, John	Songs of the Nativity	Belwin
MacDermid, James G.	Acquaint Now Thyself with Him	Forster
	Whither Shall I Go from Thy Spirit	Forster
Reger, Max	12 Sacred Songs, Op. 137	C.F. Peters
Rorem, Ned	A Christmas Carol	Elkan-Vogel
Schubert, Franz	Christmas Song of the Shepherds	
	Hymn of Praise	
	Omnipotence	
Schuetz, Heinrich	Five Sacred Songs	Concordia
	Five Short Sacred Concertos	C.F. Peters
	Now I Will Praise the Lord with All My Heart	Schott and Co.
	O God, I Will Praise Thee	Schott and Co.
	O God, My Heart Is Ready	Hinrichsen
	Three Short Sacred Concertos	C.F. Peters
	Wedding Song	Chantry Press
Thiman, Eric	Thou Wilt Leave Him in Perfect Peace	
		H.W. Gray
Vaughan Williams, Ralph	Excerpts from *Pilgrim's Progress:* The Pilgrim's Song, The Song of the Leaves of Life, The Song of the Pilgrims, The Woodcutter's Song, Watchful's Song	Oxford
Warlock, Peter	Balulalow	Oxford
	Bethlehem Down	Boosey/Hawkes

Medium Voice

Cassler, Winston	Whither Thou Goest (Wedding)	Augsburg
Sateren, Leland	To Know Thou Art (Wedding)	Augsburg
Wetzler, Robert	Two Scriptural Songs: We Wait in Hope for the Lord, The Greatest of These Is Love	
		AMSI

DUETS

Soprano/Alto

Bach, J.S. — Christe Eleison (*B Minor Mass*)

Handel, G.F. — O Lovely Peace (*Judas Maccabeus*)

Vaughan Williams, Ralph — Song of the Leaves of Life (*Pilgrim's Progress*) — Oxford

Watchful's Song (*Pilgrim's Progress*) — Oxford

Verdi, Giuseppe — Recordare (*Requiem*)

Vivaldi, Antonio — Laudamus Te (*Gloria*)

Soprano/Tenor

Elmore, Robert — On the First Day of the Week — AMSI

Soprano/Baritone

Bach, J.S. — God Forsake Not Thy Faithful
(Cantata 79: GOD THE LORD IS SUN AND SHIELD)
Lord Thy Mercy (CHRISTMAS ORATORIO)
My Friend Is Mine (Cantata 140: WACHET AUF)
'Tis Well Thy Name (*Christmas Oratorio*)

Gounod, Charles — Blessed Is He Who Comes (*Christmas Oratorio*)

Tenor/Baritone

Gounod, Charles — What Grief Can Try Me, O Lord (*Redemption*)

Mendelssohn, Felix — Now We Are Ambassadors (*St. Paul*)

ORGAN

Hymn-chorale Preludes

Most of the repertoire is from easy-to-medium difficulty. Emphasis has been placed upon more recent literature on the assumption that all have or can find the chorale preludes by the baroque masters.

Barber, Samuel — Prelude on "Silent Night" — G. Schirmer

Bingham, Seth — Twelve Hymn Preludes, vols. I, II
Gray-Belwin

Beck, Albert — Seventy-six Offertories on Hymns and Chorales — Concordia 97-5207

Bender, Jan — Fantasy on Sine Nomine — Augsburg 11-9108
Festival Preludes on Six Chorales
Concordia 97-4608

Brahms, Johannes	Eleven Chorale Preludes (ed. Biggs)
	Mercury
Cassler, G. Winston	Communion Reflections Augsburg 11-9096
	Hymn Tune Preludes, vols. I-IV Augsburg
Diemer, Emma Lou	Celebration—7 Hymn Settings
	Augsburg 11-9097
	Three Fantasies on Advent-Christmas Hymns
	Augsburg 11-9497
	With Praise and Love Sacred Music Press
Doppelbauer, J.F.	Sieben Choralvorspiele Coppenrath (Boonin)
Dupré, Marcel	Seventy-nine Chorales Gray-Belwin
Gehring, Philip	Two Folk Hymn Preludes Augsburg 11-9507
George, Graham	Two Preludes on "King's Majesty"
	Gray-Belwin St. C 898
Held, Wilbur	Built on a Rock Augsburg 11-0840
	Hymn Preludes for the Autumn Festivals
	Concordia 97-5360
	Six Preludes on Easter Hymns
	Concordia 97-5330
	A Suite of Passion Hymn Settings
	Concordia 97-4843
Johnson, David	Of the Father's Love Begotten
	Augsburg 11-0841
	A Mighty Fortress Augsburg 11-0822
	Music for Worship—Easy Trios
	Augsburg 11-9291
	Music for Worship—for Manuals
	Augsburg 11-9297
	Music for Worship—with Easy Pedals
	Augsburg 11-9295
	Wondrous Love Augsburg 11-0821
Karg-Elert, Sigfrid	Choral Improvisations Op. 65 Marks
Krapf, Gerhard	Sing and Rejoice Sacred Music Press
	Various Hymn Settings Kalmus 3606
Lenel, Ludwig	Four Organ Chorales Concordia 97-1242
Lovelace, Austin	Eight Hymn Preludes Augsburg 11-9144
Lovinfosse, Dennis	Chorale Preludes I, Lent-Easter
	Augsburg 11-9099
	Chorale Preludes II, Advent-Christmas-
	Epiphany Augsburg 11-9100
Manz, Paul	Chorale Improvisations, Sets I-VIII
	Concordia
Marpurg, F.W.	Twenty-one Chorale Preludes
	Augsburg 11-9506

Near, Gerald	Postlude on "St. Dunstan's"
	Augsburg 11-0842
Ore, Charles W.	Eleven Compositions for Organ
	Concordia 97-5019
	Eleven Compositions for Organ, Set II
	Concordia 97-5385
Peeters, Flor	Ten Chorale Preludes, Op. 68, 70, 76 Peters
Pepping, Ernst	Kleines Orgelbuch Schott
Persichetti, Vincent	Prelude on "Drop, Drop Slow Tears"
	Elkan-Vogel
Proulx, Richard	Prelude on "Land of Rest"
	Augsburg 11-0845
Read, Gardner	Six Preludes on Old Southern Hymns, Sets
	I-II Gray-Belwin
Reger, Max	Choralvorspiele Op. 67 Bote & Bock
	Choralvorspiele Op. 79b Sikorski 116
	Choralvorspiele Op. 135a Peters 3980
Roberts, Myron	Blessed Assurance Gray-Belwin GSTC 989
Rogg, Lionel	Twelve Chorales Augsburg 11-9485
Schroeder, Herman	Sechs Orgelchoräle Schott 2265
Sowerby, Leo	Advent to Whitsuntide Hinrichsen 743b
Stearns, Peter Pindar	Three Preludes on Old Hymns
	Augsburg 11-9481
Uchlein, Christopher	Dance Prelude on "Bring a Torch"
	Concordia 97-5153
Vaughan Williams, Ralph	Three Preludes on Welsh Tunes
	Stainer Bell-Galaxy
Walcha, Helmut	Chorale Preludes, vols. I-III Peters
Willan, Healey	Ten Hymn Preludes, Sets I-III Peters
Wright, Searle	Prelude on "Brother James' Air"
	Oxford 93 P. 103

Anthology
Preludes and Postludes, vols. I-III   Augsburg

Free Accompaniments—Intonations

Bairstow, Edward C.	Organ Accompaniments to the Unison Verses of 24 Hymn Tunes from The English Hymnal Oxford
Beck, Theodore	Intonations for the Hymn of the Week
	Concordia 97-4899
Bender, Jan	New Organ Settings for Hymns and Chorales, Sets I-II Concordia
	Twenty-four Hymn Introductions
	Concordia 97-5303

Bunjes, Paul	New Organ Accompaniments for Hymns Concordia
Cassler, G. Winston	Organ Descants for Selected Hymn Tunes Augsburg 11-9304
Clokey, Joseph W.	Thirty-five Interludes on Hymn Tunes Fischer-Belwin
Coleman, Henry	Varied Hymn Accompaniments Oxford
Ferguson, John	Ten Hymn Tune Harmonizations, Sets I-II Ludwig, Cleveland
Goode, Jack C.	Thirty-four Changes on Hymn Tunes H.W. Gray GB 644
Hancock, Gerre	Organ Improvisations for Hymn-singing Hinshaw
Johnson, David	Free Accompaniments for Manuals, vols. I-II Augsburg 11-9185, 9186 Free Harmonizations of Twelve Hymn Tunes Augsburg 11-9190
Manz, Paul	Ten Short Intonations on Well-known Hymns Augsburg 11-9492
Newel, J.E.	Hymn Tunes with Varied Harmonies, vols. 1-10 Edwin Ashdown
Noble, T. Tertius	Free Organ Accompaniments—100 Hymn Tunes Fischer-Belwin
Rohlig, Harold	55 Hymn Intonations Abingdon APM-256
Thalben-Bell, George	113 Variations on Hymn-tunes Novello, London
Thiman, Eric	Varied Harmonizations of Favorite Tunes Gray-Belwin
Videro, Finn	21 Hymn Intonations Concordia 97-5004

Free Organ Accompaniments to Hymns, vols. I-IV
Augsburg 11-9192, 9187, 9182, 9179

Hymn Preludes and Free Accompaniments:		Augsburg
Vol. 1	Jan Bender	11-9397
Vol. 2	Emma Lou Diemer	11-9398
Vol. 3	Philip Gehring	11-9399
Vol. 4	Austin Lovelace	11-9400
Vol. 5	Hugo Gehrke	11-9401
Vol. 6	Wilbur Held	11-9402
Vol. 7	Charles Ore	11-9403
Vol. 8	Donald Busarow	11-9404
Vol. 9	Ronald Arnatt	11-9405
Vol. 10	Richard Hillert	11-9406
Vol. 11	David Schack	11-9407
Vol. 12	Richard Hudson	11-9408

Vol. 13	Gerhard Krapf	11-9409
Vol. 14	David Johnson	11-9410
Vol. 15	Kevin Norris	11-9411

SELECTED REPERTORY FOR RECORDER

Solos (for Alto Recorder and Keyboard Unless Otherwise Indicated)
Handel, G.F. *Four Sonatas of Opus 1.* Schott RMS No. 86.
Loeillet, Jean Baptiste. *Sonata in C Major* (for soprano recorder and keyboard). C.F. Peters N. 3128.
Marcello, Benedetto. *Sonata in F Major.* Ed. Maurice Whitney. Galaxy Music No. 49.
Pinkham, Daniel. *Duet for (Alto) Recorder and Harpsichord.* E.C. Schirmer 2092.
Telemann, G.P. *Four Sonatas.* Hortus-Musicus.
Three Sonatas (The "Fitzwilliam" Sonatas). C.F. Peters N. 1139.

Duos (For Two Altos Unaccompanied Unless Otherwise Indicated)
Burakoff, G., and W. Strickland, arr. *Music of Three Centuries* (SA). Sweet Pipes SP2304.
Croft, William. *Six Sonatas for Two Trebles.* Kalmus 9006.
Gastoldi, Giovanni Giacomo. *Six Duets* (SA). Sweet Pipes SP2306.
Handel, G.F. *Chaconne for Two Treble Recorders and Keyboard.* C.F. Peters PE-6015.
Loeillet de Gant, J.B. *Six Duets for Two Trebles.* Schott 4737.
Marek, J., arr. *Christmas Recorder Duets* (SS). Screen Gems.
Mattheson, Johann. *Four Sonatas for Two Trebles* (with keyboard). Kalmus 9031.
Morley, T. *Two-part Canzonets for Voices and Instruments.* Peters H-1998. (Includes SS, SA, AT, AB.)
Neun Duett (SA). Moeck zfs 76.
Newman, H., and M. Kolinski. *First Book of Duets* (SS). Hargail H-64.
Telemann, G.P. *Six Sonatas in Canon Form for Two Treble Recorders.* Kalmus 9040.

Trios
Haydn, J. *Three Pieces for Musical Clockwork.* Associated ARS 7.
Hindemith, Paul. *Trio for Recorders from the Plone Musiktag.* Schott 10094.
Isaac, Heinrich. *Two Carmina (a 3).* Sweet Pipes SP2312.
Katz, Erich, ed. *Elizabethan Trios.* Anfor Music RCE-3.

King Henry VIII. *35 Compositions*. Ed. J. Stevens, 2 vols. Galaxy Music 4508-1 and -2.

Koch, John. *Songs and Dances*. Galaxy ARS 54.

Long, Page. *Toybox Suite* (1971). Sam Fox UM-134.

Mozart, W.A. *Recorder Ensemble: Trio*, Vol. I, II, III. Schott 12, 13, 14.

Pachelbel, Johann. *Christmas Pastorale* (Von Himmel Hoch). Schott.

Rossi, S. *Five "Sinfonie a Tre Voci."* Associated ARS-1.

Starer, R. *Ricercare for Recorder*. Fox.

Willaert, Adrian. *Four Trios*. Sweet Pipes SP2307.

Quartets (SATB, Unless Otherwise Indicated)

Adam, Joseph, arr. *Christmas Carols*. G. Schirmer 2380.

Barber, Joseph. *Bagatelles*. Sam Fox UM-150.

Chareton, A., arr. *Alman*. Anfor.

Frescobaldi, G. *Canzona*. Associated ARS 4.

German Christmas Tunes in Several Parts for Soprano and Alto Recorders. Moeck zfs 331.

Heckler, Ilse, arr. *Quartet Book for Recorders*. Moeck Verlag 2073.

Katz, Erich, ed. *Renaissance Songs and Dances for Recorders*. Associated Music. (Contains trios, quartets, and larger ensembles.)

Newman, J., trans. *Five Villancicos*. Associated ARS 39.

Poser, J. *Cantare e Sonare: Wandsbeker Tanze*. Sikorski.

Tomkins, T. *A Toy*. Faber.

Selected
Bibliography

Choral

Adler, Samuel. *Choral Conducting: An Anthology*. New York: Holt, Rinehart & Winston, 1971.

Aronoff, Frances Webber. *Music and Young Children*. New York: Holt, Rinehart & Winston, 1969.

Bamberger, Carl (ed.). *The Conductor's Art*. New York: McGraw Hill, 1965.

Bennett, Roy C. *The Choral Singer's Handbook*. New York: Edward B. Marks, 1977.

Birkenshaw, Lois. *Music for Fun, Music for Learning*. Toronto: Holt, Rinehart & Winston of Canada, Ltd., 1974.

Boyd, Jack. *Rehearsal Guide for the Choral Director*. Englewood Cliffs, N.J.: Parker Publishing Co., 1970.

Cunningham, W. Patrick (ed.). *The Music Locator*. Saratoga, Calif.: Resource Publications, 1980.

Decker, Harold A., and Julius Herford (eds.). *Choral Conducting: A Symposium*. Englewood Cliffs, N.J.: Prentice-Hall, 1973.

Ehmann, Wilhelm. *Choral Directing*. Minneapolis: Augsburg, 1968.

Espina, Noni. *Vocal Solos for Protestant Services*, 2d ed. New York: Vita D'Arte, 1974.

Finn, William J. *The Art of the Choral Conductor*. Boston: C.C. Birchard, 1939.

Garretson, Robert L. *Conducting Choral Music*, 4th ed. Boston: Allyn & Bacon, 1975.

Gordon, Lewis. *Choral Director's Complete Handbook*. Englewood Cliffs, N.J.: Parker Publishing Co., 1977.

Green, Elizabeth A. *The Modern Conductor*, 2d ed. Englewood Cliffs, N.J.: Prentice-Hall, 1969.

Hall, William D. (ed.). *Latin Pronunciation According to Roman Usage.* Anaheim, Calif.: National Music Publishers Inc., 1971.

Henderson, Larra Browning. *How to Train Singers*. Englewood Cliffs, N.J.: Parker Publishing Co., 1979.

Henneberger, Judith N. *Musical Games and Activities to Learn By*. Dallas: Choristers Guild, 1976.

Holst, Imogen. *Conducting a Choir: A Guide for Amateurs*. New York: Oxford University Press, 1973.

Hugle, P. Gregory. *Catechism of Gregorian Chant*. Glen Rock, N.J.: J. Fischer, 1956.

Hunt, Edgar. *The Recorder and Its Music*. London: H. Jenkins, 1962.

Ingram, Madeline D. *A Guide for Youth Choirs*. Nashville: Abingdon Press, 1967.

Jacobs, Arthur (ed.). *Choral Music*. New York: Penguin Books, 1979.

Jacobs, Ruth Krehbiel. *The Children's Choir*. Philadelphia: Fortress Press, 1958.

Jones, Archie N. *Techniques in Choral Conducting*. New York: Carl Fischer, 1948.

Lamb, Gordon H. *Choral Techniques*, 2d ed. Dubuque, Ia.: William C. Brown, 1979.

McKenzie, Duncan. *Training the Boy's Changing Voice*. New Brunswick, N.J.: Rutgers University Press, 1956.

Marshall, Madeleine. *The Singer's Manual of English Diction*. New York: G. Schirmer, 1953.

Mees, Arthur. *Choirs and Choral Music*. Brooklyn, N.Y.: Haskell House, 1969; reprint of 1901 edition.

Miller, Kenneth E. *Handbook of Choral Music Selection, Score Preparation and Writing*. Englewood Cliffs, N.J.: Parker Publishing Co., 1979.

Nash, Grace C. *Today with Music*. Port Washington, N.Y.: Alfred Publishing Co., 1972.

Neidig, Kenneth, and J. Jennings. *Choral Director's Guide*. Englewood Cliffs, N.J.: Prentice-Hall, 1967.

Nordin, Dayton W. *How to Organize and Direct the Church Choir*. Englewood Cliffs, N.J.: Parker Publishing Co., 1973.

Peter, Hildemarie. *The Recorder: Its Traditions and its Tasks*. New York: C.F. Peters, 1958.

Pfautsch, Lloyd. *English Diction for the Singer*. New York: Lawson-Gould Music Publishers, 1971.

Robinson, Ray, and Allen Winold *The Choral Experience: Literature, Materials and Methods*. New York: Harper & Row, 1976.

Roe, Paul F. *Choral Music Education*. Englewood Cliffs, N.J.: Prentice-Hall, 1970.

Rorke, Genevieve A. *Choral Teaching at the Junior High Level.* Chicago: Hall-McCreary, 1947.

Rowland-Jones, Anthony. *Recorder Technique,* New York: Oxford University Press, 1959.

Schafer, R. Murray. *Creative Music Education.* New York: Schirmer Books, 1976.

Steere, Dwight. *Music for the Protestant Church Choir.* Atlanta: John Knox Press, 1955.

Sunderman, Lloyd Frederick. *Some Techniques for Choral Success.* Toledo: University of Toledo, 1952.

Swanson, Frederick J. *Music Teaching in the Junior High and the Middle School.* Englewood Cliffs, N.J.: Prentice-Hall, 1973.

Thomas, Kurt. *The Choral Conductor.* New York: Associated Music Publ., 1971.

Ulrich, Homer. *A Survey of Choral Music.* New York: Harcourt Brace Jovanovich, 1973.

Wachhaus, Gustav, and Terry Lee Kuhn. *Fundamental Classroom Music Skills: Theory and Performing Techniques.* New York: Holt, Rinehart & Winston, 1979.

Wheeler, Lawrence, and Lois Raebeck. *Orff and Kodaly Adapted for the Elementary School,* 2d ed. Dubuque, Ia.: William C. Brown, 1977.

Young, Percy M. *The Choral Tradition.* New York: W.W. Norton & Co., 1971.

Church History

Bainton, Roland H. *The Reformation of the Sixteenth Century.* Boston: Beacon Press, 1956.

Baumstark, Anton. *Comparative Liturgy.* London: Mowbray, 1958.

Bieler, Andre. *Architecture in Worship.* Edinburgh: Oliver & Boyd, 1965.

Bishop, John. *Methodist Worship:* London: Epworth Press, 1950.

Book of Common Prayer, The Proposed. New York: Church Hymnal Corp.; Seabury Press, 1977.

Bowie, Walter Russell. *Story of the Church.* Nashville: Abingdon Press, 1945.

Brekke, Milo L., Merton P. Strommen, and Dorothy L. Williams. *Ten Faces of Ministry.* Minneapolis: Augsburg, 1979.

Christian, John T. *A History of the Baptists.* Texarkana, Ark.: American Baptist Assoc., 1922.

Coffin, Henry Sloane. *The Public Worship of God.* Freeport, N.Y.: Books for Libraries Press, 1972.

Dix, Gregory. *The Shape of the Liturgy,* 2d ed. Napierville, Ill.: Alec R. Allenson, 1945.

The Documents of Vatican II. New York: Guild Press, 1966.

Egge, Mandus A. (ed.). *Worship: Good News in Action.* Minneapolis: Augsburg, 1974.

Eversole, Finley (ed.). *Christian Faith and the Contemporary Arts*. Nashville: Abingdon Press, 1962.

Ferguson, George. *Signs and Symbols in Christian Art*. New York: Oxford University Press, 1977.

Gunnemann, Louis H. *The Shaping of the United Church of Christ*. New York: The Pilgrim Press, 1977.

Hageman, Howard G. *Pulpit and Table: Some Chapters in the History of Worship in the Reformed Churches*. Atlanta: John Knox Press, 1962.

Interpreter's Dictionary of the Bible. 5 vols. Nashville: Abingdon Press, 1976.

MacLeod, Donald. *Presbyterian Worship: Its Meaning and Method*. Atlanta: John Knox Press, 1965.

McManus, Frederick. *The Revival of Liturgy*. New York: Herder, 1963.

Maxwell, William. *An Outline of Christian Worship: Its Development and Forms*. London: Oxford University Press, 1936.

Meyer, Carl S. *The Church, From Pentecost to Present*. Chicago: Moody Press, 1969.

Morris, Herbert. *Church Vestments: Their Origin and Development*. New York: E.P. Dutton & Co., 1950

Reed, Luther D. (ed.). *Lutheran Liturgy*. Philadelphia: Fortress Press, 1960.

Robinson, John A.T. *Liturgy Coming to Life*. Philadelphia: Westminster Press, 1964.

Scrawley, James H. *The Liturgical Movement: Its Origin and Growth*. London: Mowbray, 1954.

Sovik, Edward A. *Architecture for Worship*. Minneapolis: Augsburg, 1973.

Spielmann, Richard M. *History of Christian Worship*. New York: Seabury Press, 1966.

Starkey, Marion L. *The Congregational Way*. New York: Doubleday, 1966.

Stuber, Stanley I. *How We Got Our Denominations*. New York: Association Press, 1965.

Thompson, Bard (ed.). *Liturgies of the Western Church*. New York: World Publishing Co., 1961.

Torbet, Robert G., *A History of the Baptists*, rev. ed. Valley Forge, Pa.: Judson Press, 1963.

Underhill, Evelyn. *Worship*. Westport, Conn.: Hyperion Press, 1979; reprint of 1937 edition.

Winchester, C.T. *Life of John Wesley*. New York: Macmillan, 1934.

Winward, Stephen F. *The Reformation of Our Worship*. Atlanta: John Knox Press, 1965.

Church Music

Abraham, Gerald (ed.). *Handel: A Symposium*. London: Oxford University Press, 1954.

American Guild of Organists. *Compensation of the Church and Synagogue Musician* (booklet). New York: American Guild of Organists, 1978.

Apel, Willi. *Gregorian Chant*. Bloomington: Indiana University Press, 1958.

Arnold, Samuel. *Cathedral Music*. 4 vols. London: 1790.

Ashton, Joseph N. *Music in Worship*. New York: The Pilgrim Press, 1943.

Barbour, J. Murray. *The Church Music of William Billings*. East Lansing: Michigan State University Press, 1960.

Blume, Friedrich, et al. *Protestant Church Music*. New York: W.W. Norton & Co., 1975.

Boyce, William. *Cathedral Music*. 3 vols. London: 1760-1778.

Cook. G.H. *The English Cathedral Through the Centuries*. London: Phoenix House, Ltd., 1957.

Davis, Walford, and Henry G. Ley (eds.). *The Church Anthem Book*. London: Oxford University Press, 1933.

Davison, Archibald. *Protestant Church Music in America*. Boston: E.C. Schirmer Music Co., 1933.

Dearnley, Christopher. *English Church Music 1650-1750*. London: Barrie & Jenkins, 1970.

DeVinney, Richard. *There's More to Church Music Than Meets the Ear*. Philadelphia: Fortress Press, 1972.

Douglas, Winfred. *Church Music in History and Practice*. New York: Charles Scribner's Sons, 1962.

Edwards, F.G. *The History of Mendelssohn's Oratorio "Elijah."* London: Novello, Ewer & Co., 1896.

Ellinwood, Leonard. *The History of American Church Music*. New York: Da Capo Press, 1970; reprint of 1953 edition.

Etherington, Charles L. *Protestant Worship Music: Its History and Practice*. Westport, Conn.: Greenwood Press, 1978; reprint of 1962 edition.

Fellerer, Karl Gustav. *The History of Catholic Church Music*. Translated by Francis A. Brunner. Baltimore: Helicon Press, 1961.

Fellowes, Edmund H. *English Cathedral Music*. London; Methuen & Co. Ltd., 1969.

Foster, Myles Birket. *Anthems and Anthem Composers*. London: Novello & Co., 1901.

Gelineau, Joseph. *Voices and Instruments in Christian Worship: Principles, Laws, Applications*. London: Burns & Oates, 1964.

Halter, Carl. *The Practice of Sacred Music*. St. Louis: Concordia, Publishing House, 1955.

Halter, Carl, and Carl Schalk. *A Handbook of Church Music*. St. Louis: Concordia, 1978.

Heaton, Charles Huddelston. *A Guidebook to Worship Services of Sacred Music*. St. Louis: Bethany Press, 1962.

Hume, Paul. *Catholic Church Music*. New York: Dodd, Mead & Co., 1956.

Hutchings, Arthur. *Church Music in the Nineteenth Century*. London: Herbert Jenkins, 1967.

Kettring, Donald. *Steps Toward a Singing Church*. Philadelphia: Westminster Press, 1948.

Larsen, Jens Peter. *Handel's Messiah: Origins, Composition, Sources*. New York: W.W. Norton & Co., 1957.

Le Huray, Peter. *Music and the Reformation in England 1549-1660*. London: Herbert Jenkins, 1967.

Long, Kenneth R. *The Music of the English Church*. Toronto: Hodder & Stoughton, 1971.

Lovelace, Austin C. *The Organist and Hymn Playing*. Nashville: Abingdon Press, 1962.

Lovelace, Austin C., and William C. Rice. *Music and Worship in the Church*, rev. ed. Nashville: Abingdon Press, 1976.

Lutheran Book of Worship: Ministers Desk Edition. Minneapolis: Augsburg, 1978.

Mitchell, Robert H. *Ministry and Music*. Philadelphia: Westminster Press, 1978.

Moore, Edgar J. *A Guide to Music in Worship*. Great Neck, N.Y.: Channel Press, 1959.

Nemmers, Erwin Esser. *Twenty Centuries of Catholic Church Music*. Milwaukee: Bruce Publishing Co., 1949.

Nicholson, Sydney H. *Church Music: A Practical Handbook*. London: The Faith Press, 1927.

O'Connell, J.B. (trans.). *Sacred Music and Liturgy*. Westminister, Md.: Newman Press, 1959.

Ode, James. *Brass Instruments in Church Services*. Minneapolis: Augsburg, 1970.

Palmer, Larry. *Hugo Distler and His Church Music*. St. Louis: Concordia, 1967.

Parry, Scott B. *The Story of Handbells*. Boston: Whittemore Associates, 1957.

Pfatteicher, Philip H., and Carlos R. Messerli. *Manual on the Liturgy; Lutheran Book of Worship*. Minneapolis: Augsburg, 1979.

Phillips, C. Henry. *The Singing Church*. London: Faber & Faber, Ltd., 1945.

Proulx, Richard. *Tintinnabulum, The Liturgical Use of Handbells*. Chicago: G.I.A. Publications, 1980.

Rice, William C. *A Concise History of Church Music*. Nashville: Abingdon Press, 1964.

Riedel, Johannes (ed.). *Cantors at the Crossroads*. St. Louis: Concordia, 1966.

Robertson, Alec. *Christian Music*. New York: Hawthorn Books, 1961.

Routley, Erik. *The Church and Music*. London: Gerald Duckworth & Co. Ltd., 1967.

———.*Church Music and Theology. (Studies in Ministry and Worship, No. 11)* London: SCM Press, 1959.

————.*The English Carol*. London: Herbert Jenkins, 1958.

————.*The Musical Wesleys*. London: Herbert Jenkins, 1968.

————.*Twentieth Century Church Music*. New York: Oxford University Press, 1964.

————.*Words, Music and the Church*. Nashville: Abingdon Press, 1968.

Schalk, Carl. *Key Words in Church Music*. St. Louis: Concordia, 1978.

Schweitzer, Albert. *J.S. Bach*. 2 vols. New York: Macmillan, 1950.

Sovik, Edward A. *Architecture for Worship*. Minneapolis: Augsburg, 1973.

Squire, Russel N. *Church Music: Music and Hymnological Developments in Western Christianity*. St. Louis: Bethany Press, 1962.

Steere, Dwight. *Music in Protestant Worship*. Atlanta: John Knox Press, 1960.

Stevens, Dennis. *Tudor Church Music*. New York: Da Capo Press, 1973; reprint of 1955 edition.

Stevenson, Robert M. *Patterns of Protestant Church Music*. Durham, N.C.: Duke University Press, 1953.

Sydnor, James Rawlings. *The Hymn and Congregational Singing*. Atlanta: John Knox Press, 1960.

Taylor, Stainton De B. *The Chorale Preludes of J.S. Bach*. New York: Oxford University Press, 1949.

Terry, Charles Sanford. *Bach: The Cantatas and Oratorios*. (Musical Pilgrim Series) 2 vols. London: Oxford University Press, 1926.

Thomas, Edith Lovell. *Music in Christian Education*. Nashville: Abingdon Press, 1953.

Titcomb, Everett H. *Anglican Ways: A Manual on Liturgical Music for Episcopal Choirmasters*. New York: H.W. Gray, 1954.

Ulrich, Homer, and Paul A. Pisk. *A History of Music and Musical Style*. New York: Harcourt Brace Jovanovich, 1963.

Werner, Eric. *Mendelssohn: A New Image of the Composer and His Age*. New York: The Free Press of Glencoe, 1963.

Whittaker, W. Gillies. *The Cantatas of Johann Sebastian Bach*. 2 vols. New York: Oxford University Press, 1959.

Wienandt, Elwyn A. *Choral Music of the Church*. New York: Free Press, 1965.

Wienandt, Elwyn A. and Robert H. Young. *Anthem in England and America*. New York: Free Press, 1970.

Hymnology

Bailey, Albert Edward. *The Gospel in Hymns*. New York: Charles Scribner's Sons, 1950.

Diehl, Katherine Smith. *Hymns and Tunes: An Index*. New York: Scarecrow Press, 1966.

Foote, Henry Wilder. *Three Centuries of American Hymnody*. New York: Archon Books 1940.

Julian, John. *Dictionary of Hymnology*, 2d revised ed. 2 vols. New York: Dover Pubns., 1957.

Parker, Alice. *Creative Hymn Singing*. Chapel Hill: Hinshaw Music, 1976.

Reeves, Jeremiah Bascom. *The Hymn as Literature*. New York: Appleton-Century-Crofts, 1924.

Reynolds, William, and Milburn Price. *A Joyful Sound: Christian Hymnody*, 2d ed. New York: Holt, Rinehart & Winston, 1978.

Routley, Erik. *An English Speaking Hymnal Guide*. Collegeville, Minn: Liturgical Press, 1979.

————.*Hymns and the Faith*. Grand Rapids, Mich.: Eerdmans, 1968.

————.*Hymns and Human Life*. Grand Rapids, Mich.: Eerdmans, 1959.

————.*Hymns Today and Tomorrow*. Nashville: Abingdon Press, 1964.

————.*Panorama of Christian Hymnody*. Collegeville, Minn.: Liturgical Press, 1979.

Ruffin, Bernard. *Fanny Crosby*. New York: The Pilgrim Press, 1976.

Sydnor, James Rawlings. *The Hymn and Congregational Singing*. Atlanta: John Knox Press, 1960.

Organ

Aldrich, Putnam. *Ornamentation in J.S. Bach's Organ Works*. New York: Coleman-Ross Co., 1950.

Armstrong, William H. *Organs for America: The Life and Work of David Tannenberg*. Philadelphia: University of Pennsylvania Press, 1967.

Andersen, Poul-Gerhard. *Organ Building and Design*. London. Allen & Unwin, 1969.

Arnold, Corliss Richard. *Organ Literature: A Comprehensive Survey*. Metuchen, N.J.: Scarecrow Press, 1973.

Barnes, William H. *The Contemporary American Organ*, 8th ed. New York: J. Fischer & Bros., 1964.

Blanton, Joseph Edwin. *The Organ in Church Design*. Albany, Tex.: Venture Press, 1957.

Clutton, Cecil, and Austin Niland. *The British Organ*. London: B.T. Batsford, Ltd., 1963.

Donington, Robert. *Tempo and Rhythm in Bach's Organ Music*. London; New York: Hinrichsen Edition Ltd., 1960.

Douglass, Fenner. *The Language of the Classical French Organ*. New Haven: Yale University Press, 1969.

Edson, Jean Slater. *Organ Preludes: An Index to Compositions on Hymn Tunes, Chorales, Plainsong Melodies, Gregorian Tunes and Carols*. 2 vols. Metuchen, N.J.: Scarecrow Press, 1970.

————.*Organ Preludes* (supplement). Metuchen, N.J.: Scarecrow Press, 1974.

Ferguson, John Allen. *Walter Holtkamp, American Organ Builder*. Kent, Ohio: Kent State University Press, 1979.

Fesperman, John. *The Organ as Musical Medium*. New York: Coleman-Ross Co., 1962.

———. *Two Essays on Organ Design*. Raleigh, N.C.: Sunbury Press, 1975.

Geer, E. Harold. *Organ Registration in Theory and Practice*. Glen Rock, N.J.: J. Fischer & Bros., 1957.

Goode, Jack C. *Pipe Organ Registration*. Nashville: Abingdon Press, 1964.

Irwin, Stevens. *Dictionary of Pipe Organ Stops*, rev. ed. New York: G. Schirmer, 1965.

Jamison, James Blaine. *Organ Design and Appraisal*. New York: H.W. Gray, 1959.

Keller, Hermann. *The Organ Works of Bach*. New York: C.F. Peters, 1967.

Klotz, Hans. *The Organ Handbook*. St. Louis: Concordia, 1969.

Niland, Austin. *Introduction to the Organ*. London: Faber, 1968.

Ochse, Orpha. *The History of the Organ in the United States*. Bloomington: Indiana University Press, 1975.

Phelps, Lawrence I. *A Short History of the Organ Revival*. St. Louis: Concordia, 1967.

Sumner, William L. *Bach's Organ Registration*. New York: Hinrichsen Edition Ltd., 1961.

———.*Eighth Music Book*. New York: C.F. Peters, 1956.

———.*The Organ*, 3d ed. New York: St. Martin's Press, 1962.

Tusler, Robert L. *The Style of J.S. Bach's Chorale Preludes*. 2d ed. New York: Da Capo Press, 1968.

Walter, Samuel. *Basic Principles of Service Playing*. Nashville: Abingdon Press, 1963.

Williams, Peter. *The European Organ, 1450-1850*. London: B.T. Batsford, Ltd., 1966.

General

Apel, Willi. *Harvard Dictionary of Music*, rev. ed. Cambridge, Mass.: Harvard University Press, 1979.

———.*The Notation of Polyphonic Music: 900-1600*, 5th ed. Cambridge, Mass.: Mediaeval Academy of America, 1961.

Bukofzer, Manfred F. *Music in the Baroque Era*. New York: W.W. Norton & Co., 1947.

———. *Studies in Medieval and Renaissance Music*. New York: W.W. Norton & Co., 1964.

Chase, Gilbert. *America's Music*. New York: McGraw-Hill Book Co., 1955.

Dart, Thurston. *The Interpretation of Music*. London: Hutchinson's University Library, 1954.

David, Hans T., and Arthur Mendel (eds.). *The Bach Reader*, rev. ed. New York: W.W. Norton & Co., 1966.

Dean, Winton. *Handel's Dramatic Oratorios and Masques*. New York: Oxford University Press, 1959.

Dent, Edward J. *Allessandro Scarlatti: His Life and Works*. London: Edward Arnold, 1960; reprint of 1905 edition.

Dolmetsch, Arnold. *Interpretation of the Music of the XVII & XVIII Centuries*. London: Novello & Co., 1946.

Donington, Robert. *The Interpretation of Early Music*. London: Faber & Faber, 1963.

Emery, Walter. *Bach's Ornaments*. London: Novello & Co., 1953.

Fleming, William. *Arts and Ideas*. New York: Holt, Rinehart & Winston, 1974.

Geiringer, Karl, and Irene Geiringer. *Johann Sebastian Bach: The Culmination of an Era*. New York: Oxford University Press, 1966.

————. *Music of the Bach Family*. Cambridge, Mass.: Harvard University Press, 1955.

Grout, Donald J. *A History of Western Music*, 3d. ed. New York: W.W. Norton & Co., 1980.

Lang, Paul Henry (ed.). *Music in Western Civilization*. New York: W.W. Norton & Co., 1940.

————. *One Hundred Years of Music in America*. New York: G. Schirmer, 1961.

Longyear, Rey M. *Nineteenth Century Romanticism in Music*, 2d ed. Englewood Cliffs, N.J.: Prentice-Hall, 1969.

Machlis, Joseph. *Introduction to Contemporary Music*, 2d ed. New York: W.W. Norton & Co., 1979.

Miles, Russell H. *Johann Sebastian Bach: An Introduction to His Life and Works*. Englewood Cliffs, N.J.: Prentice-Hall, 1962.

Moser, Hans Joachim. *Heinrich Schütz: His Life and Work*. St. Louis: Concordia, 1959.

The New Grove Dictionary of Music and Musicians (ed. Stanley Sadie). 20 vols. Washington, D.C.: Grove's Dictionaries of Music, Inc., 1980.

Pirro, Andre. *J.S. Bach*. New York: Orion Press, 1957.

Reese, Gustave. *Music in the Middle Ages*. New York: W.W. Norton & Co., 1940.

————. *Music in the Renaissance*, rev. ed. New York: W.W. Norton & Co., 1959.

Smither, Howard E. *The Oratorio in the Baroque Era*, vols. I, II. Chapel Hill: University of North Carolina Press, 1977.

Spitta, Phillip. *Johann Sebastian Bach*, vols. I, II, III. New York: Dover, 1951.

Index

Nonliturgical, 3, 7, 10, 60, 62, 71-73, 77, 220
Nunc Dimittis, 33, 38
  source, 33

Oberkirchen Children's Choir, 106
Obrecht, Jacob, 28
Offertory, 11, 25, 60, 63, 199, 203
Opera, 51
Oratorio, 46-47, 121
Ordinary, 25, 199
Orff, 112-14
  speech patterns, 112
Orff, Carl, 112
Organ, 125-26, 219
  accompaniments on, 69-70
  American, 57-58
  and heating system, 165, 172-73
  Baroque, 53, 164
  bidding on, 167
  cipher, 173
  development, 51-59
  electronic, 164, 168-69, 171
  electropneumatic action, 162-63
  English, 56-57
  finishing, 161
  free accompaniments, 68
  French, 55-56
  German, 53-55
  hymn accompaniments, 68
  Italian, 52
  maintenance, 171-73
  mechanical aids, 64
  mechanical/tracker action, 162-63
  Netherlands, 52
  placement, 162, 164-65
  practice, 171-72
  rank, 161
  reform movement, 55
  registration, 66, 70, 73
  Renaissance, 52
  Romantic, 164
  size, 162
  Spanish, 52-53
  stop, 161
  stop action, 162-63
  voicing, 161
Organ builders, 165, 170-71

Organ committee, 166
Organ consultant, 166-67, 170
Organ enthusiasts, 163
Organ recitals, 134
Organ repertory, 51-59
Organ voluntary, 71
Organist, 166
  and the director, 17
  and the organ, 164
  qualifications, musical, 176-77
  qualifications, personal, 174-75
  responsibilities, 17
Organizing the choir rehearsal, 116-17
  choir discipline, 117-18
  pacing the rehearsal, 87-88
  planning for the year, 119
  seating the choir, 118-19
Orison, 60
Ostinati, 113
Oxford University Press, 186

Pachelbel, Johann, 30, 54, 205
Paine, John Knowles, 58
Palestrina, Giovanni da, 28, 30
Palm Sunday (see Liturgical year)
Parallelism in psalms, 206
Parker, Horatio, 39, 58
Passion, 11, 42-44
Passion Sunday (see Liturgical year)
Peeters, Flor, 70
Penance, 12, 198
Penderecki, Krzysztof, 43, 47
Penitential, 62
Pentatonic scale, 113
Pentecost (see Liturgical year)
Pepping, Ernst, 43
Pericopes, 62
Personnel policies, 16-17
Peter, John Frederik, 39
Philosophy of church music, 174-75, 178, 180
Piano, 126-27
  in place of organ, 170
Pilgrim Hymnal, 24
Pinkham, Daniel, 40, 44
Plainsong, 22, 94
Plainsong hymns, 71, 94
Plainsong mass, 28

Senfl, Ludwig, 30
Senior minister, 14-16, 18
  as worship planner, 15-16
  power of, 15
Sermon, 13, 62, 200
  in worship, 15
  theme, 64
Service, 208
Service Book and Hymnal, 203
Shelley, Harry Rowe, 39
Shema, 7
Short meter, 21
Short Service, 208
Sick-leave policy, 180
Silbermann, Andreas, 53, 55
Silbermann, Gottfried, 53
Silence, 61, 70
Singing schools, 77, 219
Skinner, Ernest, 57
Social action, 13
Social gospel, 212
Soler, Antonio, 53
Southern Harmony, 24, 217
Sowerby, Leo, 39, 58, 61
Sprinkling, 13
Stabat mater, 47-50
Stainer, John, 43
Stanford, Charles Villiers, 39
Stanley, John, 56
Stanza, 68
Stations of the cross, 199
Stravinsky, Igor, 28
Study guides, 121-27
Sunday school, 218
Sursum Corda, 11
Sweelinck, Jan Pieterszoon, 53
Synagogue, 7

Tallis, Thomas, 12, 30, 77, 106, 208
Tannenberg, David, 57
Te Deum, 34-36, 71, 73-74
  source, 33
Teenage singing voice
  breathing, 96
  changing voice, 94-95
  focus of tone, 96
  harmonic sense, 98-99
  range, 97

resonance, 97
Temple liturgy, 8
Tempo, 66, 69
Ten commandments, 10
Tenebrae, 61
Text painting, 30
Thiman, Eric, 51
Titcomb, Everett, 39
Toccata, 54, 59, 61
Torah, 7
Tract, 199, 203
Trinity (see Liturgical year)
Troparia, 197
Tunder, Franz, 54

United Church of Christ, 221-23
  Hymnal of the, The, 142, 217
  Lord's Day Service, 223
  Service of Word and Sacrament, 223
  Statement of Faith, 221

Vacation time, 180
Vatican II, 201
Vaughan Williams, Ralph, 23, 28, 39, 44, 51
Venetian style, 30
Veni Creator Spiritus, 22
Venite, 36, 71
  source, 33
  text, 36-37
Verdin handbells, 152
Vespers, 71, 73, 203
Vestments, 88, 198
Victoria, Tomás Luis de, 30
Vienna Choir Boys, 106
Vierne, Louis, 56, 61
Vita, 178
Vocal problems/techniques
  breathing, 80, 96
  diction, 82
  harmonic sense, 84, 98-99
  hooty, 81
  intonation, 78, 83-84, 107-8
  placement/focus, 80, 96
  posture, 80
  range, 97
  resonance, 97
  rhythm, 84